Dear Reader:

The book you are about to read is the latest bestseller from the St. Martin's True Crime Library, the imprint *The New York Times* calls "the leader in true crime!" The True Crime Library offers you fascinating accounts of the latest, most sensational crimes that have captured the national attention. St. Martin's is the publisher of John Glatt's riveting and horrifying SECRETS IN THE CELLAR, which shines a light on the man who shocked the world when it was revealed that he had kept his daughter locked in his hidden basement for 24 years. In the Edgar-nominated WRITTEN IN BLOOD, Diane Fanning looks at Michael Petersen, a Marine-turned-novelist found guilty of beating his wife to death and pushing her down the stairs of their home—only to reveal another similar death from his past. In the book you now hold, THE FAMILY NEXT DOOR, John Glatt returns with an astonishing look at a house full of children imprisoned by their parents.

St. Martin's True Crime Library gives you the stories behind the headlines. Our authors take you right to the scene of the crime and into the minds of the most notorious murderers to show you what really makes them tick. St. Martin's True Crime Library paperbacks are better than the most terrifying thriller, because it's all true! The next time you want a crackling good read, make sure it's got the St. Martin's True Crime Library logo on the spine—you'll be up all night!

Charles E. Spicer, Jr.

Charles E. Spicer, Jr.
Executive Editor, St. Martin's True Crime Library

ALSO BY JOHN GLATT

THE
FAMILY
NEXT
DOOR

*The Heartbreaking Imprisonment of the Thirteen
Turpin Siblings and Their Extraordinary Rescue*

John Glatt

St. Martin's Paperbacks

Published in the United States by St. Martin's Paperbacks, an imprint of St. Martin's Publishing Group.

THE FAMILY NEXT DOOR

For information, address St. Martin's Publishing Group, 120 Broadway, New York, NY 10271.

www.stmartins.com

ISBN: 978-1-250-31230-3

Our books may be purchased in bulk for promotional, educational, or business use. Please contact your local bookseller or the Macmillan Corporate and Premium Sales Department at 1-800-221-7945, ext. 5442, or by email at MacmillanSpecialMarkets@macmillan.com.

Printed in the United States of America

St. Martin's Press hardcover edition / July 2019
St. Martin's Paperbacks edition / May 2020

10 9 8 7 6 5 4 3 2 1

For Audrey and Mavis Hirschberg

CONTENTS

PART THREE: THE MAGNIFICENT THIRTEEN

ACKNOWLEDGMENTS

The unspeakable crimes that David and Louise Turpin stand accused of committing against their own thirteen children are unparalleled. When Riverside County District Attorney Mike Hestrin first briefed reporters about the depths of depravity the couple had sunk to, he elicited gasps from even the most hardened reporters.

The Turpin parents, who had their children affectionately call them "Mother" and "Father," apparently lacked any conscience about the lasting mental and physical injury they were inflicting. According to the evidence, Louise would physically beat her children, and chain them to beds for months at a time. While they starved she and David dined out at good restaurants.

Although brought up in the Pentecostal Church of God, it remains a mystery how they could twist the church's teaching into madness. Chillingly, they flew under the radar, living in good, respectable neighborhoods with neighbors on either side. But no one ever reported anything untoward in the house. David Turpin officially filed papers with the California Department of Education to run his own homeschool. But none of the relevant authorities ever checked up on whether its self-appointed principal was actually teaching them.

Ten years ago, I wrote *Secrets in the Cellar*, the horrific story of how Austrian monster Josef Fritzl imprisoned his own daughter, Elizabeth, for more than twenty years, siring her seven children. In 2010, my book *Lost and Found* recounted how Phillip Garrido and his wife Nancy abducted eleven-year-old Jaycee Lee Dugard, holding her hostage for eighteen years in Antioch, California—just four hundred and twenty-five miles from the Turpins' own house of horrors.

Then in 2013 *The Lost Girls* chronicled the so-called Cleveland Abductions, where Ariel Castro snatched three young girls off the street and turned them into his sexual slaves for more than a decade. Like Jordan Turpin five years later, Amanda Berry bravely risked her life to escape and summon help to save the others.

As Cult Education Institute founder Rick Ross told me: "Who knows how many there are around the United States. This is not uncommon but we only find out about it when something horrible happens."

This book is the result of many months of research into David and Louise Turpin's lives. I started my journey in Princeton, West Virginia, tracing their roots from the beginning. Then I followed them west to Fort Worth and Rio Vista, Texas, where they had almost all their children, before finishing up in Perris, California.

There are so many people who made this book possible with invaluable help along the way. First and foremost I would like to thank forensic psychiatrist Dr. Michael Stone of Columbia University for adding his own expert analysis of this often baffling case. Child trauma expert Allison Davis Maxon provided invaluable help in understanding the full depth of damage the children suffered and the specialized treatment they will need. Renowned cult expert Rick Ross, who has been following the Turpin case from Day one, explained how super-narcissist David Turpin had first recruited Louise to form a self-styled family cult to worship him.

I would also like to thank: Jessica Barmejo, Gilbert Bolling, Dan Brodsky-Chenfeld, Jared Dana, David Downard, Janie Farmer, Dr. David Fenner, Richard Ford, Mike Gilbert, Todd Gray, Dr. Ray Hurt, Mary Hopkins, Greg Jordan, Donald Kick, Tyler Kyle, Erica Llaca, Brian McCabe, David Macher, Assemblyman Jose Medina, Lois Miller, Jeff Moore, Verlin Moye, Aaron Pankratz, Brent Rivas, Kent Ripley, Brian Rokos, Ricardo Ross, Lindsay Gatlin, Tim Snead, Bobby Spiegel, Mayor Michael Vargas, Becky Veneri, Ricky Vinyard, and Pamela Winfrey.

I would also like to thank Dolly's Diner in Princeton, West Virginia, Annie's Café in Lake Elsinore, California, and Jenny's Family Restaurant in Perris, California, for their hospitality and help, as well as Bobbie Herrera, Felipa Guerra, and the staff at Cleburne Public Library.

As always I am deeply indebted to Charles Spicer and Sarah Grill of St. Martin's Press for all their help and good advice throughout. Much gratitude too to my super-agent Jane Dystel and Miriam Goderich of Dystel, Goderich and Bourret Literary Management, my pillars who are always there with unstinting encouragement and support.

I'd also like to thank my wife, Gail, Emily Freund, Debbie, Douglas, and Taylor Baldwin, Pamela Martin, Chris Vlasak, Lenny Millen, Bernie Freund, Annette Witheridge, Ian and Helen Kimmet, Jo Greenspan, Galli Curci, Chris Frost, Roger Hitts, Danny, Cari and Allie Tractenberg, and Gurcher.

PROLOGUE

Around 5:30 a.m. on a chilly Sunday morning, seventeen-year-old Jordan Turpin and her thirteen-year-old sister, Jolinda, squeezed through their first-floor bedroom window and leaped out. It was still dark as they tiptoed through the backyard onto Muir Woods Road in Perris, California.

Fearing for their lives, the two waifish girls crept past neighbors' houses, turning right onto Presidio Lane. Suddenly, Jolinda became too scared to go through with it. She fled home and climbed back into her bedroom. Jordan was on her own.

Since moving to Perris three and a half years earlier, Jordan had rarely been outside and did not know her surroundings. She and her twelve siblings had been prisoners their entire lives. Their jailers were their own parents, who ruled with violence and torture.

Practically starved, they were only allowed one bath a year and wore the same putrid clothing for months at a time. Although officially homeschooled, many of the siblings, aged two to twenty-nine, barely had a first-grade education and lacked basic life skills.

Jordan's escape had been more than two years in the making. Several months earlier, their father's engineering job had been relocated to Oklahoma. By January 2018, the family was all packed up and ready to move; it was now or never. And Jordan finally had the means for escape: an old, deactivated cell phone her brother had given her. The teenager prayed it could still access emergency services, as she had been told.

At 5:51 a.m., her hands shaking with fear, Jordan punched in 911 and broke through to the outside world.

Seventy miles southeast of Los Angeles, Perris prides itself on being a family-oriented community with good schools, safe streets, and many children's activities. Muir Woods Road is a smart street of manicured lawns and garden gnomes where people take pride in their homes.

Outwardly, there was nothing to suggest that the house at 160 Muir Woods Road was any different. When David and Louise Turpin and their twelve children first arrived in May 2014, it had been a model home in the fashionable new Monument Park district. They were among the first families to move in.

For the next four years, the Turpins rarely went out, except to pick up their mail at the communal mailbox, and kept to themselves.

"Nobody here knew they had twelve kids," said Lindsay Gatlin, who lives a few doors away. "I thought there was just one or two."

But fifty-seven-year-old David Turpin did stand out, with his dyed-blond Captain Kangaroo haircut. Neighbors knew he worked as an aerospace engineer for Northrop Grumman, making a six-figure salary. The gleaming fleet of three cars and a fifteen-seater van in his driveway attested to that.

But behind closed doors, things were very different. David and his forty-nine-year-old wife, Louise, had turned their home into a filthy, stinking dungeon, holding their children captive. They insisted on being called *Mother* and *Father,* like in biblical times.

Confined four to a room, their severely malnourished children were frequently beaten and chained up to furniture for months at a time. Punishable offenses included washing above the wrists—"playing in the water"—stealing food, playing with toys, or even looking through the blinds.

They lived in a twilight world, sleeping during the day and awake at night. Their one meal a day was always the same: peanut butter or baloney sandwiches and burritos. The oldest, Jennifer, less than six months away from her thirtieth birthday, weighed just eighty pounds.

At Christmas, twenty-five-year-old Joshua had received a new cell phone, giving his sister Jordan his old, deactivated one. A friend online had told her it could still connect to 911.

To prove the atrocities in the house, Jordan had secretly taken two cell phone photographs of her two little sisters, shackled to bunk beds in their own filth. She had also taken a scrap of an envelope with her home address on it, as she did not know it.

"911, what's your emergency?" answered 911 dispatcher Kelly Eckley.

"Okay," Jordan replied breathlessly, "I live in a family of fifteen people, and my parents are abusive. They abuse us, and my two little sisters right now are chained up. They chain us up if we do things we're not supposed to."

In the high-pitched voice of a young child, Jordan told the dispatcher she could no longer stand hearing her two little sisters crying all night in pain because their parents had chained them so tightly to their beds.

"They will wake up at night and start crying and they wanted me to call somebody," she said. "I wanted to call y'all and help my sisters."

The stunned operator, assuming it was a small child on the line, asked her name.

"T-U-R-P-E-N," recited Jordan, misspelling it.

When asked for her address, Jordan read out numbers from the envelope she had taken, 925707774: the ZIP plus the four number code for her home.

Eckley then asked if she was near her house.

"Yeah, I think," she replied. "I've never been out. I don't go out much, so I don't know anything about the streets or anything."

Over the next twenty minutes, Jordan calmly described the inhuman cruelty that their parents inflicted on them.

"I think that my father has guns," she said at one point, adding that although she hadn't seen them, "they've talked about it."

When the dispatcher asked if the children went to school, Jordan replied no.

"Our mother tells people we're private schooled," she explained, "but we don't really go to school. I haven't finished first grade, and I'm seventeen."

Eckley asked if there was any medication in the house. Jordan said she did not know what *medication* meant.

Astonished at what she was hearing, Eckley asked where her mother was, and Jordan responded that she didn't know much about her.

"She doesn't like us," Jordan said in a quivering voice. "She doesn't spend time with us, ever. I take care of myself and my mother finds food for us, but we never talk."

She listed the ages of all her siblings, saying that the

only one "Mother takes care of right" was the two-year-old.

The house was so filthy, she said, that she would wake up unable to breathe because of the stench. Gasping for air, she would open a window for relief, risking a beating if she were caught.

"We don't take baths," Jordan said matter-of-factly. "I don't know if we need to go to the doctor."

Asked when she had last taken a bath, Jordan seemed uncertain. "Uh, I don't know," she replied. "Almost a year ago. Sometimes I feel so dirty, I wash my face and I wash my hair in the sink."

Jordan told the dispatcher that she and her siblings were being kept prisoners in the house by Mother and Father.

"[They] don't let us move out," she said. "Some of us have asked for jobs, and they said that would never happen."

After Jordan's 911 call, deputies from the Riverside County Sheriff's Department rushed to her location, where they were met by officers from the Perris Police Department.

When they first saw Jordan, they thought she was ten. The experienced officers were shocked by how badly she smelled and the black dirt that caked her skin. When she showed them the cell phone photographs of her two little sisters chained up, they went straight over to 160 Muir Woods Road to carry out a welfare check.

As soon as she heard loud knocking on the front door and saw the flashing police car lights, Louise Turpin immediately ordered the two girls to be unchained. An older sister ran into their bedroom, unlocking the padlocks and throwing the chains into a closet.

Eleven-year-old Julissa, who had been chained up, later told investigators that when she heard the knocking and saw the flashing lights, she knew Jordan had made it and they would soon be free.

When the front door was eventually opened, officers rushed inside. Although the smell was overpowering, nothing had prepared them for the unspeakable horrors inside. One of the officers was wearing a body cam with the camera rolling to record it.

Inside one bedroom, they found Jonathan Turpin still chained up. As they freed him, he acted as if it were normal. His two younger sisters, who had just been released, had white stripes on their dirty skin where the chains had been.

The other nine children were scattered all over the house in cramped bedrooms, reeking of human waste. They were all filthy, stinking, and emaciated.

"It was very dirty," said Riverside County Sheriff's Department captain Greg Fellows, "and the conditions were horrific."

All the commotion had woken up Araceli Olozagaste, who lived across the street. She peeked through her curtains to see deputies leading David and Louise Turpin out of the house in handcuffs. David was crying uncontrollably, but Louise was expressionless.

"She was just coughing," recalled Olozagaste, "acting a little weird as the police officer was talking to her. She just kept smirking at him. Then she spat twice down on the floor."

PART ONE

THE SEEDS OF EVIL

I

KING TURPIN

According to family lore, David Turpin first had "feelings" for Louise Robinette when she was ten years old and he was seventeen. The gangly six-footer showered the shy girl with attention. Their courtship consisted of secretly holding hands during fiery Pentecostal services at the Church of God in Princeton, West Virginia, which both their families attended.

Two years later, the tiny seventh grader told her grandmother that one day she would marry David and they would have twelve children.

Almost half a century earlier, David's grandfather, the Reverend King Turpin Jr., had also fallen for a sixteen-year-old girl, nearly half his age. Just two months after Nellie, the dutiful mother of his eight children, died giving birth to twins, Turpin married his children's nurse, Bertha Lee Church.

The day after Christmas 1932, the charismatic Pentecostal preacher made a deal with her father: to swap Bertha for his flashy Studebaker Big Six car.

"My dad traded me for the car," she would admit many

years later. "King said that if he hadn't given my dad the car, he wouldn't have got me."

Over the next eighteen years, Bertha would bear him eleven more children, for a total of nineteen, though five died in infancy.

Although physically small, the Reverend King Turpin Jr. is a larger-than-life icon in the Turpin family. David's elder brother, the Reverend J. Randolph "Randy" Turpin, is the family genealogist, and in 2010, he wrote and self-published their grandfather's biography: *A Man Called King*. It was intended as an inspiration to all future generations of Turpins.

Born in 1903 in Chattanooga, Tennessee, the "Little King," as he was fondly known, grew up in dire poverty in an often-violent home. His mercurial father, King Turpin Sr., was a strict disciplinarian, losing his temper at the slightest provocation. He would chase the mischievous little boy and his younger sister, Minnie, around the house, brandishing a white-hot poker or throwing rocks at them. When he caught them, they would receive a brutal whipping.

On one occasion, he took away their only pairs of shoes as a punishment, making them walk barefoot through the rough rural countryside. On Sundays, he gave them back for church so the neighbors wouldn't talk. But as soon as they got home, he confiscated them again for another week, saying they could wear shoes when they learned to behave.

King Turpin Sr. often left his two young children home alone for weeks at a time while he roamed the Tennessee countryside doing odd jobs to scratch out a meager living.

"We were living by ourselves," Minnie remembered many years later. "We pulled ourselves up . . . we had a pretty hard life."

After one particular savage beating, the Little King and Minnie ran away to escape their violent father. A family friend took them in and then called King Sr., who came to collect them.

In 1915, when the Little King was twelve, the Tennessee welfare authorities intervened. The state's early version of Child Protective Services found the two Turpin children had been seriously neglected and placed them in separate Chattanooga orphanages. The Little King was soon released into the care of an uncle, but Minnie wasn't so lucky. She spent two years at the orphanage before she was placed in the custody of another close family member, becoming pregnant when she was thirteen.

At eighteen, King Turpin Jr. moved to Knoxville, Tennessee, where he found work in a cotton mill. In August 1921, he married Nellie Griggs, who soon bore him a daughter, Agnes. King Jr. moved his new family to Lynch, Kentucky, and became a coal miner. Soon afterward, baby Agnes died after accidentally swallowing calcium carbide, which her father used to light his miner's helmet lamp.

Family legend has it that King Turpin Jr. was miraculously converted to the Pentecostal religion at a prayer meeting in Lynch, Kentucky. He suddenly heard a loud voice from the heavens shout, "It's a-comin'! It's a-comin'! It's a-comin!"

"At that moment," wrote his grandson Randy, "the power of the Holy Ghost rushed from the top of his head down to his feet, and he began to speak in tongues."

After his epiphany, King Jr. became a lay preacher, going down into the mines with his banjo and Nellie at his side, spreading the Pentecostal gospel message.

They had two more children, James Jackson and Robert, in quick succession. In 1927, Nellie bore King's fourth child, Willie, who died a year later of gastroenteritis. On the baby's death certificate, a doctor noted, "The family never gave any medication; they believe in divine healing."

King Jr. moved his growing family to Arizona, where he became a minister of the Church of God, a radical Pentecostal sect that believes the Bible is the direct word of God. Founded in 1886, Church of God followers believe in baptism with the Holy Ghost, which is manifested by speaking in tongues. King Jr. would often speak in tongues during his services as the Holy Ghost took over his spirit.

"The gift of tongues and the gift of interpretation were frequently manifested," wrote Randy, an ordained bishop in the Church of God.

In his book, Randy recounts an early church service where his grandfather spoke in tongues in one language before moving on to a completely different one and then interpreting in both. A multilingual member of the congregation stood up, announcing the Reverend Turpin had been speaking in perfect Spanish and Greek, neither of which he knew.

In 1932, the Reverend King Turpin Jr. moved his growing family two thousand miles east to Rock House Mountain in southern West Virginia. Soon after they arrived, Nellie died during childbirth, and Turpin immediately married sixteen-year-old Bertha Lee Church.

Thirteen months later, she bore him a son, James "Jim" Randolph Turpin—David and Randy Turpin's father.

Over the next few years, King Jr. moved his family around West Virginia, preaching in various Pentecostal churches and working as a coal miner. He also built a home church onto his house in McDowell, West Virginia, inviting the whole neighborhood to his daily prayer meetings.

"Everyone knelt to pray," wrote Randy in his biography. "Frequently in these times together, King and Bertha would speak in tongues, interpret tongues and prophesy . . .

demonstrations of God's power were part of their every-day life."

Jim Turpin grew up in the strict Pentecostal religion, which he practices to this day.

"As far back as I can remember," he recalled, "I always loved Jesus."

All through his childhood, Jim attended services led by his parents. At the age of twenty, he witnessed his father delivering a message in tongues. It was followed by an interpretation with a special message to Jim: "Soon you will see mighty works of God performed."

Soon afterward, a Church of God evangelist held a series of tent revival meetings in the neighborhood. King and Bertha brought Jim to one of them.

"The altar call was given," wrote his son Randy, "and Jim went forward in response. He felt the spirit of God come upon him. He knew, in that moment, he had been saved. It was King and Bertha's prayer that all of their children be saved."

In June 1955, Jim married seventeen-year-old Betty Jean Rose, settling down in a modest house on New Hope Road in Princeton, West Virginia. Set deep in the heart of rural Appalachia, the small town, with a population of just 6,400, is known as the "Jewel of the South." In the late nineteenth century, coal mining and the newly built railroads combined to create a lucrative new industry and make Princeton rich.

"Princeton was built on the coal industry and the railroads through here," explained *Bluefield Daily Telegraph* reporter Greg Jordan. "This is the area where a lot of the coal industry got started in the United States in a big way."

In May 1958, Jim and Betty Jean had a baby boy they named James Randolph, whom they called Randy. Three years later, on October 17, 1961, they were blessed with their second and last child, David Allen.

Every summer, David and Randy would visit their grandparents in Ohio, where they were now living. The Reverend King Turpin Jr. would play an important role in David's and Randy's childhoods, instilling in them a love of the Pentecostal church and its teachings.

"King did more than just play with [us]," recalled Randy. "He took time to impart spiritual treasures into [our] lives. At times . . . his eyes would glisten with tears, his face would become radiant, and he would start speaking in tongues."

During long summer nights, the aging preacher sang them songs he'd learned in the 1920s, strumming along on his banjo. One of David's favorites was "Long Boy."

"I remember he used to call me 'Long tall grandson,'" said David. "I have very, very fond memories of Grandpa."

One summer, his grandparents moved into their Princeton house while Bertha had two hip replacements in a nearby hospital. During their extended stay, King Jr. would make his two young grandsons memorize some of his favorite scriptures from the Bible and then recite them in front of him.

Every Sunday, the Turpin family attended the Princeton Church of God on Oliver Avenue, where they became close friends with Allen "Wayne" Robinette, his wife, Phyllis, and their three daughters, Louise, Elizabeth, and Teresa.

"We were a big church family," said Teresa. "My dad was a preacher, [and] David's family grew up with our family . . . so Louise and David have known each other all their lives."

2

"HE'S SO CREEPY"

Louise Robinette's family had lived in Princeton, West Virginia, for more than a century. Her maternal grandfather, John Thomas Taylor, was a highly decorated World War II veteran who served in Europe and Africa. A first class gunner in the U.S. Army, Third Armored Division, he received a Silver Star, five Bronze Stars, a Purple Heart, and a Good Conduct Medal.

In December 1945, the handsome twenty-one-year-old returned to Princeton a war hero. He became a coal miner but was ambitious and didn't intend to stay down in the mines for long. Taylor was a member of the Church of God and served as its chaplain for military funerals. It was through the church that he met and soon married Mary Louise Harmon, the daughter of a Pentecostal minister. They went on to have four children: Eugene, Glenn, Phyllis, and James.

But John Taylor's broad, toothy smile concealed a ruthless ambition. Utilizing his heroic war record, he soon became a powerful player in Princeton politics as an American Legion lobbyist. He made his fortune helping

real estate developers overturn the newly set up Veterans
Emergency Housing Program.

In 1945, the United States faced a severe housing
shortage due to a drastic cut in the number of homes being built. Returning veterans were hit the hardest, and it
was impossible to buy new homes.

To solve the problem, President Harry S. Truman appointed Wilson W. Wyatt, the former mayor of Louis-
ville, Kentucky, to the newly created federal post of
housing expediter. The goal was to provide affordable
housing for all, and Wyatt planned to give returning war
veterans preferential treatment so they could get back on
their feet.

"We cannot [welcome] our veterans [home] with a
half-hearted housing program," Wyatt explained.
"[There] is nothing but confusion and blasted hopes for
the homeless veterans."

But the sweeping new plan was bitterly opposed by
the real estate industry, as it cut into their profits. In Mercer County, John Taylor would fight it tooth and nail, as
his loyalty now lay with the real estate tycoons.

In late January 1949, he made headlines in the *Bluefield Daily Telegraph* for forcibly ejecting a Veteran of
Foreign Wars representative from an American Legion
meeting at the Statler Hotel in Bluefield.

"All veterans organizations are supposed to be inter-
ested in housing," read the article. "But an interesting
tip-off on the American Legion's position occurred the
other day when Legion lobbyist John Thomas Taylor
kicked a Veteran of Foreign Wars (VFW) housing officer
out of the meeting."

During the meeting, Taylor became incensed as the
VFW representative stood up to talk about the new federal
housing policy to benefit veterans.

"John Thomas Taylor was pointing in his direction and

sputtering furiously," stated the article. "'Get him out of here!' he shouted."

Another Legion official tried to calm him down.

"'I don't care,' he yelled. 'I'm running this meeting and I want him out of here,'" the article continued.

The VFW representative duly left, and the meeting continued behind closed doors, with some powerful real estate lobbyists, including the vice president of the National Association of Home Builders, in attendance.

"The Legion long has been accused of playing hand-in-glove with the real estate boys," read the article, "especially when it comes to sabotaging Wilson Wyatt's far-sighted housing program."

A few months later, the powerful real estate lobby forced the suspension of housing price controls, and Wilson Wyatt resigned.

Over the next few years, John Taylor built houses and car lots all over the Princeton area. He opened the first Shell gas station in Mercer County, which was a big success.

"He was very wealthy," said his granddaughter Elizabeth Robinette Flores. "He built, with his own hands, [his] home and a Shell gas station."

His Shell station on Athens Road became a well-known local landmark, the only place to gas up for miles around. And Taylor took great pride in serving his customers personally.

"It was a thriving business," remembered Lois Miller, who as a little girl used to buy gas there with her mother and aunt. "When you pulled in, John Taylor cleaned your windscreen and checked your oil while he pumped your gas. And I remember gas being nineteen cents a gallon."

But it was common knowledge that Taylor was lecherous.

"He was very creepy," recalled Miller, who now runs the Mercer County Historical Society, "and he'd play with your hand when you handed him money. He would just rub your hand and look at you kind of goofy-like while you're trying to get away from him."

Whenever they went to the Shell station, Miller's mother would keep the window up, handing her daughter the gas money for Taylor.

"The same thing happened to my aunt when she bought gas," said Miller, "but they had to get gas there, as there was nowhere else."

A few years later, a friend of Lois's took a summer job at Taylor's Shell station.

"She told me he had molested her when she worked for him," said Miller. "She said, 'I don't even want to discuss him. He's so creepy!'"

On Monday, January 3, 1966, Joseph Maxfield was unloading gasoline at the Shell gas station when it caught fire, turning him into a human fireball. The thirty-eight-year-old tank truck driver suffered first-, second-, and third-degree burns over 85 percent of his body. He was rushed to Princeton Memorial Hospital in critical condition.

The story made the front page of the *Bluefield Daily Telegraph,* and John Taylor, now forty-two, told the reporter that the deliveryman had been unloading gasoline for about twenty minutes when he took a break, possibly to smoke a cigarette.

"Taylor reported the flames shot 20 to 30 feet into the air from an open hole leading to the underground gasoline storage tanks," read the story. "He could offer no explanation for the fire, but theorized that fumes around the truck ignited."

Taylor explained that neither he nor his employees smoked cigarettes but the tank driver did.

A few days later, Joseph Maxfield, who was married with four children, died in Princeton Memorial Hospital of his burn injuries.

To the outside world, John Taylor was a good churchgoing pillar of the Princeton community. But behind closed doors, he was molesting his own daughter, Phyllis. It was a dark family secret that would remain hidden for the next sixty-five years.

All through her childhood, Phyllis Taylor had been sexually abused by her father, unable to tell anyone. Her mother had no idea what was going on. The young girl felt trapped in the family home and was desperately looking for a way out.

At the age of seventeen, Phyllis started dating Allen "Wayne" Robinette, a skinny nineteen-year-old who had recently graduated from Princeton High School. Studious with a gift for figures, Robinette, who had grown up in the Green Valley trailer park and worked as a lay preacher, sported a crew cut and wore a pair of fashionable horn-rimmed glasses. It was a whirlwind romance. When he proposed marriage, Phyllis immediately accepted.

On July 20, 1967, the young couple applied for a marriage license at the Mercer County Courthouse. Nine days later, they married in a traditional double-ring ceremony at the Princeton Church of God, which they regularly attended and where Allen occasionally preached.

John Taylor proudly walked his daughter down the aisle. The attractive brown-haired bride wore a floor-length white silk gown, with delicate lace decorations on the bodice and train. She had a matching white floral headpiece with a cascading veil and carried a Killen daisy nosegay bouquet. The groom wore a smart black suit and striped tie with a white rosebud boutonniere.

After the ceremony, the guests went back to John Taylor's house for the reception, featuring a three-tiered wedding cake topped with wedding couple dolls for good luck. A report of the nuptials of the wealthy man's only daughter made the society wedding page of the *Bluefield Daily Telegraph*.

Exactly nine months later, on May 24, 1968, Phyllis and Allen had a baby girl, whom they named Louise Ann, after her grandmother. The cherubic baby was christened at the Church of God.

3

THE HONOR STUDENT

In 1974, thirteen-year-old David Turpin started at Glenwood Junior High School, just a few miles from his home. Mike Gilbert was in David's class, and they would spend the next five years as friends.

"Our junior high was really small," said Gilbert, "so of course you knew everybody. David was very intelligent but kind of quiet and kept to himself. He was nerdy and always did well at school with good grades."

Even as a young teenager, David stood out from the other boys. Almost six feet tall, he towered over most of his classmates and always dressed very conservatively.

"He had really short hair and wore dress clothes most of the time in junior high," recalled Gilbert. "He even wore a bow tie on occasions as a fashion statement. We're talking about the 1970s, when everybody else had long hair and bell-bottom pants. David wasn't like that."

The two ninth graders soon bonded over chess, which David was obsessed with. He taught Gilbert how to play during gym class, when the teacher wasn't looking.

Said Gilbert, "He already knew how to play chess, and he beat me one time in three moves. But he taught me something, and nobody has ever beaten me in three moves since then."

On November 27, 1977, the Reverend King Turpin Jr. died in a Fremont, Ohio, hospital at the age of seventy-four. He had been in the hospital for a few weeks due to failing health; all his years down the mines had caught up with him.

"Tubes were running into Grandpa Turpin's body," wrote Randy, who visited him a few days before he died, "including oxygen tubes in his nostrils. Grandpa was fighting for every breath."

David later penned a tribute to his grandfather for his brother's biography.

"I mostly remember him as smiling, joking around, laughing, carrying on . . . really just a lot of fun to be around," he wrote. "We all really lost a lot when he died."

In 1976, David followed Randy to Princeton High School, where he and Mike Gilbert began to grow apart.

"He had his own group of friends," said Gilbert. "When we moved on to high school, he got a little wild and started wearing blue jeans."

The Princeton High School yearbooks contain many photos of David's achievements in various clubs over the years. A group picture from a Bible club picnic in the fall of 1976 shows fifteen-year-old David with a new Prince Valiant fringe, staring at the camera with a wry smile.

By the following year, David was the club's treasurer and sits in front of the other members in the yearbook photo. Underneath is its mission statement: "The purpose of the Bible Club is to encourage Christian Fellowship during and after school. Along with fellowship comes the frolicking fun that Bible Club members enjoy in each other's company."

Bible club activities included bell-ringing for the Salvation Army, hosting a Thanksgiving dinner for an underprivileged family, and organizing a Christmas party.

Bluefield Daily Telegraph reporter Greg Jordan, who has covered the Princeton area for more than twenty years, said Bible study plays a vital role in Mercer County schools.

"It's been said you can't throw a rock around here without hitting a church," he explained. "It's a very churchgoing community, and the local schools study the Bible as literature."

David also regularly made the school's "B or Better" honor roll and was cocaptain of the five-member Princeton High School chess team, which competed against schools all over West Virginia.

"He was just kind of goofy and nerdy," remembered David Downard, who was also on the team. "He was very quiet and always had this funny grin and [would stand] with his hands tied together behind his back."

Another member of the chess team, Tony Veneri, still talks about an incident on the drive back to Princeton after a tournament.

"One of the other chess club members, Phillip Wright, was driving and going a little fast," said Tony's wife, Becky, who has heard the story numerous times. "And David, who was usually quiet and easygoing, became very anxious and screamed, 'Oh, Phillip! Slow down! You're going to kill us!'"

By his senior year, David Turpin had decided he wanted to be an engineer and was an active member in the Princeton High School science club.

The straight-A student won first place in the annual Mercer County Science Fair and joined the prestigious

West Virginia Junior Academy of Science. He was also a huge fan of the hit TV show *Star Trek,* strongly identifying with Mr. Spock, perhaps the inspiration for his new hairstyle.

"[David] and his friends were *Star Trek* fans, or Trekkies," said Gilbert, "and they would make jokes about that."

The 1979 Princeton High School yearbook has a humorous picture of the cocaptain of the chess team—the spitting image of Leonard Nimoy's character—gazing longingly at a sports sneaker.

"David Turpin surrenders his king to an Adidas," read the tongue-in-cheek caption.

The teenager also loved cars, which would become a lifelong passion. His father, Jim, helped him to customize his old Honda Civic.

"He and his dad put a big old pair of air horns on it with an air [compression] tank," recalled Gilbert, "like his little Honda Civic was an eighteen-wheeler or a tractor trailer. He would pull up behind you blowing those air horns and scare you, because it was coming out of such a little vehicle. He loved to blow that horn, and he'd be laughing and scaring people."

Every Saturday night, David drove his Honda into downtown Princeton, dressed in slacks, a dress shirt, and a bow tie.

"Back in those days, the big thing was cruising," Gilbert said. "Everybody would go out on a Saturday night and just drive back and forth through town. You would see [David] there cruising and sounding off his air horns."

Now retired, Mary Hopkins taught both Turpin brothers algebra at Princeton High School. She remembers David being an excellent student.

"He had a sense of humor," she said. "He would smile and say funny things, and I would see the twinkle in his eye. But he was pretty serious about what he was doing, and he did well."

Tim Snead, who took biology and Spanish with David, said David never had a girlfriend and didn't take part in any social activities.

"He really didn't socialize a lot," said Snead. "He seemed like a geek, but he was very intelligent."

David graduated from Princeton High School in the class of 1979, with a grade point average of 95.6585. He had also been awarded a coveted scholarship to study electrical engineering at Virginia Tech.

At his graduation ceremony, David wore a mortarboard and robes and was presented with a "top twenty student" award. The 1979 yearbook explained the accolade.

At every high school there are always groups of students known as the "brains." They are the ones that actually do all their homework every night . . . and always have a tremendous stack of books to carry home. Consequently, the top twenty are truly the "tops."

In his graduation picture, a smiling David Turpin wears a smart fawn-colored suit and a flashy striped tie, with his Mr. Spock haircut. His numerous group affiliations and career ambitions are listed below his photo. In addition to being cocaptain of the chess team, treasurer of the Bible club, and a science club member, he was in the Spanish club and the school's a cappella choir. His goal for the future was "to take up a career in electrical engineering and invent the light bulb."

His life motto, he said, was "Never do today what you can put off until tomorrow."

It was around the time of his graduation that David was first attracted to ten-year-old Louise Robinette. David's and Louise's parents had been close friends for many years; David had actually held Louise when she was a little baby. Both families' lives revolved around the Princeton Church of God. David's brother, Randy, worked there as a pastoral minister, and their mother, Betty Jean, taught Sunday school. Louise Robinette was one of her pupils.

After their 1967 wedding, Allen and Phyllis Robinette moved into a small house at 102 B Ray Street. It was there that Louise grew up as a Taylor—in one of Princeton's most respected families. Her grandfather, John Taylor, was already a wealthy man from his Shell gas station and various property deals. Her uncles Eugene and Glenn Taylor were also successful in their own right; Eugene owned the Clearview Trailer Park, and Glenn was a self-employed brick mason.

Tragedy struck the family in 1974 when Louise's youngest brother, James, was seriously injured in a motorcycle accident. He was on the way to nearby Athens High School for a date with his girlfriend, Sharon, when his bike skidded off the road.

"James got his leg cut off from the knee down," said Lois Miller, who was in Sharon's class. "I wasn't too crazy about Sharon dating him. I thought he was too wild."

In 1978, Louise celebrated her tenth birthday, and Allen Robinette shot video of his daughter opening presents in her bedroom. With her long dark hair in a headband and wearing a white ruffled shirt with a Peter Pan collar, the little girl looked like she didn't have a care in the world.

Later that day, there was a party with a birthday cake, and her grandfather—affectionately known in the family as Papaw—was photographed with Louise and her little eighteen-month-old sister, Elizabeth Jane.

However, the reality of the Robinettes' household was less than picture-perfect. After her own abusive childhood, Phyllis Robinette showed little interest in being a mother, leaving Louise to bring up her red-haired baby sister.

The Robinette home was a battleground with Phyllis and Allen's constant arguments. Some of Elizabeth's earliest memories are of Louise trying to shield her from their parents' raging fights.

"There was fighting between my parents and yelling and screaming," said Elizabeth. "I remember Louise covering my ears and planting my face in her chest . . . so I wouldn't have to hear or watch it. She was very, very protective."

Beginning when Louise was a tiny child, Phyllis would regularly drive her over to her father's house. For years, John Taylor, now in his midforties, had allegedly been molesting his daughter. Now he turned his attention to his pretty young granddaughter, and Phyllis allowed it—in return for money.

"He was the family leader," said Elizabeth. "He had money, so when my mom needed money, she ran to [him]."

It was always the same. At some point during the visit, Papaw would whisper to Louise that they were going into the other room for "a tight hug."

Years later, female family members would reveal what had really happened in their grandfather's house.

"He molested my mom all her life," said Louise's youngest sister, Teresa. "We begged my mom not to take us there some days, and she would take us anyway. He was very, very wealthy."

Their grandfather's alleged abuse was a closely guarded family secret, and the girls were told never to talk about it.

"That's how we're programmed," Elizabeth explained. "We know how to mask very well [and] not show what we're feeling."

Like David, Louise also attended Glenwood Junior High School and then Princeton High School.

"She was kind of quiet and kept to herself," remembers Richard Ford, who was in Louise's class at Princeton High School. "She didn't have many friends, and she was picked on a little bit. It was kind of strange. She isolated herself from everybody else. I don't remember ever seeing her out. Most of the students would go to the mall on the weekends or the ball games."

The sole mention of her in the 1984 yearbook is as vice president of the Bible club. Her yearbook photograph shows Louise dressed in an all-American crewneck, her long, dark, curly hair cut into bangs.

Elizabeth remembers her older sister being very unpopular and constantly ridiculed by her schoolmates.

"She didn't have any friends," said Elizabeth. "She was made fun of a lot. She never had any control in her life growing up."

Allen Robinette, who worked as a draftsman doing blueprints for the Joy Manufacturing Company, would often drive his daughter home from school. He appeared to have had no idea of Louise's struggle to fit in.

On Friday, March 25, 1983, he photographed her holding schoolbooks, writing underneath, LOUISE "DADDY'S GIRL" COMING FROM SCHOOL.

In 1982, Mary Louise Taylor caught her fifty-eight-year-old husband raping their fourteen-year-old granddaughter, Louise, on their living room couch. Furious, she picked up a frying pan and chased him out of the house. Within days, she had filed for divorce, and Taylor moved into a new house at Bailey Hollow Road, right behind his Shell station.

To avoid scandal, the horrific incident was never reported to the police.

"It was a very small town, and everybody knew him," explained Elizabeth. "We had to keep our family name [and] be uppity-up for the town of Princeton. So we can't go to the authorities."

Elizabeth's younger sister, Teresa, who was a year old at the time, would only learn the real reason for her grandparents' divorce after she had become another victim of Taylor's sexual abuse.

"There was never any justice," said Teresa. "The family told us girls . . . to keep quiet. We didn't want to ruin the family name, and he had all the money."

A year later, Louise started secretly dating twenty-two-year-old David. Phyllis was aware of the relationship but was too scared to tell her husband, as the evangelical preacher would never have approved of his young daughter dating an older man.

"My mom was like, 'Oh, it's David Turpin, the Turpin boy,'" said Elizabeth. "'He's a good boy.'"

Louise confided to Elizabeth that she was going to marry David as soon as possible and have twelve children. He was going to be a rich engineer, she told her sister, earning $100,000 a year and giving her everything she had ever dreamed of.

Child trauma specialist and therapist Allison Davis Maxon, nationally recognized as an expert in children's mental health, said that child incest victims may, as adults, feel powerless or worthless, and can "attract" partners who abuse them or their children.

"When a young girl has grown up being constantly victimized and perpetrated on," explained Maxon, "it's not uncommon, unfortunately, for her to grow up to marry a perpetrator and/or a pedophile, because that's the relationship dance she knows. It's really about attachment. When a child has learned that connection means pain, trauma, and abuse, he or she learns the dance of victimhood.

"The child typically internalizes a belief system that they are unworthy, dirty, 'less than,' 'bad,' and/or deserve to be punished. So it's not uncommon for children who have suffered intense abuse and trauma to grow up and find a partner that will treat them according to what their belief system dictates: 'I'm worthless, bad, and deserve to be punished.'"

Now in his first year at Virginia Tech, David was majoring in electrical engineering and was an excellent student. He was also a member of Eta Kappa Nu, an elite international electrical and computer engineering honor society. Past members include Apple cofounder Steve Wozniak, Larry Page and Eric Schmidt of Google, and Yahoo! founder Sabeer Bhatia.

Most weekends, David would drive home from the Virginia Tech campus in Blacksburg, Virginia, to visit his girlfriend, Louise, but they always had to sneak around so her father wouldn't find out that they had become more than friends.

"My mom hid that from my dad . . . and let Louise see him behind [his] back," explained Teresa. "He didn't think that it was appropriate for them to be alone without adult supervision."

Phyllis encouraged the relationship, admiring the Turpin family's devout Christian values. But her husband, now working in the Mercer County Assessor's Office, would never have approved. His daughter was only fifteen and below the age of consent; any sexual contact between the couple would have been statutory rape.

In 1984, David Turpin graduated Virginia Tech with a bachelor's degree in electrical engineering. In both his junior and senior years, he was awarded the prestigious Marshall Hahn Engineering Scholarship. In the yearbook, he's pictured with a tuxedo, a bow tie, and a big grin. He projects the look of a confident young man who is really going places.

As David began sending off his résumé to blue-chip companies, Louise started tenth grade at Princeton High School.

"She was a tiny little girl and looked like she was about ten," recalled her shorthand teacher, Pamela Winfrey, who had been in Louise's father's graduating class. "I guess she was fifteen or sixteen, but she was a really quiet girl."

But younger sister Teresa said Louise was highly manipulative, and Teresa would later realize that acting shy and dutiful was part of Louise's act.

"Obedient in front of them," explained Teresa, "but behind their back, no. Louise was going to get her way no matter what."

Elizabeth said her sister was headstrong and always got what she wanted.

"It was her way or no way," Elizabeth explained, "and if she had to sneak around to do it, she would."

David soon found an engineering job with the U.S. defense contractor General Dynamics in Fort Worth, Texas. He asked Louise to elope with him, promising to buy her whatever she wanted.

Louise immediately agreed, and they began secretly planning their new life together.

Elizabeth now believes that Louise was also desperate to escape her grandfather's sexual abuse, which had worsened since his divorce. Phyllis was bringing her three daughters over to his new home regularly, allowing her father to abuse them and then taking his money.

But whenever Papaw asked Elizabeth for a "tight hug," Louise would insist on taking her place.

"She would always push me out of the way and say, 'I'll go,'" remembered Elizabeth. "She was very protective."

When their grandmother discovered Phyllis was still allowing her daughters to be molested, she demanded Phyllis stop taking them over.

"And my mom would just say, 'That's my father,'" said Elizabeth.

4

THE RUNAWAYS

That Christmas, Louise gave little sign of her imminent departure. On Christmas Day, she was photographed with her grandmother, sitting on a checkered couch in the living room beside a fully trimmed Christmas tree with presents underneath.

But by mid-January, David Turpin had devised an elaborate scheme to whisk the sixteen-year-old off to Fort Worth, Texas, so they could marry. It was a big secret. Louise told only Elizabeth and a friend in her shorthand class at Princeton High School, swearing them to secrecy.

The night before leaving, Louise called Elizabeth into her bedroom, saying she had something important to tell her. She came in to find her older sister packing a duffel bag. Then Louise asked how Elizabeth would feel if she married a rich man and had a baby.

"You could come over and hold it," said Louise, adding that they would all live together in a big house, with a nice car and lots of money to spend.

"Wouldn't that be fun," she said, "and I could buy you what you want."

Then she made Elizabeth promise not to tell anybody.

Early the next morning, Louise said good-bye to her parents and went off on the school bus as usual. David's plan called for him to masquerade as her father so he could sign her out of school.

That morning in shorthand class, Louise seemed nervous, waiting for her boyfriend to arrive. She repeatedly asked her teacher, Pamela Winfrey, for permission to go to the restroom so she could check if he was there yet.

"She said, 'Can I be excused?'" recalled Winfrey. "And she left and then came back to class. Then just a few minutes later, she said, 'Can I be excused again?'" and then she left. She asked two or three times to be excused. And then she left and I never saw her again."

When Louise didn't return to class, Winfrey asked the other pupils if Louise was sick.

"Then one of the girls told me, 'Well, she's planning on running off and getting married to David Turpin.' I was totally amazed. But by then, it was too late to stop her."

David Turpin had disguised himself to look older, donning a fake mustache and a cowboy hat. He had then parked outside the front entrance of Princeton High School and marched into the office, announcing he was Allen Robinette and Louise had to leave with him immediately. Nobody questioned him further, and he officially signed her out of school.

A few minutes later, David Turpin and his underage girlfriend were heading west out of Princeton for their eleven hundred–mile journey to Fort Worth.

When Elizabeth arrived home alone that afternoon, her mother presumed Louise had missed the school bus, so she drove to Princeton High School to collect her and was informed that her husband had checked her out hours earlier.

So Phyllis called Allen Robinette to find out what was happening, and he "flipped out," saying he had not signed out their daughter. He then called the school, who told him that a tall man with a mustache and hat had left with Louise hours earlier.

"Daddy was frantic," said Elizabeth. "Mommy was frantic, so they went to the police station and reported Louise missing."

Over the next several days, there was no word from Louise. Her parents blamed each other for her running away. Allen was furious with his wife for encouraging the relationship with David, saying it was all her fault.

"I remember the chaos in the house when she eloped with David," said Teresa. "Our whole family being in the house and my parents fighting and crying."

A few days later, a police officer picked up the runaway couple in Fort Worth and made Louise call her parents to say she was all right. Ironically, it was her mother who wanted to press charges against David for kidnapping. When David's parents heard the threat of legal action, they were livid, since their son would face prison for transporting a minor across state lines. They begged the Robinettes not to press charges.

After his initial fury when Louise had gone missing, Allen now had "mixed emotions." As an evangelical preacher, he decided it was better to let them quietly marry, as extramarital sex went against his strict Church of God beliefs. His attitude was that Louise had made her choice and should now go off with David and live her life.

"He got on the phone and told Louise, 'You're now an

adult [and] can take care of yourself. If this is what you want, you go for it,'" said Teresa.

It was only after Allen Robinette agreed to give written permission for his sixteen-year-old daughter to marry David that the couple drove back to Princeton.

On February 11, 1985, Louise and David Turpin were married at a small, quiet church ceremony in Pearisburg, Virginia, thirty-five miles east of Princeton. Only close family members attended. The bride wore a mid-calf-length conservative white dress, with a high mock turtle neckline and slightly puffed long sleeves. She had a simple white flower corsage. The groom wore a loose-fitting, brown three-piece suit with a striped tie and his usual grin.

Immediately after the wedding, the newlyweds returned to Fort Worth to begin their new life together.

There was no wedding report in the *Bluefield Daily Telegraph,* and few of Louise's classmates even noticed she had suddenly dropped out of school mid-semester and never graduated.

"She was supposed to be in my graduating class," said Richard Ford. "She just disappeared."

At the beginning of their marriage, David was making good money in his new job at General Dynamics, keeping his promise that they would live well. Although she still sent Elizabeth letters regularly, Louise turned her back on Princeton. She wanted nothing to do with her miserable childhood, blaming her family for her grandfather's sexual abuse.

"When she first left home, she was mad and resented Mommy a lot," explained Teresa. "She resented the whole family because they kept the secret."

With Louise gone, her parents' arguments became even worse. Eight-year-old Elizabeth and her three-year-old sister, Teresa, would hug each other to try to escape the continual fights.

Then Phyllis started an affair with a local man.

Late one night, after her father had gone to bed, Elizabeth heard her mother talking to somebody on the phone. She instinctively knew something was wrong. She woke up her father, telling him that her mother was on the phone with a stranger.

Allen picked up the phone and listened to the conversation for a few minutes before slamming it down. Then he confronted Phyllis, demanding to know who she was talking to. When she claimed it was only her father, he knew she was lying and berated her for being unfaithful.

Things got so heated that Phyllis finally called her father for help. John Taylor rushed straight over and ordered his son-in-law out of his own house, threatening to call the police if he didn't leave.

Allen did leave. He filed for divorce the next day.

With Allen out of the picture, John Taylor started spending more and more time at the B Ray Street house. By then, he was also molesting Teresa, his youngest granddaughter. Without a husband to support her, Phyllis became more and more reliant on her father's money to feed and clothe her children, so she allowed Papaw to molest them whenever he wanted to.

"She sold us to a wealthy pedophile," said Teresa. "He would slip money into my hand as he molested me. I can still feel his breath on my neck as he whispered, 'Be quiet.' He would come to the car after every time and hand my mom money. And he thought that made it okay."

Without their big sister to protect them, Elizabeth and

Teresa would now have to endure their grandfather's despicable behavior alone.

Soon afterward, Phyllis became pregnant by her new boyfriend, Billy Lambert, and they got engaged. Allen, who had recently been appointed chief deputy assessor of Mercer County, approved, believing the relationship gave Phyllis some stability. Lambert also got along well with Elizabeth and Teresa.

Then, days before the wedding, Billy was driving home from work when he suffered a brain hemorrhage. His car went over a cliff, and he died instantly. When Phyllis gave birth to his son months later, she named him Billy Jr.

Meanwhile, in Fort Worth, David and Louise Turpin were thriving. David was working as a computer engineer on the F-16 Fighting Falcon, one of the most popular military supersonic jet fighters. It was a high-paid job, and the couple often ate out at pricier restaurants around town. They spent weekends at the historic Fort Worth Stockyards, going to the rodeo and Wild West shows.

In 1987, David and Louise moved to Brea, California, for his job. Just thirty-three miles southeast of Los Angeles in Orange County, the scenic city is famous for its public arts program, which attracts tourists from all over the world. The Turpins loved the warm Mediterranean climate, with the average temperature in the eighties.

The Turpins found a modest two-bedroom apartment at 800 South Brea Boulevard. Though Louise still resented her family for her traumatic childhood, she embraced any opportunity to boast about her affluent new life. She wrote letters back to Princeton, vividly describing their beautiful home, fleet of cars, and frequent trips to Disneyland. She promised to fly her mother and sisters out soon to visit, all expenses paid.

Back in Princeton, her family's situation was less fortunate. After her fiancé's tragic death, Phyllis Robinette turned to prostitution to survive. She would leave Elizabeth and Teresa home alone all night to care for their baby brother while she turned tricks downtown on seedy Mercer Street. Sometimes she took the kids with her, leaving them in the car while she entertained her clients.

Janie Farmer taught Elizabeth and Teresa in Mercer Elementary School. She could see the neglect the children suffered, eventually becoming their surrogate mother.

"I found them to be a sad, needy family," recalled Farmer. "I hate to talk bad about their mother, because I think she did what she could, but she couldn't do a lot."

Each morning, the two Robinette sisters came to school looking unkempt with bad personal hygiene. They were made fun of by their classmates.

"They were not clean and kind of raggedy-looking," Farmer said. "When the other kids would go out to play, they basically stayed by themselves. They seemed to be sad children."

Farmer, who was good friends with their father, as they were both staunch Democrats, was surprised by how Phyllis always tried to keep her daughters away from Allen.

"The girls got to visit their father," recalled Farmer, "but he didn't seem to be allowed to be in their lives as much as he wanted."

Although Phyllis never attended any parent-teacher meetings, she suddenly started visiting Mercer Elementary School for another reason; she had developed a crush on David Lee, the African American school custodian.

"She was smitten . . . infatuated," said Farmer. "She would come to the school just to see the custodian."

Most evenings, Phyllis would drive her little girls back to the school, leaving them in the car while she went in to see her new boyfriend.

"They dated," said Elizabeth, "but it wasn't normal dating. He cleaned the school at night . . . and we would keep him company while he cleaned."

Before long, the two were virtually living together, leading to even more instability for Phyllis's family. Janie Farmer became so concerned for the girls that she confronted Phyllis.

"She'd say, 'Well, I'm doing the best I can,'" said Farmer. "And for all purposes, she probably was. But the girls never spoke to me about abuse or anything like that."

Although Farmer eventually lost touch with Elizabeth and Teresa when they both graduated to middle school, David Lee would stay in the Robinettes' lives a while longer. Over the next four years, Phyllis would give birth to two of his children, McCeary and Alene Lee, before the couple finally drifted apart.

PART TWO

THE FAMILY

5

"I THOUGHT THEIR LIFE WAS PERFECT"

In the fall of 1987, Louise Turpin became pregnant. She and David were delighted. Louise had always told her family that she wanted a dozen children, and now she was on her way. The following summer, David photographed his twenty-year-old wife wearing a checked shirt and proudly displaying her eight-month-pregnant belly. She sent the photograph back home to Princeton, where her proud father duly wrote, LOUISE ANN ROBINETTE TURP, JULY 1988, at the bottom.

A few days later, on July 28, Louise gave birth to a little girl, whom they named Jennifer Dawn. Over the next few weeks, Louise would send a stream of photos of herself and David posing with their baby daughter at Disneyland and other scenic places in Southern California.

That Christmas, true to her word, Louise paid for her mother and siblings to come to California and meet her new baby. They took the Amtrak train from Princeton to Brea, where David and Louise met them at the station.

"It was so cool," remembered Teresa, who was six at the time. "She took us to her house. It was very clean and well kept."

For the next three weeks, the Robinettes stayed with the Turpins, going on lavish day trips to Disneyland, Universal Studios, and the Movieland Wax Museum.

"We saw the Hollywood sign," said Teresa, "and the world's biggest tree with a tunnel cut through it. It was a trip I will never forget."

In early 1990, David Turpin was transferred back to Fort Worth by General Dynamics, soon to be taken over by the huge defense contractor Lockheed Martin. He moved Louise and their now eighteen-month-old daughter into 3225 Roddy Drive, a spacious, modern, four-bedroom, two-bathroom house in the fashionable Meadowcreek neighborhood on the outskirts of Fort Worth. They left a storage unit full of their belongings back in California, which was later auctioned off for nonpayment.

Finally, Louise and David were ready to introduce their little daughter, Jennifer, to Princeton, West Virginia. On August 6, 1990, the *Bluefield Daily Telegraph* featured a birthday picture of the Turpin toddler on the Lifestyles: Keeping in Touch page.

"Jennifer Dawn Turpin celebrated her 2nd birthday July 28," read the caption below. "She is the daughter of David and Louise Turpin of Fort Worth, Texas, formerly of Princeton. Grandparents are Wayne Robinette, Mr. and Mrs. James Turpin, Phyllis Robinette, all of Princeton. Great-grandparents are John and Louise Taylor of the Athens Road."

David Turpin was now earning a six-figure salary in his highly specialized engineering job. Soon after moving in, Louise invited her mother and siblings to visit. It was the start of a series of much-anticipated annual trips that the Robinette family would make to Texas over the next decade, with Louise and David paying for everything.

"She was paying for our airfare out there every year," said Teresa. "My mom couldn't afford that."

And when they arrived, David and Louise were more than generous hosts, taking them all out to the Fort Worth Stockyards and Six Flags over Texas and dining at the best restaurants.

"It was the highlight of our year," said Teresa, "because that's when we got to do the fun things."

But she never really got to know her brother-in-law, David, who always seemed very distant during the visits.

"He was very quiet," remembered Teresa. "He . . . always sat back and watched and observed. He was very, very . . . smart. Book smart. The nerdy type."

Back in Princeton, Allen Robinette had given up preaching and had been elected Mercer County surveyor, running his own office in the Mercer County Courthouse on Main Street. He was very active in the West Virginia Democratic Party.

"Everybody liked [Allen]," said his friend Verlin Moye, a Mercer County clerk. "He did a lot of complex tax formula work [with] land tables and that kind of thing. He specialized in the appraisal end of the assessor's office."

Robinette would proudly talk about his son-in-law, David, saying he was making big money for a defense contractor. But he never mentioned how his daughter, Louise, had run away at sixteen to elope, leading to his bitter divorce.

"I just really didn't know that they had a falling-out over that," said Moye. "[Allen] just never did divulge any of his personal life to me."

Still deeply religious and active in the Princeton Church of God, Allen started every county commission meeting with a prayer. When he wasn't busy assessing taxes, he collected celebrity autographs and NASCAR memorabilia. His prized collection included every American astronaut and many U.S. presidents and world figures.

A few years later, the *Bluefield Daily Telegraph* would run a story about Allen Robinette's impressive collection of celebrity autographs. With the headline TRUE COLLECTORS NEVER KNOW WHEN TO SAY WHEN, there was a photograph of Louise's father, in which he wore a checked shirt and overalls, standing by his collection.

In the article, Robinette boasted that he now had more than three thousand autographs in his collection, including almost every American astronaut. He said his first ever autograph had been Republican presidential candidate Barry Goldwater, who lost to Lyndon Johnson in 1964.

"I was a student [in] high school and a Goldwater admirer," explained Robinette. "I wrote him and he replied. That is how I started collecting."

With prized autographs of every president from John F. Kennedy to George Bush, Robinette had strong views about anyone trying to profit from selling famous people's autographs.

"He had an extensive, impressive collection," recalled Moye. "Mother Teresa, Gandhi, and Princess Diana . . . just anybody and everybody. It was just amazing to me."

But while Allen Robinette held one of the most important jobs in Mercer County, his ex-wife and two youngest daughters were now destitute and living in a homeless shelter in Tennessee.

On February 3, 1992, Louise Turpin gave birth to a baby boy. He was named Joshua David. From then on, all their babies' Christian names would begin with the letter *J*.

Soon after Joshua was born, David and Louise Turpin

iled chapter 7 bankruptcy. Despite David's high salary, the couple had been living beyond their means and had maxed out their credit cards, racking up substantial debt. Louise had also recently discovered a passion for gambling and had been losing heavily.

But she never admitted any financial problems to her family, always pretending that everything was fine. And during her family's annual visit, Louise was as generous as ever.

"It was a pride thing," explained Teresa. "She was the only one of us that had made it in the world . . . I believe she was ashamed to tell us anything bad had happened."

6

MEADOWCREEK ELEMENTARY SCHOOL

In July 1993, Louise met her family at Dallas / Fort Worth International Airport, heavily pregnant with her third child. Once again, Louise insisted on paying for everything. Being homeless, Phyllis and her daughters were delighted to be staying in Louise and David's house on Roddy Drive.

"That house was beautiful," said Teresa. "It was fun and happy."

On November 3, Louise gave birth to a baby girl named Jessica Louise at Texas Health Harris Methodist Hospital Southwest Fort Worth. There was a brief mention in the *Fort Worth Star-Telegram* that the new baby's parents were "Louise Ann and David Allen Turpin of Fort Worth."

In the spring of 1994, the *Telegram* invited readers to send in some of their favorite family photographs, accompanied by a short sentence about their mother, for an upcoming feature to celebrate Mother's Day. David and Louise Turpin entered a number of photographs, resulting in three appearing in the newspaper.

In one photograph, Louise is pictured with Jennifer, Joshua, and baby Jessica in their backyard, playing with their pet dog, Blackie. In another, David and Louise pose with Jennifer as a baby, along with her paternal grandmother, Betty Turpin.

"My mother is very special and we love her very much," read David's caption below.

The third, which was around five years old, showed Phyllis Robinette holding her newly born son, Billy Jr. Next to them stood David with Louise, holding Jennifer.

"There is no other like my mother," read Louise's caption. "She's the best."

Fifteen months later, eight-year-old Jennifer Turpin started first grade at Meadowcreek Elementary School, just a few blocks from her home on Roddy Drive. Every morning, Louise would drive her to school and then collect her in the afternoon.

From the start, the frail-looking girl was cruelly taunted by her peers. Not only was she a couple of years older than everybody else in her class, but she had poor personal hygiene. She wore the same white-and-purple floral puffy top to school each day, and her long, greasy brown hair, crudely cut into bangs, was never brushed. She was also missing her two front teeth, as her adult ones had not come in yet.

"She was definitely criticized," recalled Jared Dana, who was in Jennifer's class. "She used to wear the same smelly clothes every day; a pair of beaten overalls and a purple shirt. A lot of the time, she'd take foil out of candy bars to do up her hair."

Her classmates would hold their noses when she passed by. Dana, who was also bullied, was one of the few kids who would talk to her.

"I was a pretty shy kid as well," he recalled. "I wouldn't say we were drawn toward each other, but we talked on occasion. Jennifer was genuinely nice. I don't think she ever had a mean bone in her body. On a dare, I once kissed her on the cheek, and I was ridiculed horribly for it."

He still remembers the little Turpin girl as being unusually hyperactive and excitable.

"She was very full of energy at school," Dana said. "On field days, she was always super-excited and would be the first one running in front of everybody."

Aaron Pankratz was also in Jennifer's first-grade class and still remembers her "really long, unkempt hair" and "hand-me-down dresses."

"She struck me as being really poor," he said, "and I remember being weirded out by her. I really just avoided her for the most part . . . she was more of an outcast."

On December 17, 1995, Louise Turpin gave birth to her fourth child, Jonathan Wayne, at Texas Health Harris Methodist Hospital Southwest Fort Worth. He was a healthy baby weighing eight pounds, eight ounces, and was twenty and a half inches tall.

His proud parents sent a photograph of baby Jonathan to the *Fort Worth Star-Telegram*, which subsequently appeared in the birth announcements column.

"He joins his older siblings," it read. "Jennifer, 7, Joshua, 3, and Jessica, 2."

In June 1996, Louise and David brought their four children back to Princeton for a family visit. They proudly showed them off, assuring close family members there would be many more to come. The children were all dressed in identical clothes, right down to their shoes.

"They would all walk in a straight line," recalled Teresa. "They were like a school rather than a family. I just thought she was overly strict with them."

Once again, David and Louise paid for everything,

taking everyone out for lavish meals at different restaurants every night. And both their families were duly impressed by the luxurious lifestyle David, Louise, and the kids seemed to enjoy. It seemed that Louise really had found her Prince Charming and was living the American dream.

"We thought she had the perfect life," said Louise's half brother Billy Jr. "Any time they wanted something, they did it. I thought they were just a normal, happy family."

During their visit, Elizabeth, who was now studying at Lee University in Cleveland, Tennessee, asked if she could spend the summer with them in Fort Worth. David and Louise readily agreed, and when they left to return home, Elizabeth sat in the back of the van with the children.

As they drove through Louisiana, David suddenly took an exit off the interstate. Louise announced they were going to a casino to gamble, asking Elizabeth to look after the children while they were away. But first she made her sister promise never to tell anyone in the family they gambled, as it was against their religious beliefs.

"I was in shock," remembered Elizabeth. "We were all raised up in a strict Christian home and taught that gambling was a sin."

A few hours later, as the children slept in the back of the van in the casino garage, David returned. He seemed very upset, complaining that Louise had a serious gambling problem and refused to stop even though she was losing heavily. Then he went back into the casino, saying he hoped they would have enough gas money to reach Fort Worth.

Several more hours passed before David brought Louise back to the car. They had obviously been arguing.

"Louise was upset," said Elizabeth, "and yelled, 'I'm not a child! Stop bossing me around!'"

_____

Former Princeton High School teacher Pamela Winfrey
would often think back to the day she had unwittingly excused Louise Robinette from class so she could elope with
David Turpin. She regularly shopped at the Walmart in
Bluefield, where Phyllis Robinette now worked as a cashier.

"One time I mentioned to Phyllis that I had taught
Louise on the day she'd left," said Winfrey, " and asked
her about it. She said it was because of [Louise's] dad that
she got married. I told Phyllis I was amazed how brave
and gutsy she was to run off. I would never have the nerve
to do anything like that."

When Elizabeth moved into 3225 Roddy Drive, she was
initially delighted to be reunited with Louise. They enjoyed spending time together, playing board games, listening to music, and watching movies. But Elizabeth
soon realized just how strict Louise and David were
with their young children, especially Jennifer.

"They had to ask permission to go to the bathroom,"
said Elizabeth. "They had to ask permission to eat."

Elizabeth never saw her sister or brother-in-law dis-
play any affection or tenderness toward their children.
During the summer Elizabeth lived there, she never
once saw them kiss their children or even hold them.
They never read them a book, tucked them into bed, or
gently rocked baby Jonathan to sleep.

Elizabeth was also puzzled by Louise's almost ritu-
alistic mealtimes. After placing the plates of food on the
table, she would call the children down to eat one at a
time. And for some reason, Louise was always harder on
Jennifer than any of the others. Before being allowed to

eat, the first grader had to look her mother in the eye and smile, and then wait for it to be returned.

"And then [Louise] would say, 'Okay, sit down,'" Elizabeth said. "And then she would literally just sit there . . . waiting for permission to eat. And then [Louise] would tell her, 'Okay, you can eat.'"

After Jennifer had finished eating, her mother would tell her to stand up, look at her, and smile before sending her back to her bedroom.

"It was like a secret code," recalled Elizabeth, "at every meal."

Jennifer and her three siblings were confined to their rooms for long periods of time and were never allowed any contact with their aunt unless Louise was present.

"She didn't want me talking to the kids," explained Elizabeth, "and they weren't allowed to talk to me without permission."

Louise told Elizabeth it was to "protect" her children, as she didn't want her beliefs "rubbing off on them."

Although she felt uneasy about how David and Louise were treating their children, the nineteen-year-old never challenged them.

Elizabeth also noticed how they both had bad tempers. Usually soft-spoken, David would fly into a rage at the least provocation.

"David would get set off if Louise did something he didn't like and get really mad," said Elizabeth. "When I lived there . . . he didn't want us doing anything together without him. She knew not to do it because he would just flip."

Years later, Jennifer Turpin would tell investigators that she had witnessed her father losing his temper and physically attacking her mother. Eventually, David promised to stop, but it is unknown whether or not he did.

According to Rick Ross, an expert on cults and the founder of the Cult Education Institute, it was in Fort Worth that David Turpin began molding his family into a twisted cult, using his warped version of Pentecostal teachings as a foundation. He viewed himself as a charismatic leader, with Louise as his second-in-command.

Over the next few years, as their family expanded, David and Louise introduced a set of elaborate rules and punishments, conditioning the children into absolute obedience and dependency. The children were required to call them *Mother* and *Father*.

"What we call 'cult brainwashing' is actually a synthesis of coercive persuasion or thought reform," explained Ross. "And they develop influence techniques, either by trial and error, instinctively, or they read books and figure it out."

Ross said family cults were all about power, control, and domination.

"The father figure simply wants to turn his family into essentially a group of devotees," said Ross. "And there is no legitimate reason to leave. You don't grow up and move out."

He said there was nothing new about family cults like the Turpin family.

"Who knows how many there are around the United States?" he said. "This is not uncommon, but we only find out about it when something horrible happens."

Soon after moving to Fort Worth, Elizabeth found a summer job at a local store. Louise insisted on driving her to and from work, laying down a strict set of rules for her to follow. She was not allowed to have any friends, use their home phone, or even tell anyone where she lived. It was if she had now been recruited into the family cult.

"Louise was a very private person," explained Elizabeth. "I was told if I broke the rules, I would be kicked out."

That summer, Elizabeth observed David and Louise at close quarters, learning the strange dynamics of their relationship. Outwardly, her sister appeared to be in control and to make all the decisions as David quietly watched with his arms folded. But then Louise would always look at him for affirmation.

"They'd make eye contact," said Elizabeth, "and she'd say, 'Right, David?' And David would either say, 'Right,' or he'd say, 'Well . . .'"

Elizabeth said it was Louise who would decide whether or not to punish the children for some infringement of her growing set of rules. Then David would carry it out.

Elizabeth was also becoming uncomfortable with her brother-in-law's increasingly inappropriate behavior. He began teasing her about an ex-boyfriend, saying that he must have gotten excited when she went swimming in her skimpy bikini. One day in the kitchen, David and Louise opened up about their relationship. David admitted having had "the hots" for her sister since Louise was ten years old, when he had made "a pass" at her.

Soon after this revelation, Elizabeth was taking a shower when Louise picked the bathroom lock with a coat hanger. Then she and David came in to watch.

"That was real inappropriate," said Elizabeth, "and made me feel very uncomfortable. [They] would come in and watch me shower and make me get out in front of him."

As she self-consciously dried herself off, they began laughing at her embarrassment.

"I was red from head to toe," said Elizabeth. "They

tried to [pretend] it was a joke. Like they weren't doing anything wrong."

From then on, David and Louise often watched Elizabeth in the shower, telling her she was beautiful. Although Elizabeth hated it, she had no alternative. She insists that David never laid a finger on her.

Forensic psychiatrist Dr. Michael Stone, a professor of clinical psychiatry at Columbia University, explained that incest victims often have no sexual boundaries.

"They tend to have various sexual abnormalities," said Dr. Stone. "They were raised by people who violated rules, so there's no rules. Some of them become wildly promiscuous, and others feel that sex is dirty and disgusting after what happened to them. But there is usually some abnormality."

Toward the end of the summer, Louise discovered her sister had befriended a fellow worker and regularly ate lunch with him. She was furious. After dropping Elizabeth off at work one day, she never returned to pick her up. Elizabeth was frantic and kept calling Louise, who refused to answer the phone. She spent the night sleeping on a bench at a nearby Walmart.

For the next three nights, Elizabeth slept outside, going to work in the same clothes. Finally, Louise answered the phone, telling her sister to go home to Tennessee. It was only after Elizabeth threatened to call the police that Louise allowed her to come back and collect her things.

On May 21, 1997, Louise was back at Texas Health Harris Methodist Hospital Southwest Fort Worth, giving birth to their fifth child, a baby girl they named Joy Donna. The bouncing baby girl weighed seven pounds, seven ounces, and was twenty and a half inches tall. The *Fort Worth Star-Telegram* printed her photo in its birth announcements column.

"She is welcomed by her brothers and sisters, Jennifer, 8 years, Joshua, 5 years, Jessica, 3 years, and Jonathan, 18 months," read the caption David had provided.

Three months later, Jennifer started second grade at Meadowcreek Elementary School. Her hygiene had deteriorated even further.

"She smelled just like dirty clothes and urine," recalled classmate Jessica Bermejo. "She always wore the same clothing . . . so she probably just never took it off, I guess."

But her aunt Teresa, who had recently visited, vividly remembered seeing a row of expensive dresses in Jennifer's closet that had never been worn.

"[They] didn't even fit her anymore," said Teresa. "The tags hadn't even been taken off . . . $200 and $300 dresses."

While the expensive dresses gathered dust in her wardrobe, Jennifer wore the same dirty long-sleeved white shirt and purple pants each day.

The nine-year-old, now confined to her bedroom for hours at a time, also seemed unnaturally hyperactive, constantly doodling and playing with her hair. She also began exhibiting disturbing behavior in front of her classmates.

"She would touch her private area," Bermejo said. "I don't know if it was itching, and it could have been because she was dirty as well."

Jennifer also said things that made everyone uncomfortable.

"She was talking about things that could indicate sexual abuse," Bermejo reflected. "Things that were inappropriate for that age. I just kind of brushed it off."

Jared Dana remembers a teacher sending Jennifer to the principal's office for rubbing her pubic area, but apparently, no action was ever taken to investigate if there was a problem at home, and the Texas Department of Family and Protective Services have no record of the Turpins.

When Jennifer was in third grade, there was a lice outbreak at Meadowcreek Elementary School, and everyone blamed her.

"I actually was one of the kids that got lice," said Bermejo. "It was a big deal that a lot of people got lice too. The kids were calling her the Cootie Girl, because everyone knew that her hygiene was [bad]."

Taha Muntajibuddin and his twin sister, Nuha, were also in third grade with Jennifer and observed how badly she was treated.

"She was often made fun of by the other third graders," wrote Muntajibuddin on Facebook, "because her clothes would sometimes look as though they had been dragged through mud, which she would also smell like on most days."

One day, Jennifer was humiliated when a teacher ordered her to remove an old Hershey bar wrapper, which she was using as a scrunchie to tie up her long, dirty hair.

"I distinctly remember my entire third-grade class scoffing at her," Muntajibuddin wrote.

But even though she endured so much ridicule, the good-natured girl was always friendly.

"She tried to socialize," said Bermejo, "but people just didn't want to play with her and stayed away from her. I reached out to her a few times, but I was an introvert as well."

———————

On June 15, 1998, Louise gave birth to her sixth child, Julianne Phyllis, at Texas Health Harris Methodist Hospital Southwest Fort Worth. The healthy baby weighed eight pounds, fourteen ounces, and was twenty-one inches tall.

"She is welcomed by her brothers and sisters," read her birth announcement in the *Fort Worth Star-Telegram,* alongside a photograph.

A month later, Louise, David, and their four oldest children drove east to Princeton for a family visit. It was an unhappy stay, and Louise made no secret of how much she hated Princeton.

"She went to see the family one last time," Elizabeth later told Dr. Oz, during an interview on his popular television show. "She had [told me] that she wasn't going back there. She wanted [to] let Mommy and Daddy see their grandkids."

Teresa believes her oldest sister was traumatized by that final visit, as all her childhood nightmares flooded back.

"She was so hurt," explained Teresa. "Being there made her sick. Made her resentful."

It would be the last time Louise and David ever set foot in West Virginia, and there would be no more all-expenses-paid annual visits for the Robinette family.

As Christmas approached, the Turpins were in dire financial straits. Although David was earning good money working for Lockheed Martin, he and Louise regularly drove to Louisiana to gamble, and she was still losing badly.

Since getting kicked out of the Turpin home, Elizabeth had dropped out of college and gotten married. She eventually reconnected with Louise, and they talked on the phone regularly. During the calls, her sister often spoke about her love of gambling and how David disapproved. She said she loved "the rush" gambling gave her and couldn't stop.

In late December, Elizabeth called her sister's cell phone. Louise said she was out Christmas shopping and would call back. Several hours later, she did, boasting that she was maxing out all her credit cards to buy as much as she could before they were declined. At that moment, she told her sister, David was in the garage stacking up all the children's presents.

She then proudly announced they were about to file for chapter 7 bankruptcy. The bank was foreclosing on the Roddy Drive house, as they had fallen so far behind in mortgage payments.

When Elizabeth questioned whether bailiffs would seize all their possessions after they filed for bankruptcy, Louise laughed. She explained that although they would lose their house, they could still keep everything else bought on credit. Under chapter 7 rules, they would even be able to keep their cars if they started paying off what they owed.

Louise assured her shocked sister that all their debts would be written off, so they wouldn't have to pay for anything. When Elizabeth called this dishonest, Louise argued that they were only doing it so their children could have as many clothes and toys as possible in the future. It was only good sense, she said, to exploit the system before filing for bankruptcy.

When Elizabeth replied that it sounded more like stealing, Louise slammed down the phone.

In spring 1999, the bank foreclosed on the Roddy Drive house and evicted David, Louise, and their six children.

Without any explanation, Jennifer stopped coming to Meadowcreek Elementary. She would never return to public school.

"One day she just never came back," said Jessica Bermejo. "I thought that was odd. Later, I tried looking her up, but I never found anything. She had fallen off the grid."

None of the other Turpin children would ever see the inside of a classroom, as their father had decided to homeschool them. This would avoid any probing questions from teachers and parents about the Turpin family's unusual lifestyle. Louise, who had dropped out of high school at sixteen to marry David, would be their teacher.

Cult expert Rick Ross believed that the next stage of the cult came when David and Louise withdrew their children from the outside world, setting up an alternative caricature of one within their own increasingly unstable home.

"He used those techniques to manipulate their minds and create unreasonable fears about the outside world," said Ross. "And instill the kind of dependence, obedience, and submission that [he wanted]."

Ross said that although David Turpin was clearly the instigator and leader of the cult, Louise willingly went along with it.

"This is an example of a group that is dominated by a patriarchal figure," said Ross, "and the mother has some responsibility as well. But David Turpin was like a god in this family. He became an object of worship, and to disobey him was the cardinal sin. And the children had no life, other than what he allowed them to have."

After the Turpins moved out, the new owners of 3225 Roddy Drive were so appalled at the deplorable state the house had been left in that they took photographs. There was a terrible stench, and all the floors and carpets were caked in grime. There were also large dark stains covering the walls of every room, which appeared to be feces.

7

RIO VISTA

At 10:31 a.m. on July 27, 1999, Louise Turpin gave birth to a seventh child, a healthy baby girl they named Jeanetta Betty. Once again, the baby was born at the Texas Health Harris Methodist Hospital Southwest Fort Worth in downtown Fort Worth.

The following week, the *Burleson Star* duly printed a birth announcement sent in by the proud father on its Look Who's New in the World of Babies page. Strangely, it listed the Turpins as living in Burleson, Texas, where they only had a post office box.

"David and Louise (Robinette) Turpin of Burleson announce the birth of their daughter, Jeanetta Betty Turpin on Tuesday, July 27, 1999. She weighed 6 pounds, 3 ounces and measured 18¼ inches long.

"She is welcomed by her siblings: Jennifer, 11; Joshua, 7; Jessica, 5; Jonathan, 3; Joy, 2; and Julianne, 14 months."

It would be the last birth announcement David and Louise would ever send off to a newspaper.

Several days after Jeanetta's birth, the Turpin family moved into a house at 595 Hill County Road in Rio Vista, Texas. Forty miles south of Fort Worth, the nearest town of Cleburne seven miles away, Rio Vista was well off the beaten track. With a shrinking population of just 744, it was the perfect place to disappear from the world.

A largely agricultural community, Rio Vista produces cotton, hay, peanuts, and dairy cattle. Neighbors often live miles apart, and everybody minds their own business. In the summer, the hot, muggy temperatures can be almost unbearable, and the winters are cold and windy.

Although Rio Vista had its own school system, none of the Turpin children were ever enrolled. They were now totally off the radar.

It was here that David and Louise would brainwash their children into total, unquestioning obedience.

David and Louise created a bubble around their children, controlling every single aspect of their lives. David reigned like a god, introducing a harsh set of rules they must live by or suffer the terrible consequences. With Louise's help, he brainwashed them into fearing the world outside so they would never try to escape. They ordered the children to never tell anyone their names or speak about what happened inside the house, as it would contaminate the family.

"[He had] isolation and control of the environment," explained Rick Ross. "He created an echo chamber, in which only [his] thoughts and [his] ideas [were] dominant. And then you have all of the family reinforcing everything that you say."

Even finding the redbrick house on Hill County Road presented quite a challenge. Route 174 south from Cleburne suddenly turned into a bumpy gravel path, with cows grazing on either side. The new Turpin home was a 2,300-square-foot, single-story ranch house with a double-pitched metal roof and a large barn to the side. The four-bedroom, two-bathroom home fronted a huge thirty-six-acre spread of rural farmland, dotted with mesquite trees. The property featured a producing gas well, for which David Turpin would receive $577.92 a month for mineral rights. It was also a commutable distance to the Lockheed Martin plant in Fort Worth, where David still worked.

Directly opposite the Turpins on Hill County Road lived Ricky Lee and Shelli Vinyard and their two young daughters. When Shelli first saw her new neighbors moving in, she was excited to see children the same age as hers in such a desolate place.

"Out here, there's no one around," Shelli explained. "[I was] looking for some fun myself and then somebody for the kids to play with."

When Shelli walked across the road and knocked on the front door to welcome the Turpins to the neighborhood, there was no answer. She could hear a baby—Jeanetta—crying inside. Eventually, she gave up and went home, wondering what was going on.

"They were extremely mysterious," said her husband, Ricky, who works as a tree cutter. "We tried to talk to them, but they wouldn't answer the door, even though we lived straight across the road."

Eventually, their two daughters—Ashley, then aged ten, and her younger sister, Barbara—saw Jennifer, Joshua, and Jessica outside and tried to talk to them.

"[They] were walking up and down the street," Ashley remembered. "Joshua had a stick in his hand and was poking at rocks on the ground. We live in the country out here, so I was excited to have a group of kids to play with."

The three Turpin kids refused to give their names, cryptically saying the girls would have to pay attention and work it out themselves.

"We had to guess them, basically," said Barbara, "and the kids didn't like that either."

Nonetheless, over the next few weeks, they all became friends, playing together in the Turpins' backyard and around their property. The three Turpin siblings all stayed unusually close to each other.

"We played in the creek that runs by their house," said Ashley, "catching frogs and minnows and throwing rocks—normal kids' stuff. Running around, just being crazy and having fun."

But whenever Ashley asked about their parents or where they went to school, the kids went blank.

"They really didn't talk about their parents or family," said Ashley. "Every time I innocently asked them about their parents, they would sort of shut down."

During the ten years they lived across the road, Ashley rarely saw Louise or David Turpin.

"The mother always dressed modestly," she recalled. "The father had an intimidating presence, but quiet. He never said anything."

Ricky Vinyard was also curious about his new neighbors but not at all surprised they were distant and unfriendly.

"Out here, everybody pretty much keeps to themselves," he observed. "My best friend, that neighbor up there, I didn't know him for the first four years."

Every morning, he'd see David leave for work in his Mustang, and later Louise would head out with some of the kids, driving a large minibus to town and back.

"They'd come in from work," recalled Vinyard. "They'd go get their groceries [but otherwise] they never left the house. Never outdoors."

Ashley only went inside the Turpin house twice, each time entering through the back door.

"There were animal cages and newspapers strewn

about on the floor in piles with feces on it," Ashley remembered. "They had dogs, cats, and goats [and] even though the house smelled of poop . . . I really didn't think anything about it. We lived out in the country, [so] it was no big deal to have animals in your house."

But she was never allowed past the kitchen and dining room area, into the children's bedrooms. And although the Turpin kids were "really friendly," if they ever saw her mother outside, they went silent. They also appeared to be under strict instructions never to walk past the Vinyard house.

"Whenever we would come close to [our] house," said Ashley, "they would turn and start going back toward their property. [They] didn't want to come past our house. We would pretty much just [play] in their yard all the time."

If they ever needed to go past the Vinyards' house, the Turpin kids would take a long, circuitous route to avoid it. They would walk up a hill at the edge of their property before coming down again farther along Hill County Road.

One day, Shelli Vinyard spotted Jennifer and Jessica walking down the road. She came over and introduced herself as Ashley's and Barbara's mom. Then she asked their names.

"And it got weird," Shelli recalled. "The older girl was like, 'Well, if you pay attention to what we say, maybe you can figure out what our names are.' And the younger girl turned around and goes, 'No! Don't! Don't!' She looked scared, like they were going to get in trouble."

The next time Ashley went over to play, Louise answered the door. Apparently, she had found out that Shelli had been asking questions and said the children could no longer come out and play. Then she shut the door.

"I'm just like, 'Wow, I can't play with my friends

anymore,'" remembered Ashley. "We live so far out in the country, and they're the only kids on the whole street that I had to play with. And now I couldn't."

The next day, Ashley came back and knocked on the front door, hoping one of the Turpin children would answer and explain what was going on.

"And I knocked and I knocked and I knocked," she said, "and nobody ever answered."

She peeked through a window and saw baby Jeanetta lying in her playpen, crying.

"Nobody else was there," said Ashley. "She'd be there for hours, all day, all night, unsupervised."

Now living off the grid, Mother and Father's abuse of their seven children escalated. What had started as neglect in Fort Worth turned increasingly violent over the next decade in Rio Vista.

"It started with slapping, hitting, [and] throwing around the room," reported Riverside County deputy district attorney Kevin Beecham. "And it aggravated to belts."

At first, Mother and Father whipped the children with the leather end of David's belt, using the metal buckle if they still didn't behave. Then they began using a wooden paddle or an oar. The offending child would have to drop his or her pants and lie down on the bed. They would then be beaten with the oar on their lower back, buttocks, and the backs of their upper legs.

Years later, their oldest son, Joshua, would describe being beaten with the oar as "the worst of the worst."

If this still didn't work, Mother and Father would use what Joshua called "the switch"—a metal tent stick with fiberglass wrapped around it and metal tips on the end. Both parents carried out the beatings, but Joshua prayed

Mother would do it, as she didn't have Father's strength. These savage beatings often injured the children, who would cry out in pain.

But there was no one to hear them.

Their parents also laid down strict rules for the children to follow, allegedly following the tenets of the Pentecostal religion in which David and Louise had been raised. But there was nothing in any religion that forbade washing and taking showers to keep clean.

"None of the victims were allowed to shower more than once a year," said Riverside County district attorney Mike Hestrin. "One of the reasons for the punishments [was] if the children were found to [have] wash[ed] their hands above the wrist area, they were accused of 'playing in the water' and they would be chained up."

Cult expert Rick Ross said these unnatural punishments were all about David Turpin's need to control his children.

"The father had a kind of philosophy," said Ross, "but it wasn't really about religion at all. The Pentecostal religion had little, if any, meaningful relevance to what he was doing."

Shelli Vinyard recalls noticing how the Turpin siblings' hands were pale white, compared to their thin arms.

"The rest of them were dirty," she said. "[From] the wrist down was the only clean part of them."

Soon after they moved in, David converted the living room into a makeshift schoolroom, with a row of eight school desks. His parents, James and Betty Turpin, who visited Hill County Road several times, said their grandchildren had "very strict homeschooling," learning long scriptures from the Bible by rote. Some of the older ones even memorized the entire book.

The prosecutor said that some of the Turpin children could barely read and write and learned from educational posters with letters of the alphabet and numbers. They also had phonics books, and religious posters with selected teachings were pinned to the wall.

Jennifer, age 29, who only had a third-grade public school education, taught her younger siblings as much as she could, but years later, some of them hadn't got past the first half of the alphabet, according to prosecutors.

The children were so badly fed that their growth became stunted, and they would suffer permanent physical and cognitive damage. There were also questions of whether David and Louise were making them fast.

Sixteen years later, David's brother, Randy, by then the president of Valor Christian College in Columbus, Ohio, would self-publish a book called *21 Days of Prayer and Fasting.*

"Fasting and prayer go hand in hand," Randy wrote. "Fasting is a good way to open our hearts for the Holy Spirit to reveal areas of pride. Recognizing and eliminating pride is a key to entering God's best for your life."

Randy claimed that after three days of fasting, people are no longer hungry and have a heightened awareness of God.

He defined fasting as "voluntarily depriving oneself of physical nourishment in order to accomplish a spiritual purpose . . . putting to death fleshly desires." He also warned how "bodily appetites" lead us away from God.

His book also provided a road map for the three-week fast, along with a journal to be filled in each day.

"Learn how to deal with cravings for food," he advised. "Keep a notepad on hand for this purpose. By making a list of meals and food items you are craving, it is a way to postpone the thought or desire. When you write it down you are telling yourself, 'I can think about this another time.'"

It was around this time that David and Louise started

providing journals for their children, encouraging them to keep daily records of their lives, according to the D.A. However, there is no direct evidence that the children's near-starvation diets were in any way connected with this Pentecostal religious practice or influenced by their uncle.

In November 2000, Louise gave birth to her eighth child, Jordan.

David began dabbling in farming. He bought some cows, chickens, goats, and three enormous pigs, but since the pigs were never fed enough, they terrorized the neighborhood in search of food.

"The pigs were huge—three-hundred pounders," recalled Ricky Vinyard. "And they kept escaping because he refused to feed them."

On numerous occasions after the pigs escaped, Vinyard would cross the road to warn David.

"And I'd beat and beat and beat on the door," he said. "I never could get hold of anybody. These people didn't want any human contact."

One day, a large dumpster appeared in the Turpin front yard, into which they started throwing their trash. Over the next few years, their concerned neighbors watched the rubbish pile higher and higher until it was an overflowing health hazard.

While all their neighbors took care of their properties, 595 Hill County Road was an eyesore.

"They had a pretty good spread out there," said Ricky, "but they didn't do anything with it. They never mowed the lawn. They didn't do anything but huddle up in the house."

Vinyard would often see his neighbor shooting off his gun outside. One day he watched, aghast, as Turpin placed a can in his driveway by the road, walked back to his house, and began firing at it.

"I caught him standing in his driveway with a pistol shooting toward the road," said Vinyard. "It kind of spooked me out."

After Mother ordered her children not to play with Ashley and Barbara, the family went into virtual lockdown. The siblings started sleeping during the day and were only allowed to leave their rooms to use the bathroom and go into the kitchen one at a time to eat. The children were apparently allowed to clean their teeth, although none of them had ever seen a dentist.

"At night . . . every light in the house was on," remembered Ashley, "but all the curtains were drawn shut. That house was silent all day long."

Every night, she could hear the Turpin children playing out back where they couldn't be seen, but over time, they came out less and less.

"They were keeping night hours," said Shelli. "It was completely a ghost town during the day. I was getting concerned at that point. Something's going on over there. Something's not right."

The Vinyards often considered contacting the authorities for suspected abuse, but Ricky always had reservations.

"We discussed it," said Ricky, "and we didn't want to have the repercussions with them. Also, I knew he had a pistol."

8

DL4EVER

In the summer of 2001, four-year-old Joy Turpin was bitten in the face by the family's white-and-black border collie. More than a day passed before David Turpin called 911, and emergency responders rushed her to the emergency room at Cook Children's Medical Center in Fort Worth, where she got stitches. The Turpin dog, which had not been vaccinated for rabies, was taken to a local veterinarian and put down. The incident was reported to the Hill County Sheriff's Office, but no officers were ever sent to 595 Hill County Road to investigate further.

"Nobody," said Hill County chief deputy Rick White, "had anything that led them to believe that there were any concerns."

That Christmas, James and Betty Turpin spent the holidays in Rio Vista with their eight grandchildren. It was the first of two visits they would make over the next several years. Later, they maintained they never saw anything untoward during their stay, and all the children seemed fine.

In a family photo dated January 4, 2002, the Turpin grandparents pose on the living room sofa, flanked by

David and a grinning Louise, with her arm around her mother-in-law. One of their small daughters hovers in a doorway behind them like a ghost.

A few months later, fifteen-year-old Billy Lambert came to visit. His half sister Louise was now pregnant with her ninth child, James. He was impressed by their apparently affluent lifestyle.

"They didn't want for nothing," he later told *Sunday Mirror* reporter Chris Bucktin. "David had a good job in the airplane industry in Texas and was well paid."

The highlight of his visit was his brother-in-law taking him to the Lockheed Martin plant in Fort Worth, where he worked.

"He worked in Air Force One when Bill Clinton was president," said Billy.

Billy liked David, whom he found very generous and who always tried to make him laugh, but during his visit, he observed how strictly David and Louise had trained their children. On family trips to the Fort Worth Stockyards and Six Flags, Billy watched the identically dressed children line up in single file, standing at attention, before they were allowed to board the minibus.

"It was military-like," recalled Billy. "Everything was so regimental . . . and everything they did had its own routine. Any sign of dissent and they would be punished."

Billy also saw the classroom in the living room, where David and Louise supposedly homeschooled their children.

"There was schoolwork there," said Billy. "I did see some books and four or five desks. There were papers, reading tests, math, equations. I didn't watch Louise physically teach them, but there was some evidence of schoolwork there."

During his stay, Billy found all his nieces and nephews remote and standoffish.

"The oldest just seemed like she didn't want to hold a conversation with you," he explained. "She didn't really want to make eye contact. They just didn't seem like they wanted to go out there and play."

It was the last time he would ever be invited to Rio Vista for a family visit.

In early 2003, one of the Turpins' starving pigs escaped and waddled onto Ricky Vinyard's uncle's property, devouring fifty-five pounds of dog food under the carport. The giant pig then charged Ricky's uncle, who fired his pistol into the air to scare it away. His uncle filed a complaint with the Hill County Sheriff's Office, who dispatched a deputy to investigate. The officer interviewed David Turpin outside his house but never went in. After Turpin agreed to replace the dog food, the case was dropped.

In a subsequent report by the Hill County Sheriff's Office, it was noted that Turpin had "penned" the hog after it escaped and would ensure it never got free again.

Soon afterward, one of the Turpins' cows escaped and wandered onto neighbor Nellie Baldwin's property. When she walked over to inform them, no one came to the door.

A few months later, Louise gave birth to her tenth child, Joanna. It was a milestone for the Turpins, who sent photographs of their new baby back to Princeton, along with their annual Christmas card. Allen Robinette took great satisfaction in having so many grandchildren, although he had never met some of them. He would often talk about them to his colleagues in the Mercer County Assessor's Office.

"He was really proud about how large the family was,"

recalled his friend and colleague Verlin Moye. "He spoke to me when they had just had their tenth child, and I told him that I couldn't imagine a family that large. But he mentioned that David made good money, so he was able to have a large family."

After the family moved to Rio Vista, Allen Robinette had only visited them once. It had been during the summer, and he was not used to the withering Texas heat.

"I remember him being impressed with the new surroundings," said Moye, "and being able to see his grandkids. He was a family man, and he cared for them deeply. He loved them."

That was the last time he ever saw Louise, David, and his grandchildren, but they continued to talk regularly on the phone.

Louise frequently sent photographs of her ten children to family members. The children were always smiling and well dressed in matching clothes. Teresa, who hadn't seen her oldest sister for five years, thought her nieces and nephews looked very thin. When she asked her sister about it, Louise explained that David was "lanky" and their children took after him. Teresa accepted her explanation.

"The pictures we got always looked like healthy kids," she explained. "They always had smiles. They were always dressed in the nicest of clothes."

David and Louise often ate out at Applebee's Grill and Bar, a few miles away in Cleburne. They were regulars at several local restaurants, although they always dined alone. Their children stayed home.

"We saw the parents out at Applebee's a couple of times when we would go out on date night," said Shelli Vinyard. "She looked slim in a pair of jeans and a vest. She'd be with her husband but not with the kids."

Louise and David also loved going to Billy Bob's Texas

rodeo show at the Fort Worth Stockyards. Once they posed for a souvenir photo, riding a bull together in full cowboy gear, which they used on the family Christmas card.

That Christmas, Louise and David went on a shopping spree, buying ten expensive new children's bicycles. They lined them up under the carport with the price tags on the handlebars and stickers on the wheels for all the neighbors to see. There they remained, unridden, for years, as the sun bleached all the stickers.

"It was disgusting," said Ricky Vinyard. "There was a lot of money spent on toys that were never used."

Shelli said that even when the children ventured out at night to play, they never touched the bicycles.

"And they just sat and rotted," she remembered. "No one ever played with them."

Louise actually boasted to family members about the top-of-the-line bicycles they had bought their kids as Christmas presents.

"We were led to believe that the kids had all these bikes and nice clothes," said Billy Lambert. "They always said that anything their kids wanted, they had."

In May 2004, a gleaming new Clayton double-wide mobile home—worth $63,000—suddenly appeared on the Turpin property. David Turpin pulled it through a fence and onto his land, parking it 150 yards behind their house. He laid an aboveground water line from the house to the trailer, as well as electric cables with a meter.

Then David and Louise and their ten children moved into the trailer, leaving their house empty. It was now uninhabitable, garbage and feces strewn everywhere.

"You never saw them again," said Ashley. "As I got older, I realized, 'There are a lot of kids over there growing up or half-grown-up. What are they doing?'"

Barbara Vinyard could still hear the younger Turpin children playing in their yard at night. She decided to make one final attempt to befriend them, taking her jump rope across the street and knocking on their trailer door.

The door was opened by a rail-thin girl with long brown hair. She looked as pale as a ghost, staring at the visitor.

"Her eyes just got real wide," Barbara remembered. "She closed the door back in my face."

A few minutes later, the girl emerged from the back of the trailer and approached her.

"[She] looked at me," said Barbara, "and then ran back away into the house, through the back door."

Soon after the move, Louise gave birth to their eleventh child, a baby girl named Jolinda. Once again, Louise sent photos of the newest Turpin baby to family members, saying how blessed she and David were to have so many children.

That summer, James and Betty Turpin returned to Rio Vista for a five-day visit to see their grandchildren. It was a brutally hot day, over a hundred degrees, when they arrived at the Turpin trailer and knocked on the door. There was no answer.

When Ricky and Shelli Vinyard saw the well-dressed elderly couple waiting outside in obvious discomfort, they invited them into their house until David and Louise returned.

"It's blistering hot here in August," said Ricky. "They looked like regular people, and we let them in to use the facilities."

Shelli remembers the Turpin grandparents as being "strange in an uptight way." She became uncomfortable when Betty started asking whether she religiously instructed her children.

"The grandparents came here to use the facilities," she remembered, "and she was like, 'Well, I hope you spend a lot of time with your children, reading and praying and all this hands-on stuff.' I felt like I was being grilled in my own home."

An uncomfortable silence set in. Finally, the senior Turpins stood up, saying they were going to drive around in their car and wait for Louise and David to come home.

A few days later, David and Louise came over to thank the Vinyards for looking after their parents and brought them some cupcakes.

In 2006, David and Louise Turpin's twelfth child was born. They named her Julissa. The proud parents celebrated by setting up a new email address, lessbythedozen@gmail.com, a spoof on the Steve Martin comedy *Cheaper by the Dozen*, which had come out two years earlier. Louise had finally achieved her childhood ambition to have twelve children. She even had a personalized car plate made for their Mustang—DL4EVER.

The Turpins now had twelve kids in just seventeen years—but ten years would pass before they had another.

Soon after Julissa was born, Elizabeth Flores suffered a miscarriage and telephoned her big sister for support.

"Louise [told] me that she had a couple of miscarriages herself," Elizabeth later wrote in her memoir. "'I know how you feel,' she said while crying. 'It's like losing a part of yourself.'"

9

LORD OF THE FLIES

After moving into the trailer, Father built a makeshift cage to imprison any children who dared to break his rules. The large metal cage was seven feet wide by five feet tall and divided in half to accommodate two offenders. It had thick pegboard siding with holes in it, the type usually found in a garage for hanging tools. There was a five-inch gap at the bottom where food could be pushed through.

According to prosecutors, Mother and Father started locking their children in the padlocked cage for days at a time. But before long, Jonathan, now eight, discovered how to escape by lifting the bottom up and crawling out.

To prevent this, Father brought in a dog kennel with a padlock. The three-by-three-foot metal kennel was far too small for the children to stand up in.

Joshua, then a lanky sixteen-year-old, would later tell investigators how he was locked up in the kennel for a day after Mother caught him watching a *Star Wars* video.

A free video-calling service called Skype had recently been introduced, and Louise began making regular Skype calls to her family back east. It was the first time they had ever seen all her children, although Louise would never let them talk to more than two at a time.

"She would bring in one or two," said Teresa, "and then she would send them out and tell them to send down so-and-so. They were friendly, but it was a very weird conversation every time, because they weren't real talkative."

Over the next few years, Louise became increasingly reluctant to let the family talk to the children on Skype. It was as if she didn't want them to see the children.

"It got really strange," said Teresa. "She would just start making up excuses of why she couldn't video chat."

Louise would explain how she and David were too busy looking after all their children, promising to Skype them the following weekend.

"And then it just never happened," said Teresa. "Then seven to eight years passed, and we didn't video chat or anything."

At some point after moving into the trailer, Mother and Father abandoned their children for four years. They found an apartment forty miles south in Benbrook, Texas, taking Julissa and Jolinda with them.

Jennifer and Joshua were put in charge of their eight younger siblings. Every few days, David would arrive at the trailer to drop off frozen food. Louise never visited.

The ten remaining Turpin children had to fend for themselves, a real-life version of William Golding's 1954 novel, *Lord of the Flies*. In the book, a group of British adolescents are stranded on a remote island after their plane crashes. They soon become savages, turning on one another as they try to survive on the tropical island by themselves.

Over the next few years, the children lived in appalling conditions in the trailer, which was overflowing with excrement and rubbish. Under the parents' orders, the children were still forbidden to wash above their wrists. Their pet animals defecated inside, and the smell was often unbearable in the long hot summers. There was also no medical treatment for any of the children if they hurt themselves. Jonathan still has three scars on his head from living in the cramped trailer and bumping into various pieces of furniture.

Although they now lived almost an hour's drive away, Mother and Father still completely controlled their children over the phone. Joshua was ordered to change diapers and Jennifer put in charge of preparing basic meals for her siblings. The two oldest children were also instructed to punish any of their brothers and sisters who broke their parents' rules, by locking them in cages. "Time-outs in the cage is how [Joshua] described it," said Wade Walsvick, a senior investigator for the Riverside County District Attorney's Office. "He said if he didn't do it, he would then be put in the cage."

Cult expert Rick Ross said this is typical family cult behavior.

"The family members spy on each other," he explained. "When you are a child in a family cult, you are raised, from your earliest memory, embedded in this kind of system. And you know nothing else. These children are typically homeschooled. They don't have contact with the outside world, unless it's managed by their father—by their leader. And so the other children are going to monitor you, and they will inform on you."

For more than three years, Joshua and Jennifer were both torn by having to maintain their parents' reign of terror in the trailer. Eventually, they both tried to escape.

During an emotional interview with Investigator Walsvick in 2018, Joshua attempted to explain how he had once tried to confront Mother and Father but became too overwhelmed by fear to continue.

"He wanted to rebel," Walsvick would later testify, "and he tried to tell me about a conversation between his mother and his father where they instilled this fear. He could not finish the conversation."

After composing himself, Joshua told Walsvick, "I chose to take the correct path and try to keep my siblings alive."

Early one morning, Jennifer actually managed to escape from the trailer in a desperate attempt to live outside the family. She ran across neighboring properties, scaling several fences, before doubling back to Hill County Road to summon help.

Shelli Vinyard was taking her daughter Barbara to school when she saw Jennifer running toward her.

"She was coming out of the woods behind me," said Shelli, "which means she would have had to have snuck out of her house."

A neighbor then stopped her pickup truck, and Jennifer climbed inside.

"From what I was told," said Shelli, "she didn't seem to know who the president was."

The terrified girl refused to give her name or age, asking how she could get a job, an apartment, and a car.

The neighbor drove Jennifer into town, where she attempted to get a job. But without a driver's license or any identification, she never stood a chance.

"She had no real prospects," said deputy DA Kevin Beecham. "No socialization whatsoever. So what did she do? She called her mother. And her mother came, picked her up, and took her away."

Ricky Vinyard still remembers the incident, which was the talk of Hill County Road at the time.

"It was terrifying," he said.

   Neither the Hill County Sheriff's Office nor the Texas
Department of Family and Protective Services have any
record of it.
   Sheriff Rodney Watson said the runaway Turpin girl
should certainly have raised red flags at the time.
   "A lot of people will dismiss some things that they
hear as just crazy talk, which is sad," he said in 2018.
"We could have stopped a lot of years of suffering."

At around 1:30 p.m. on Saturday, October 6, 2007, five-
year-old Mikey Vinyard was playing outside his parents'
house, when his father, Ricky, backed up his car. The
little boy suddenly ran out behind him, and Vinyard accidentally hit him. Mikey was rushed to Harris Methodist
Walls Regional Hospital in Cleburne, where he was pronounced dead on arrival.
   The tragedy shocked Rio Vista and made the front
page of the *Cleburne-Times Review*. Even David and
Louise, who happened to be in town at the time, visited
their grieving neighbors.
   "When my son passed away, they actually came over
here and made a condolence call," said Shelli Vinyard.
"I was in bed . . . and didn't get to talk to them, [but] my
husband and kids, I think, talked to them. They would act
a little social, but they wouldn't get real social."

10

"SOW THOSE WILD OATS"

On May 24, 2008, Louise Turpin celebrated her fortieth birthday and had a midlife crisis. She and forty-seven-year-old David now decided to start investigating new religions, including snake-handling and witchcraft. They began drinking alcohol in bars and decided to try an open marriage. The mother of twelve suddenly got a makeover, cutting off her long hair and dyeing it red and wearing heavy makeup.

"Louise had never drunk a beer or smoked a cigarette or done a drug . . . in her whole life," Teresa told *MailOnline* reporter Martin Gould. "Then one day, just as she was turning forty, she called and told me she and David were going to have a drink."

A few hours later, Louise called back.

"She was drunk for the first time in her life," said Teresa. "She was very giggly. I was in shock."

Louise also informed her sisters that she and David no longer went to church, as they were "tired" of it.

"They didn't want to bring their kids up in church," said Elizabeth. "They don't trust church people."

Louise said they were now examining other religions,

including Catholicism, Mormonism, and the Mennonites. She added that they were also practicing witchcraft, collecting Satanic books, and contacting spirits with a Ouija board.

Around this time, the couple also started taking twelve hundred–mile gambling trips to Las Vegas.

"She told me that the older children were helping her take care of the younger children," said Teresa, "so her and David could sow those wild oats that they didn't sow when [they] were younger."

Elizabeth was shocked by Louise's new hedonistic attitude to life.

"She started partying in her forties," she said, "acting like a teenager [and] doing things that normally in our family we don't do."

A few months later, Louise called Teresa to announce that she and David had become swingers and were driving seven hundred miles east to a hotel in Huntsville, Alabama, for a rendezvous with a man they had met on the internet.

"She [said she] was going to sleep with him," said Teresa, "and that David was okay with that. I told her I thought it was a mistake."

When they got to the hotel, David dropped off his wife. He waited in the car as she went up to the room and had sex with the stranger. Louise had the man record them making love, using a video camcorder she had brought with her so David could watch it later. She also posed for provocative photographs in the bathtub, wearing sexy lingerie.

Back in Texas, Louise posted some of the photos on her MySpace page.

"My mom got so mad at Louise," remembered Teresa. "[She] got very, very upset over those pictures. [Louise] said, 'It's our life.'"

According to Elizabeth, Louise detailed how she had sex with the man in the Alabama hotel room, and how he he had been rough with her.

Exactly one year to the day after hooking up with the stranger, they drove back to Huntsville, Alabama, checking into the same hotel as before. On the way there, Louise called Teresa to boast about their latest sexual adventure.

"She thought it was funny that David was taking her back to the exact same hotel room," said Teresa, "so David could sleep with her in the same bed . . . that she had slept with this man in. [It's] even worse and even weirder."

Louise was also becoming obsessed with snakes. She was now attending a snake-handling church, and she started going to the annual rattlesnake roundup festival in Sweetwater, Texas.

"Louise was attracted to that," said Elizabeth. "Women dancing with rattlesnakes around their necks. Snakes give you power."

Louise boasted that she loved eating rattlesnakes. She would skin them before cooking and said they were delicious.

The Turpins were now living the high life, running up thousands of dollars of debt on dozens of credit cards. They spent freely during their gambling trips to Las Vegas and would stay at Caesars Palace. They bought expensive computer games and lavish toys that were never unwrapped. Louise often bragged to her family about their luxurious lifestyle and how David treated himself to a brand-new Mustang every year.

During a two-month period in 2009, Louise and David bought a Ford Econoline van and a Ford Focus, worth almost $30,000, on credit.

"I couldn't understand," wrote Elizabeth, "how they could afford to drink, party, go on vacations, visit amusement parks and gamble."

However, when Elizabeth fell on hard times, Louise was there to protect her younger sister, just as she always had. A year earlier, Elizabeth had caught her own husband, Jonathan Flores, having an affair. He had then walked out of their eleven-year marriage while she was pregnant, moving in with his new girlfriend. Jonathan took their six children, but Elizabeth eventually won custody of them.

Now living in Texas, a desperate Elizabeth called Louise for help before her baby was due. Although it had been months since the sisters had last spoken on the phone, Louise immediately came to her rescue.

"When I had the baby, she came to the hospital," said Elizabeth. "She went every single day to the NICU to visit the baby."

Louise would wait until her little niece was off the feeding tube and hold her. After being discharged from the hospital, Elizabeth was homeless, ending up at a Salvation Army shelter with her new baby. Then Louise stepped in.

"[She] was there for me in my separation and bought me a house," said Elizabeth, "and supported me when my husband wasn't anywhere there for me."

For the next few months, Louise paid all her bills, hiring a lawyer to win back custody of her other children. Every weekend, she would visit Elizabeth at her new home.

"We would go out to eat," Elizabeth recalled. "She would take me shopping for clothes. It was amazing."

On one visit, Louise wanted to bring in her Ouija board, which she kept in the trunk of her car. When Elizabeth refused, saying it was dangerous and evil, her sister laughed. She said that she and David only did it when they were staying in hotels and never in front of their children. She also claimed she had asked the Ouija board if she was going to have a thirteenth baby, and it had said yes.

A couple of times, Louise brought two children along with her, but Elizabeth said she never saw anything to make her suspect any "child endangerment issues," or that they had abandoned their other children alone in the trailer.

After counseling, Elizabeth and Jonathan reunited after a two-and-a-half-year separation, and they are now bringing up their seven children in Tennessee.

In early 2010, David Turpin lost his job at Lockheed Martin. Once again, they were deep in debt, but that didn't stop David from treating himself to a $22,000 Ford Mustang on credit. But their creditors were catching up with them, and it became a common sight to see repo men knocking on the door of the Turpin trailer.

"The repo guys started coming up," remembered Ricky Vinyard. "They put a bounty on them because they bought a van and a Mustang and quit paying for them. They basically stole them because they knew they were already in trouble. They were preparing to skin out."

On April 5, Johnson County Sheriff's deputies arrived at the Hill County Road property, officially serving the Turpins with civil papers. Wells Fargo had foreclosed on the property for nonpayment of mortgage.

A month later, David and Louise Turpin returned to 595 Hill County Road for the first time in years. They loaded their twelve children into the van, taking as many personal possessions as they could. They left all their pet dogs in the house, along with their pigs, goats, and chickens. Then they drove off into the night and never came back.

Because the Turpins were so reclusive, it was some time before their Hill County Road neighbors noticed they were no longer living there.

"One day, they just vanished," said Ashley Vinyard. "We didn't realize it for several weeks, until bill collectors were knocking on our door asking about the Turpins. They had brand-new cars that were being repossessed, and debt collectors were looking for them because they were foreclosing on the property."

One day, Ashley, her father, and a neighbor decided to go into the trailer to see just how their mysterious neighbors had been living for the last ten years.

"We went up there and knocked on the door," said Ricky, "and we could hear the dogs indoors barking. So it was like, 'Man, we've got to let these dogs out.'"

When they opened the door, the Turpins' two pet Chihuahuas ran out and hid under the house.

"They wouldn't come out," said Ricky. "So we went in. The smell was rancid."

All the carpeting had been ripped out, and the floors were covered in feces and urine. The dogs had apparently survived by eating dirty diapers and drinking from the toilets, which were now empty.

As they entered the bedroom, the stench became overpowering. It had been set up like a barracks, with six bunk beds stacked in a row. None of the beds had mattresses, but Ricky noticed ropes tied to some of the headboards.

"At the time," said Ricky, "I didn't think nothing of it."

They ventured into the filthy living room. It looked like it had been used as a makeshift schoolroom, with eight small desks and educational posters tacked on the walls. There was a broken chalkboard. Scattered around the floor were an array of religious pamphlets and books.

"It looked like a cult house," Ashley remembered. "It was kind of scary. Like preparing for Armageddon . . . because the devil [controls] the government. Social media is evil. It's all corrupt."

As they walked through the trailer, they noticed that all the doors, closets, toy chests, and even the refrigerator shared a disturbing feature.

"Everything was padlocked," said Ricky. "When [we saw this] we're like, 'Oh my god. What were they doing?'"

The trio left the stinking trailer to take a look at the house where the Turpins had lived for the first five years. They walked past an abandoned old Ford pickup, which had been used as a dumpster and was overflowing with wiener sausage cans, potted meat, and diapers.

"It had been there so long the bags had withered," said Ricky, "and the trash was actually falling out and the critters were getting in there and eating."

Ashley heard a baby kitten crying inside, which they pulled out and took home with them.

"The dumpster smelled of death," said Ashley. "Who knows what was buried in it."

The back porch door of the redbrick ranch house was wide open, so they walked in. The pungent smell was overwhelming.

"It's knee deep in filth," Ricky recalled. "Dirty diapers piled waist high. There's computers, toys, and trash. The toys are still in the boxes. They've never been opened. They had Mattel toys for the baby and Pirates of the Caribbean stuff, as well as a TV in the mulch. You could see the rats jumping in and out of the stuff."

In the kitchen, they found a dead cat on the stove and a dead dog on the floor, as well as several other animal corpses lying around.

"And once we saw those corpses," said Ricky, "it's like, 'Let's go. Let's get out of here.'"

It took the mortgage company three months to clean up the Turpin property and make it halfway presentable. The trailer was then repossessed by Vanderbilt Mortgage and Finance and eventually removed from the backyard.

When the Hill County Road property was finally put on the market, the real estate agent made prospective buyers sign a "hold harmless agreement" before they could view it, to indemnify the bank if they became sick.

The house was eventually purchased by Nellie Baldwin and her son Billy as rental property. Nellie, seventy-eight, was a neighbor of the Turpins and knew them by sight. She had always wondered what had happened to them.

"The house was in really bad shape," said Billy. "It was just nasty. The flooring in the bathroom was rotted out. There was feces on the floor and a lot of diapers around. We spent about $30,000 on it to get it livable."

His mother, who had been buying rental properties for decades, was shocked when she went in to try to clean it up.

"They had smeared feces on walls," she said. "The living room and every room just had a terrible odor."

After a busy day of cleaning the house, Nellie would pour a couple of gallons of bleach on the floors to make the stench more bearable the next day.

Soon after taking possession, the Baldwins noticed some unusual vents in the master bedroom closet, where some of the Turpin children might have been imprisoned. Billy also found some old Polaroid photographs taken before the Turpins left. One showed a rope tied to the end of a metal bed rail in the children's bedroom. Another captured some children's drawings on a bedroom wall of what appeared to be a pregnant woman.

II

MURRIETA

On June 4, 2010, David and Louise Turpin moved their twelve children to Southern California. Thirteen-year-old Joy Turpin memorialized the event in her journal, writing that they had "crossed into California." One week later, the Turpin family moved into a beautiful new house in Murrieta, sixty-five miles north of San Diego.

Built in 2002, 39550 Saint Honore Drive was a spacious 2,470-square-foot, five-bedroom family home with three bathrooms and a loft. There were two large living rooms downstairs, and Louise and David took the master bedroom upstairs, while their twelve children occupied the other four rooms, none of which faced the street. There was also a beautiful fitted kitchen, strictly off-limits to the children.

Their new house, which they were renting, lay in a trendy Vintage Reserve neighborhood of stucco and tile-roofed homes in Murrieta, Riverside County—midway between San Diego and Los Angeles.

Louise told her family that they were moving to Southern California for David's work in the aerospace industry—but in reality, he had been unemployed for the

last few months. Their sole income was the monthly
royalties—$577.92—that David still received for the
mineral rights to the well on his now-foreclosed Rio Vista
property. The payments would continue until March 2011,
when the royalty company realized he no longer owned
the well.

Although they survived on credit, Louise painted a totally different picture of their life in sunny California to
her family. She boasted about their new annual pass to
Disneyland for the whole family and personalized car
plates reading DSLAND.

"They were the most perfect family I had ever seen,"
said Teresa. "She always had nice homes and nice cars. I
even said, 'Oh, Louise got the fairy tale. She's been married to her husband since she was sixteen. They've got all
this money.'"

Over the next several years, Teresa and Billy made
plans to visit Louise in California and get to know their
nieces and nephews, many of whom they had never met,
but the trips were always canceled at the last minute.

"[Louise] would always come up with an excuse," explained Teresa. "That she had had a bad dream about the
flight [or] one of the kids got sick."

Once, she invented an elaborate story about how one of
their daughters had gotten into trouble, and she and David
were too "aggravated" to host a family visit.

Over the next few months, Louise started distancing
the children even further from her family, now only allowing her siblings to speak to their nieces and nephews one
at a time. Teresa worried that the children's homeschooling did not allow them to go out and meet new friends
and learn social mores. They always seemed uncomfortable and difficult to talk to on Skype.

"I was always concerned that they weren't going to be
socially developed," she said.

Louise began making excuses as to why she and the kids could no longer Skype weekly. She would explain how busy she was caring for so many children. Finally, she broke off all contact.

In fact, homeschooling was virtually nonexistent. Louise would teach the children using phonics books for a few days before losing interest. Years would pass between lessons. To ensure that the Riverside County authorities never questioned why none of the Turpin children attended school, David Turpin officially opened the City Day School, designating himself as principal. On October 1, 2010, he filed the California Department of Education's Private School Affidavit, under penalty of perjury. He wrote that his City Day School at 39550 Saint Honore Drive, Murrieta, had eight students—from the second to the eleventh grade. Under the religious column, he wrote that it would not be affiliated with any denomination.

"This is a private full-time school," read the signed affidavit, "that offers instruction in several branches of study required to be taught in public schools of the state that offers this instruction in English and that keeps attendance records."

From then on, Mother and Father were officially homeschooling their children, with no legal obligation to send them to state school. Because the City Day School had more than six students, it was subject to an annual inspection by the local fire marshal to check that it was up to safety and fire standards.

But for the next seven years that David Turpin ran his private school, there would never be one inspection.

After the move to Murrieta, Louise and David's abuse of their children escalated. Instead of being a fresh start, the Murrieta house became their new prison. Mother and Father confined their children to different rooms and began tying them to furniture with ropes as punishment. But David and Louise treated the older siblings far better than the younger ones, perhaps trying to breed resentment and jealousy among the children; Joshua got a camera, and Jennifer was even allowed to have a smartphone. Mother and Father felt confident that their cultlike control was strong enough that the siblings would never try to use these limited luxuries to escape.

When Louise reentered her children's lives after her radicalizing "midlife crisis," prosecutors say she seemed to take over as the dominant physical abuser. She always seemed angry, and all the children were terrified of her. She only allowed them out of their rooms to use the restroom, eat, and brush their teeth. All exercise was banned.

Jordan would later tell police that in Murrieta, they would spend twenty hours a day in their rooms, waking up at around 11:00 p.m. and then going back to bed at 3:00 a.m. The rest of the time, they slept.

They were fed minimal food on a schedule and had no access to televisions, radios, or newspapers, leaving them with zero understanding of the outside world. But Mother and Father still encouraged them to keep daily journals.

"The abuse and severe neglect intensified over time," said Riverside County DA Mike Hestrin, "and intensified as they moved to California."

Soon after moving into the house, things began to go missing from Mother and Father's bedroom. The adolescent girls, starting to explore their burgeoning womanhood, took to borrowing Mother's makeup and trying on her clothes. When they were caught, Father decided to chain up all twelve children and teach them a lesson. Years later, Jennifer told an investigator that her father had said putting everyone in chains was the only way to stop it. But Mother objected, saying they should only chain up the culprits, and she knew exactly who they were.

Mother labeled the children she suspected of stealing, or being disrespectful, as "suspects." And Jonathan Turpin, then fifteen, was the chief one. It began after he took Joshua's camera and hid it in the trash can as a joke, but it was accidentally thrown out. He was also a "suspect" for stealing food.

As punishment, his parents hog-tied him, but he was able to bite through the ropes to escape. Then they started chaining him to the bed rail with padlocks. When Jonathan managed to slide the chains off, Mother and Father started using thicker, heavier chains. Over the next six and a half years, Jonathan would be chained up for weeks or even months at a time, causing permanent spinal damage.

Mother could turn violent at any perceived slight. She disciplined her daughters by giving them a "pitching," literally throwing them around the room by the hair. She would also choke them, hit their heads hard with her fists, or slap them in the face.

On one occasion, Mother threw Joanna down a flight of stairs. She had caught the seven-year-old in her room and became incensed. She started yelling and throwing the little girl around the bedroom. Then she pushed her down the steps. Joanna lay at the bottom of the staircase, dizzy and crying in pain. Her neck and back hurt for days afterward, but she never received any medical attention.

A few days after David Turpin opened the City Day School, Louise posted a photograph on Facebook of her and David posing in front of the Cinderella Castle at Disneyland. David, with a goofy grin, wears a Disneyland T-shirt that reads, HAPPIEST MEMORIES ARE HERE. A smiling Louise has a red T-shirt featuring Grumpy, one of the seven dwarfs. Presumably their children were back in Murrieta.

The middle-aged couple had recently opened a Facebook account in the name "louise-davidturpin." Their profile picture showed them lovingly gazing in each other's eyes. David and Louise began to post a series of carefully posed photographs, using their kids as models for what seemed to be their big new project—conquering Hollywood with a hit reality TV series.

The Turpin parents were both avid fans of TLC's reality show *Kate Plus 8,* which followed the lives of Kate and Jon Gosselin and their sextuplets and twins. It was one of the most popular shows on cable TV at the time, becoming even more so after the Gosselins' contentious divorce. Making it big as reality TV stars, Louise had already informed her family, was one of the main reasons for their move back to California.

"Louise used to say how they would be perfect for TV," Billy Lambert told *Sunday Mirror* journalist Chris Bucktin, "and would often mention they would be bigger than the reality show *Kate Plus 8.*"

The Turpins trained their children to walk in a line with military precision, in the order of their ages, with Father at the front and Mother at the back. All the girls wore identical dresses, and all three boys had their father's Captain Kangaroo haircut. And perhaps looking to upstage the Gosselins' octet even further, forty-two-year-old Louise was now trying to have another baby.

In late 2010, David and Louise posted a picture on Facebook, showing them with their twelve smiling children.

They were all standing in a field, dressed in bright red shirts and holding their homeschool graduation diplomas, which Louise had ordered online. They all look painfully thin, except for David, who had a paunch.

A friend on Facebook asked if the children were all theirs.

"Yes all 12 are our children," David-Louise Turpin replied, "and we are very proud of them."

In January 2011, David Turpin found a job as a computer engineer in San Diego with leading aerospace and defense contractor Northrop Grumman. The highly specialized job at the Goldentop Road plant paid $143,000 a year and required a forty-four-mile commute each way on Interstate 15. He was working the 2:00 p.m. to 10:00 p.m. shift, so traffic would be light at that time of day. It would also suit his family's nocturnal lifestyle.

Soon after the Turpins moved into 39550 Saint Honore Drive, their new neighbor, Mike Clifford Jr., who lived directly opposite with his parents, began to notice strange things happening across the road between midnight and 3:00 a.m.

"We'd see them marching backward and forward [along the corridor] military-style," Clifford, aged thirty, remembered. "The lights would be on and the window blinds would be open. They were odd. There was something definitely not right."

His sixty-year-old father, Mike Clifford Sr., also saw the children marching in circles for hours all through the night.

"I'd come home," he said, "and anywhere [between] twelve thirty to three in the morning, there's kids marching between those two rooms up there. It looked like they were doing a loop . . . just like they were in the military."

Clifford Jr. said he only saw any of the children during the day once, when two of the Turpin sisters came out to check the mail.

"I tried to say hi," he said, "but they looked straight ahead, went to the mailbox, and went back [into the house] like zombies, completely monotone. No personality or social skills or anything."

The Cliffords thought the children were either disabled or autistic and that was the reason why they stayed inside the house.

Over the next few months, the Cliffords also noticed their mysterious new neighbors driving in their van late at night.

"They would load up their kids at about one in the morning," said Mike Sr. "The garage doors would just pop open, and half a dozen kids would get into the van, and then they'd drive off."

This happened every couple of weeks during the three years the Turpins lived in Murrieta. The Cliffords often wondered if they were "selling the kids, sexually or whatever," but they never contacted the authorities—another missed opportunity for the children to be rescued.

When the Turpins first moved in, some of the neighborhood kids would go over to their house and ask them to play, but when there was no answer, they gave up.

"I always thought they were some kind of a cult," said Mike Jr., "or that the parents were psychotic. What kind of parents don't let their kids play outside?"

On Thursday, April 28, 2011, David Turpin's grandmother Bertha Green died in Gary, West Virginia, at the age of ninety-five. The sixteen-year-old child bride of the Reverend King Turpin Jr. had remarried Hobart Green and then outlived him by twenty-one years.

Although David Turpin did not attend her funeral, he did post a tribute online in the Engle-Shook Funeral Home & Crematory guestbook.

"Grandma meant love to me," he wrote. "I always knew she loved all of her grandchildren. We will miss her, but she has finally reached her reward. My family and I are sorry that we could [not] be there today. David, Louise, Jennifer, Joshua, Jessica, Jonathan, Joy, Julianne, Jeanetta, Jordan, James, Joanna, Jolinda, Julissa."

12

"SO MANY LITTLE
BRIGHT-EYED DREAMERS"

In early July, the Reverend Randy Turpin, now an ordained bishop in the Church of God, flew to California with his wife, Kerry, and their five children to visit his brother. The highlight of the trip was the two families going to Disneyland together.

Randy's second-eldest daughter, Miranda Joy Turpin, was the same age as her twenty-year-old cousin Jennifer. They had last seen each other in the mid-1990s, when they were six. The only other Turpin cousin she had met was Joshua, so she was particularly excited to meet her other ten cousins. Miranda, an apprentice horse trainer who lived in Maine, memorialized her visit to the Turpins on her blog called Dream Chaser.

"We went to California," she wrote, "to visit my Uncle and Aunt and their 12 kids. We have always lived a continent apart and considering the size of both our families . . . we were never able to visit each other."

Upon entering the Turpin house, Miranda wept tears of joy.

"We walked into their home and I saw my 12 beautiful cousins for the first time," she wrote. "It was truly a dream come true. I cried, and it takes a lot for me to cry."

She described her cousins as the "sweetest" and "most well behaved" kids she'd ever met, saying she was "blessed" to be part of their family. Their trip to Disneyland, she said, was "unforgettable."

"It was amazing to be in 'The Place Where Dreams Come True' with so many bright-eyed dreamers," wrote Miranda.

During her visit, Miranda bonded with her cousin Jennifer, saying she was "the sweetest, most pure-hearted person" she'd ever met. Jennifer told her that she dreamed of being a professional singer one day. Miranda thought she had a naturally beautiful voice and an "amazingly creative imagination."

"Jennifer told me that she has written 141 songs," wrote Miranda, "[which] she sings regularly to her younger brothers and sisters."

Jennifer allowed her cousin to video record some of her favorites, which Miranda later posted on her blog, along with a photograph of the two of them. She wrote that she was "truly blown away" by her cousin's voice and her "great lyrics."

Jennifer then sang what she described as her "worst" song. It was called "Have Faith," and Miranda found the lyrics so "uplifting and catchy" that she caught herself humming it in the shower the next morning. Jennifer told her that she was the first person outside her immediate family who had ever heard her sing.

"She only ever sings for her brothers and sisters," wrote Miranda, "and never has a chance to sing outside the house. Because of this, there is an amazing purity to her songs and her heart shines through so brightly because she is not trying to impress anyone and she has no reason to fear what others think of her."

During the visit, Jennifer even wrote a song for her cousin she entitled "Miranda."

"It's number 142!" Jennifer told her.

At the end of their visit, Miranda told Jennifer about her Dream Chaser blog, asking permission to post the videos of her songs on it.

"Her face just lit up," recalled Miranda.

A couple of weeks later, Randy Turpin posted a family photograph on Facebook of the whole Turpin family posing in front of the Disneyland Cinderella Castle.

"A memory that I will hold on to for the rest of my life," read his caption. "It was so great being with you guys."

Exactly one week later, David and Louise Turpin filed for chapter 7 bankruptcy, owing almost a quarter of a million dollars to scores of creditors. They hired a bankruptcy lawyer named Ivan Trahan, going to his nearby Temecula office for a consultation and paying him $2,700 for his services.

Louise proudly told the attorney about their twelve children and how they loved Disneyland. He thought they were "a very nice couple."

Chapter 7 is designed for debtors who are unable to pay off their existing debts. As joint debtors, Louise and David Turpin would have to undergo a "means test" to determine if they were eligible to have their debts wiped out so they could start afresh. They would also be allowed to keep cars and other property, considered exempt under U.S. bankruptcy law.

According to their filing, the Turpins owed $240,564 to sixty-three creditors and had assets of just $149,492. They claimed $100,696 in exemptions, including David's 401(k)s from Lockheed Martin and Northrop Grumman; their three Ford vehicles; Louise's clothing and jewelry;

and $500 worth of DVDs. They listed their respective oc-
cupations as engineer and homemaker and their depen-
dents as three sons and nine daughters.

The eighty-three-page bankruptcy document reveals
just how profligate the Turpins' spending had become.

Their debts included $88,421 on twenty-seven credit
cards; $1,102 to AT&T on unpaid cell phone bills; $396 for
pest control; and $140 to Bob's Rural Garbage for trash
service back in Texas. The Turpins also owed $45,283 for
their repossessed double-wide trailer and $40,079 for
their foreclosed farm in Rio Vista.

They listed their monthly expenses as $8,938, in-
cluding $2,500 for food, $1,300 for transportation, and
$350 for clothing.

As part of the requirements for chapter 7 bankruptcy,
Louise and David Turpin both completed an online course
in personal financial management. Both passed.

A few weeks later, the Turpins signed an agreement
with the United States bankruptcy court, agreeing to re-
pay the Ford Motor Company $424.31 a month over the
next four years, putting David's 2010 Ford Mustang up as
collateral. All their other debts would be erased.

In a reaffirmation agreement, Louise Turpin explained
how they had now cut their monthly expenses by more
than $2,000.

"We started using coupons," she wrote, under penalty of perjury, "and being more conservative in our
spending."

At the end of October, David Turpin officially registered
his City Day School with the California Department of
Education for a second year. Then he and Louise drove to
Las Vegas to renew their wedding vows after twenty-six
years of marriage.

Despite their claims of "cutting back," the couple
spared no expense for the occasion. The bride got a complete makeover, chopping off her long brunette locks to
go blonde and buying a new wedding dress. Unlike the old-
fashioned, conservative dress Louise had worn in 1985,
this time she selected a far sexier one. It was a spaghetti-
strap gown, fitted over the bodice with lightly gathered
layers of fabric over the long full skirt. David purchased a
classic tuxedo with a wing-collar shirt and black bow tie.

For the ceremony, Louise had booked the Hound Dog
Package at A Elvis Chapel, right off the Las Vegas strip.
For $325, they would receive a package that included the
chapel's resident Elvis impersonator, Kent Ripley, singing three of the King's songs; a limousine to and from
their hotel; a copy of Elvis and Priscilla's original license
certificate; and a video and fifteen digital prints, taken by
a professional photographer during the service.

David and Louise arrived in Las Vegas on Friday,
October 28, checking into the Circus Circus Hotel, Casino & Theme Park. They had left their twelve children
back in Murrieta.

On Saturday morning, they put on their wedding outfits in their hotel room before getting into their stretch
limo for the five-minute drive to A Elvis Chapel. When
they arrived, they were met at the door by Kent Ripley,
wearing a gold lamé jacket and sporting a young Elvis
haircut and sideburns. It would be the first of three Turpin
marriage renewals that fifty-two-year-old Ripley would
conduct over the next four years.

"They came in by themselves," he remembered. "David's haircut was just unusual, and listening to him talk,
I had the impression he was a rocket scientist. So I was
thinking . . . he's a very smart guy."

Before the ceremony, the Turpins told him about their
twelve children, whom they homeschooled.

"I joked to myself," said Ripley, "'This is the Brady Bunch times two.' I mean, that's a big family."

The ceremony took place at the altar beneath fake Grecian columns. The happy couple held hands and gazed lovingly into each other's eyes as they renewed their vows. As Ripley sang "Love Me Tender" to a prere- corded music track, an emotional David gave Louise a ring. They then slow-danced to "Can't Help Falling in Love," followed by a rousing rendition of "Viva Las Vegas" to finish the ceremony.

That night, the newly remarried couple went out drinking and gambling. Louise later told her sister Eliza- beth that she got so drunk she could barely stand up. Fi- nally, at around 6:00 Sunday morning, David told her to stop gambling, as she was losing so heavily, and a drunken Louise furiously lashed out at him.

"She . . . made a scene," wrote Elizabeth. "That's when the security guards got involved . . . and literally escorted her out."

Six weeks later, the United States bankruptcy court offi- cially discharged David and Louise Turpin, writing off almost all their debts and leaving them with a clean fi- nancial slate.

13

"LOUISE TURPIN IS A SUPER MOM"

That Christmas, James and Betty Turpin flew to Murrieta to visit their grandchildren. Years later, the Turpin grandparents, then both in their late seventies, would describe the children as healthy and well adjusted.

"They were joyous to see us," said their grandfather. "The kids were fine. They weren't skinny or nothing. They were 'sweetie' this and 'sweetie' that to each other."

The grandparents stayed at the Turpins' home and were delighted to see their son David's "happy family." During their visit, they ate out at restaurants and went to Disneyland, where they were impressed to see how well organized the children were.

At each Disneyland attraction, the dozen Turpin children would automatically line up in a row—the oldest to the youngest—with David at one end and Louise at the other. Heads turned as they all waited in line, wearing their identical Disney-themed outfits.

"That shows you," their grandmother later explained, "how particular they were about keeping the kids together and organized."

Betty Turpin would later say that her son David had

told her how God had called on them to have so many
children.

"I feel they were model Christians," said Betty.

Though the trips to Disneyland were a rare chance for the
twelve Turpin siblings to interact with the real world,
child trauma expert and licensed family therapist Allison
Davis Maxon said it would have been frightening for
them to suddenly leave their world of extreme deprivation and find themselves in Disneyland.

"It's just so foreign to them," said the clinician based
in Orange County, California. "For them, it would be like
literally being on a different planet. This is not the world
they have known for their entire existence . . . for them, it
must have been really terrifying."

She explained how confusing and disorientating it
would be for them to see other happy families enjoying
themselves, while they lived in a world of total darkness
and suffering.

"I would use the analogy," said Maxon, "that you and
I live in the world of light. We live on the earth's surface,
and they live a mile underground. No sunlight. No joy. No
laughter. No birds. Nothing. What do they think about
when they come to the surface? They would think, *That's
a world I don't know. I see all these people talking,
laughing, playing, and enjoying life and each other. I
see these things, but I don't know what they are. I can't
even wrap my mind around what they are, because my
world is a mile underground. There is only suffering and
pain. And it's dark, and it hurts.*"

Years of torture and near starvation had stunted the
siblings' cognitive and physiological development, making the whole experience hard for them to take in.

"They may really struggle," she said, "being in a

world that feels overstimulating to them. All those sights, sounds, smells, and sensations you and I can filter could feel overwhelming and overstimulating due to the intense and chronic deprivation they experienced. The average adult brain can easily filter out most unnecessary sensory input. When the human brain is chronically under-stimulated and deprived of age-appropriate sensory input for most of its growing-up years, developmental mile-stones are not reached and can result in delays in social, cognitive, and emotional development."

It must have been devastating, Maxon said, when Mother and Father brought them back to their prison after their day out. Returning to their subterranean world of pain, near starvation, and torture, it must have felt ee-rily familiar and terrifying at the same time.

"Their world was like a living hell," she said.

Over the next few weeks, David and Louise posted photo-graphs from their trip to Disneyland on Facebook, elicit-ing responses from their online friends. One shows the children posing outside the cinema in Main Street USA, the gateway to Disneyland. In another, David, in a black Darth Vader T-shirt, Louise, and their children are all pictured smiling with Princess Jasmine. Another shows them happily posing with Eeyore from Winnie-the-Pooh.

"Blown away," posted Louise's cousin Tricia Andreas-sen, "how I have my hands full with just one and look at you!"

"Louise Turpin is a super mom," wrote her aunt Eilene Harris. "I really couldn't have handled it. KEPT BUSY FROM MORNING UNTIL NIGHT WITH MY FOUR."

In June 2012, David Turpin opened a Twitter account, @DavidTurpin, describing himself as a family man.

Several months later, he retweeted a tweet from the

Disneyland Resort, the only account he was following. "Hooray! It's Mickey's Birthday today! Watch all the wonderful greetings that came in and keep the celebration going! #HappyBirthdayMickey."

Three months later, Mercer County chief deputy assessor Allen "Wayne" Robinette retired after twenty-six years in his job. The *Princeton Times* ran a story on his retirement in the September 30 edition with the headline FA-MILIAR FACE: ROBINETTE LEAVES POST AT COURTHOUSE TO SPEND TIME WITH FAMILY.

Alongside the story was a photograph of the sixty-four-year-old former West Virginia Democrat of the Year, in his courthouse office with an American flag behind him.

In the article, Robinette said he was hoping to fulfill a lifelong dream and visit his daughter Louise.

"I'm planning to travel out to California to see my daughter and her family," he said. "She has twelve children."

Robinette said he wanted to retrace the 1940s trip his father had made to California by steam train.

"[My dad] bragged on that trip the rest of his life," said Robinette. "Getting to do the same thing would be pretty fun. But if I can't do it by train, I'll fly."

A few weeks later, he bought a plane ticket to California and flew there without telling Louise. But when he called her from San Diego International Airport, Louise refused to give him her address and told him to go home.

"[Dad] was so hurt," said Elizabeth Flores. "He'd got the ticket and he was going to surprise her, and she told him not to come."

On October 17, to celebrate David's fifty-first birthday, the couple posted a photograph on their joint Facebook

account of their recent Las Vegas wedding renewal, posing with Elvis impersonator Kent Ripley.

"Love this pic!" wrote their former obstetrician Donna
Cox Kolar, who'd become a close friend when the Turpins
lived in Fort Worth. "Happy B Day."

"Thank you!" replied David-Louise Turpin. "I miss
you and your office staff very much. Haven't had much
desire to reproduce without you around."

"Thanks. We miss you and yours too," Dr. Kolar wrote.

On March 9, 2013, Louise Turpin's grandmother died at
the age of eighty-eight. Mary Louise Taylor Smothers,
known to the family as Mamaw, had divorced John Taylor more than thirty years earlier after catching him raping Louise. She had since remarried, remaining in
Princeton, West Virginia, where she was still a regular at
the Church of God.

John Taylor was among the mourners at the open-casket
funeral. It was the first family gathering he had attended in
many years.

"When he walked into the funeral home and I saw
him, I got the shakes," said his niece Tricia Andreassen,
who says he molested her when she was seven years old.
"And within three minutes of seeing him walk in the
room, I walked out in fear. I couldn't even be in the same
room as him."

After the funeral, Tricia—Louise, Elizabeth, and Teresa's first cousin—started talking regularly with Elizabeth about the abuse they had all suffered as children. It
would be the basis of their close enduring friendship as
they tried to break the secret cycle of abuse in their
family that had gone on for generations.

"None of us girls, sisters or cousins had talked about
it," wrote Elizabeth in her book, *Sisters of Secrets.* "Tricia

told me she had told her parents and my Mamaw. But the
only advice they had given her was, 'Just stay away from
him.'"

That spring, all the Turpin children fell ill, most likely
due to their unhygienic living conditions. Mother and
Father briefly relented and took them all to Loma Linda
University Medical Center for treatment, something they
apparently had never done before. The children were
carefully briefed about what to tell the doctors, so no one
would suspect there was anything untoward going on at
home. After they were treated, Mother and Father brought
the siblings back to their filthy house to recover.

On June 27, Louise secretly opened a new Facebook account under her maiden name, Louise Robinette. In her
profile picture, the forty-five-year-old mother of twelve
looks more like a teenager, with heavy makeup and a
seductive smile. She wears a figure-hugging tank top
over a low-buttoned floral shirt. Her new Facebook page
was the polar opposite of the family-friendly David-
Louise Turpin account, leading to speculation that she was
using it to meet men. It seemed that she was no longer
satisfied by the swinging lifestyle and wanted to strike
out on her own.

    "I don't know if David knew about it," said her sister
Elizabeth, who was shocked when she stumbled across it.
"Apparently, it was used for a dating site [and] she used . . .
her maiden name."

14

VIVA LAS VEGAS

On Monday, September 2, David and Louise Turpin returned to Las Vegas for their second wedding renewal ceremony to mark their twenty-eighth anniversary. This time, they brought all twelve children with them.

Several weeks earlier, Louise had purchased A Elvis Chapel's top-of-the-line "Viva Las Vegas" concert package for $1,195 plus taxes. She had paid a nonrefundable $400 deposit, guaranteeing $60 tips each for the Elvis impersonator, limo driver, and photographer. And she requested that Kent Ripley officiate as he had done before.

"The second time they came, they had the big package," recalled Kent Ripley. "Like a wedding followed by a concert. I got to sing and dance with the kids."

Now a redhead, Louise had bought a revealing new white satin wedding gown. It boasted a wrapped strapless long-line bodice and a long-flowing split skirt with frothy tulle truffles. David would wear a tux and bow tie, sporting a pink floral buttonhole.

Their nine daughters, now aged between eight and twenty-five, received identical homemade pink tartan dresses, white tights, and white Mary Jane shoes. Their three sons, aged between nine and twenty-one, would wear loose-fitting dark suits, white shirts, and red ties. In the official A Elvis Chapel video, all the siblings look painfully thin in their ill-fitting outfits, which are hanging off them.

Before leaving Murrieta, Mother and Father had given the children their first bath in months and washed their hair. Then they drove to Las Vegas, staying in a pair of adjoining rooms at Circus Circus.

The next morning, they all rode in style to A Elvis Chapel in a stretch limousine. As soon as they arrived, Louise told Ripley something that unsettled him.

"Louise made a comment that stuck in my mind," he explained. "She [said that] she's been following my career. And it was odd because she mentioned a couple of events that I did, not necessarily weddings."

Louise had closely researched him online, mentioning several corporate events Ripley had performed outside the chapel.

"She followed me, as in Kent Ripley," he said. "What I found unusual is the fact that she's got twelve kids and has time to watch my career." Though her fixation struck him as odd, he brushed it off. "Sometimes we need outlets, things to do in our lives to relax."

The dozen identically dressed Turpin siblings entered the building in single file. David and his three sons headed into the chapel, while the nine girls lined up at the back entrance, Louise bringing up the rear.

In their own twisted way, Louise and David may have viewed the A Elvis Chapel wedding video as a pitch for their potential reality TV show, as the children all seemed well rehearsed, knowing exactly where to stand in relation to each other.

"We are live in Las Vegas," announced Ripley in his best Elvis impression. As a prerecorded backing track began playing, Ripley, in his gold Elvis lamé jacket, started singing "Love Me Tender."

Louise and her nine smiling daughters then walked into the chapel, stopping for photographs along the way. "Elvis," singing into a classic RCA microphone, took the blushing bride's hand and walked her down the aisle, where David waited at the altar.

In the pews to the left of the altar sat the girls, with the boys to the right. Nine-year-old James held a small white pillow with two gold rings on it.

"Ladies and gentlemen, put your hands together for Ma and Daddy," "Elvis" announced as all the children applauded. "David and Louise. Twenty-eight years of happiness, love, and laughter are being celebrated today. Because today we get to celebrate your love."

Ripley asked Louise to give her white flowers to one of her daughters and hold her husband's hands so the wedding ceremony could begin.

"David and Louise," he began, "the two of you . . . made promises to each other, to honor, to cherish and to protect. To share your hopes, to share your dreams. We are celebrating today . . . because you have kept the promises for twenty-eight years."

As his children applauded, David teared up with emotion and Ripley handed him a tissue to wipe his eyes. Then Mother and Father solemnly exchanged vows, pledging to be each other's "best friend" and "soul mate" forever.

He then beckoned the ring bearer, James, up on stage, telling him to stand by his parents.

"David, it's time to take the ring for your wife," said Ripley solemnly, "and place it on her ring finger."

As they swapped vows, Father had all the children laughing at his impromptu Elvis impression, repeating the word *baby* numerous times, using the King's inflections.

"Now, Louise," continued Ripley. "You take the ring

from your king—and I mean King David. I'm going to ask you to slip it on his ring finger."

As David placed the ring on his bride's finger, dabbing his eyes with a tissue, one of his daughters can be heard off camera shouting, "Don't step on my foot!"

The Elvis impersonator had the happy couple join hands and repeat their vows together. "David and Louise," he continued, "we know that the two of you share a very special love. A bond that goes beyond everything."

Ripley sent "dear brother James" back to his seat, giving an Elvis signature hip swivel to the children's applause.

"Live from Las Vegas," he declared, "I now pronounce the two of you . . . still will be husband and wife. David, you may now kiss your beautiful wife."

David and Louise shared a long, slow kiss, and the Elvis concert began.

Ripley sang "All Shook Up," gyrating his hips Elvis-style on the small circular stage. Then he launched into "Burning Love," having the Turpin children sing the chorus "Just a hunk, a hunk of burning love," one at a time into the microphone.

Next, the three youngest Turpin daughters—Joanna, Jolinda, and Julissa—took the stage to dance "Hound Dog" with him, then he summoned Julianne, Jeanetta, and Jordan to the stage for a hip-swiveling rendition of "Teddy Bear." At the end of the song, he asked their names, saying it was nice to meet them.

Although the smiling children enthusiastically joined Ripley onstage for the performance, there was something hollow about them. It was as if they had no idea how to respond to all the attention.

Ripley then beckoned "Mom and Dad" up to the stage, handing them each a pair of sunglasses. He asked them to look into each other's eyes and see a "beautiful future" in front of them.

As their smiling children looked on, David promised never to leave Louise at "Heartbreak Hotel or any hotel," be cruel to each other, or step on their blue suede shoes. At Ripley's prompting, David self-consciously raised up his left hand, awkwardly swiveling it Elvis-style, as he promised to always be Louise's "hunk of burning love."

"It's Daddy!" shouted Ripley enthusiastically, shaking David's hand to the children's wild applause.

Then they slow-danced to the "Hawaiian Wedding Song," as David openly wept with emotion.

As they left the stage, Ripley told David to take as many of those "happy towels" as he needed to wipe his eyes.

Later, he invited the boys onstage for a medley of Elvis songs. During "Jailhouse Rock," he encouraged a rail-thin Jonathan—whom Ripley mistakenly called James—to awkwardly dance the twist in his baggy suit.

Towering over his sons and looking uncomfortable, Father did his best to join in as they danced to "A Little Less Conversation."

For the finale, Ripley brought everyone onstage for "Can't Help Falling in Love." As their parents slow-danced, staring into each other's eyes, their dazed-looking kids surrounded them. They all looked completely overwhelmed and exhausted from Ripley's electric performance.

"God bless each and every one of you," said Ripley. "Thank you for allowing me to be a part of your memories. Now we're going to have fun with this one."

To the strains of "Viva Las Vegas," "Elvis" led everyone in a conga line around the chapel, the youngest child at the front and David at the back. Then they returned to the stage for a final photo opportunity, waving goodbye to the camera.

"Ladies and gentlemen," said Ripley, "I wish you the

very best until we meet again. God bless you, and Elvis has left the building."

After the ceremony, Kent Ripley asked David and Louise how they coped with so many children. During their conversation, they seemed to be attentive parents, expressing excitement about an upcoming trip to Disneyland.

"I asked them questions about where they go," he remembered. "I mean, how do you transport twelve kids? They used a big van . . . a bus. Well, he works seven days a week, and she takes care of the kids. That was the impression."

Though all the children looked very thin, Ripley thought it was because they were "so active" as a family.

"They went here, they went there," he explained, "so when you're active you seem to stay a little thinner than heavier. That was my thoughts. I don't know if kids are healthy or not. I'm an entertainer."

Later, he would ponder if the younger Turpin children even knew who Elvis was.

Two weeks later, David and Louise posted their official wedding renewal video on Facebook, as well as some photographs of them and the children with "Elvis."

"I watched your wedding video," commented one Facebook friend. "It was great. Your children are so well behaved. I am so proud of you Louise and David. You have a great family."

15

PERRIS

That Thanksgiving, according to Jordan, David summoned her into the television room upstairs. All her siblings were in their rooms, and Louise was out of the house. He beckoned her over to the recliner he was sitting on, and when she got close, he pulled her pants down.

"I didn't like that," Jordan told him, and she pulled her pants up. Ignoring her, he pulled them back down and lifted her onto his lap. But before he could go any further, they heard Louise arrive home and come up the stairs. Jordan jumped off his lap and pulled her pants up just before she walked into the room.

Later, David ordered her never to tell anybody what had happened.

Over the next several years, David would continue his inappropriate advances on his underage daughter.

"Forcible kissing," she later told an investigator. "He would try and force kisses on my mouth."

In April 2014, Mother caught fourteen-year-old Jeanetta playing with her Barbie doll and ordered her to stand in the corner of the upstairs bathroom as punishment. After a couple of hours, Jeanetta became "light-headed and dizzy." She was unable to stand and felt a tingling in her fingers. When Jeanetta shouted that she felt sick, Louise was on the phone and ignored her. Jeanetta then asked her sister Joanna to tell Mother she wasn't feeling well, and Jeanetta got into trouble for interrupting the phone call.

Finally, Jeanetta collapsed on the bathroom floor. When she came to, she was covered in blood, with a fractured chin and broken teeth. She still felt woozy and did not know what had happened.

When Louise finished her phone call, she came upstairs to find Jeanetta in terrible pain. It was another hour before she took her to Loma Linda University Medical Center, instructing Jeanetta to say she had slipped on a wet bathroom floor. At the hospital, doctors took an x-ray and found the teenager had suffered a hairline fracture to her jaw. She was treated and told to come back for a checkup in a couple of days. But she never did.

One month later, David and Louise bought a brand-new four-bedroom, three-bathroom house in Perris, California, for $350,000. Despite having multiple discharged bankruptcies on their record, they still arranged a thirty-year mortgage for $344,446 from the Federal Housing Administration.

A few days after signing the mortgage, the Turpin family moved to 160 Muir Woods Road, a ranch-style family home in a new development called the Sequoia at Monument Park. They left the Saint Honore Drive house in such a deplorable state that it had to be fumigated.

Their new home was just north of Murrieta and still in Riverside County, adding only a few minutes onto David's daily commute to Northrop Grumman. The brown, tile-roofed, stucco house, sporting an entryway and garage, was a model home in the new development, full of trimmed lawns and landscaped gardens.

Perris—pronounced like Paris, France—is a bedroom community halfway between Los Angeles and San Diego. With a mostly Hispanic population of around seventy-six thousand, the cost of living in Perris was far lower than Murrieta, and the poverty rate was almost 25 percent, one of the highest in Riverside County.

Perris is best known as a world-class sky-diving center, where well-heeled parachutists gather to try to break records. During free falls, skydivers enjoy perfect views of Monument Park, about a mile away from the town's luxurious private airport.

"This is one of the premier skydiving centers in the world," said the manager of Skydive Perris, Dan Brodsky-Chenfeld. "We do 150,000 jumps every year, and people come from all over the world."

But Mother and Father would never let their children leave their new home to watch the adventurous skydivers falling from the skies. Their beautiful new home would become yet another prison for their twelve children and fall into rack and ruin.

Once they moved to Perris, Louise's violent abuse knew no bounds. With David working long hours at Northrop Grumman, Louise was now solely in charge of punishing the children. She would slap them around and beat them for the slightest infringement of her rules, regularly chaining up "suspects" for long periods of time as punishment for stealing food and other perceived offenses. And she always made sure the heavy metal chains were bound tightly around their wrists so they couldn't wriggle out, leading to heavy bruising.

Mother encouraged her favorites—Jennifer, Joshua, Julianne, and Jeanetta—to spy on their siblings, handing out gifts and other incentives as payment, possibly in an attempt to foster distrust and drive the children apart. These "hall monitors," as she called them, were the only ones allowed out of the house to accompany Mother on shopping trips and other chores.

They also guarded the kitchen around the clock to stop their hungry siblings from stealing food or sneaking into Mother's bedroom. Later, Jordan would refer to the quartet as "their real children," as they were treated far better than the others. Joshua watched television with his parents, and Jennifer even had social media accounts on her cell phone before it was taken away after she downloaded an app Mother didn't approve of.

Like they had in Murrieta, David and Louise forced their children to live a nocturnal existence, yet another method of control.

"They would go to sleep at four or five in the morning [and] sleep all day," Riverside County district attorney Mike Hestrin would later explain. "When the rest of the world is up and active, they're sleeping. Then they would get up and do whatever activities they were going to do throughout the night."

Again, Mother and Father confined their kids in different parts of the house. The younger sisters—Jordan, Julissa, Joanna, and Jolinda—shared one bedroom. The middle sisters—Julianne, Jeanetta, Joy, and Jessica—shared a second. Eventually, Jeanetta would sleep out in the hallway. The third bedroom, at the other side of the house, was shared by Jennifer, Joshua, Jonathan, and James. Louise and David had the master bedroom.

Each bedroom had two sets of bunk beds. There were padlocks on many of the beds so a "suspect" could be chained up as punishment.

None of the siblings were allowed to leave their bedrooms without Mother's or Father's permission. The only other rooms in the house they were allowed in were the bathroom and kitchen / dining room area, when it was their turn to eat.

The siblings' schedule depended on what shift Father happened to be working at Northrop Grumman. It was dark when they woke up and dark when they went to bed.

Though exercise was strictly forbidden, Jordan would walk back and forth in her bedroom for hours at a time, trying to strengthen her unused muscles. She told police that she had to be careful not to get caught, as she was supposed to be sitting down. When she wasn't pacing in her room, Jordan played with her Barbie dolls and wrote songs and stories in her journal.

"She told me she had problems with her back," said Riverside County Sheriff's Department deputy Manuel Campos. "When she would wake up, her head felt weird. She described it as *oozing* and *vibrating*."

The only times all the siblings socialized with one another was when Mother and Father were both out of the house. Then they could sneak out of their rooms and hang out. There was Wi-Fi and a landline in the new house, but by then, they were too terrified of Mother and Father—and the overwhelming, overstimulating world outside—to ever try to escape.

The siblings were fed lunch and dinner during their waking hours. Eventually, this was combined into a single meal, as they were not up long enough to eat two. Under Mother's direction, mealtimes had developed into a strange, elaborate ritual.

All meals were prepared by Jennifer, who, after getting Mother's permission, called her siblings down one at a time in strict order. They would eat standing up by the kitchen counter, drinking water out of the faucet. Every meal consisted of either a peanut butter sandwich, a baloney sandwich, or a burrito and chips. After they finished eating, they returned to their bedroom, and Jennifer would wait until Mother signaled that the next sibling could come and eat.

While their children starved, Mother and Father feasted on pizza, Jersey Mike's, and hearty Mexican food. They brought in mouthwatering pumpkin and apple pies, leaving them on the counter as their starving children watched the pies turn moldy and eventually get thrown away.

The siblings were still only allowed one bath a year and were filthy, never changing their soiled clothes or getting clean bedclothes. While they were chained up, oftentimes the children soiled themselves.

Strangely, David and Louise still encouraged them to keep daily journals and even brought in two Maltese dogs as pets, who they fed far better than their children.

"What was going on in their minds?" asked forensic psychiatrist Dr. Michael Stone, wondering at the Turpin parents' motives. "That they didn't allow them to bathe or use the toilet so they would stink. And why is it that they themselves didn't mind the odor? This is something very strange that is close to the edge of madness."

The idea of parents only allowing their children to have one bath a year on special occasions like Mother's Day, Dr. Stone said, was a special kind of torture.

"It's almost like psychotic," he said. "These [people] are crazy and yet they seem not to be crazy. He's finished college and has a good job. It's as if they have some sort of paranoid, weird philosophy."

Dr. Stone posited that they had initially based their methods off certain passages in the Bible before rejecting their Pentecostal roots to explore more obscure religions once they'd solidified complete control over their children.

"Little by little, you might discover," he explained, "that

they had a very bizarre reason for not letting the kids [wash or be hygienic]. As if they were doing God's work in some fashion."

Soon after moving to Perris, Louise became pregnant with her thirteenth child. She announced the news on Facebook, beside an old picture of the family at Disneyland.

"In 9 months we will have a new little one to add," read the caption.

That summer, Allen Robinette was diagnosed with dementia, and Elizabeth Flores moved to Princeton, West Virginia, to take care of him. Since his retirement two years earlier, and Louise's refusal to allow him to see his grandchildren, his health had declined rapidly. The once portly man had lost a huge amount of weight and was wasting away.

"It was sad," said his friend Verlin Moye.

By the time Elizabeth arrived from Cleveland, Tennessee, her sixty-five-year-old father was unable to look after himself. She was granted power of attorney and began selling off his possessions, including his valuable autograph and model car collections and NASCAR memorabilia.

Over the next eighteen months, Elizabeth sold his home and auctioned off everything he owned. Then Louise accused her sister of misappropriating their dying father's money.

"She called [our family] bashing me," wrote Elizabeth in her book, *Sisters of Secrets,* "and saying she knew I was stealing Daddy's money, which I was not. It was so hurtful."

According to Elizabeth, their bedridden father would often ask to speak to Louise on the phone, but she would not take his calls. She also refused to give her new address to any family member, a clear sign of her increasing paranoia and mental instability.

In October, David officially registered his new Sandcastle Day School with the California Department of Education. He signed an affidavit that the private nonreligious school had eight pupils, once again listing himself as the principal.

There would be little to no homeschooling in Perris for the children, who, with the exception of Jennifer and Joshua, were still at the kindergarten level. Jolinda, now eleven, had worked her way up to the letter *I*.

On the rare occasions Mother did teach her curriculum, she could become violent.

"If they didn't do straight lines or stay within lines," said lead investigator Thomas Salisbury of the Riverside County Sheriff's Office, "Mother would pull their hair and throw them across the room."

Before long, Mother stopped giving lessons entirely, leaving the children in educational limbo.

However, inexplicably, she did enroll Joshua, now twenty-two, in a music course at the nearby Mt. San Jacinto College in Menifee. Over the next three years, he would also take courses in algebra, English fundamentals, public speaking, freshman composition, and guitar. Amazingly, he was an honor student, taking up to fifteen credits a semester and earning As in many of his classes.

Each day, Louise would drive her rail-thin son, who had thick black glasses and his father's bangs, seven and a half miles to the college. She would escort him across campus from the parking lot to his classroom and then wait outside in the hallway. When the lesson had finished, she would walk him back to the car for the drive home.

Angie Parra, who was in Joshua's class, described the tall, painfully thin student, who wore the same clothes each day, as a "sweet" but "odd introvert" who kept to himself.

"I could see sadness in his face," she recalled. "His eyes . . . he never wanted to make eye contact with anyone."

At one class potluck, Parra watched Joshua scarf down as much food as he could as if he were starving.

"[He was] famished," she said. "It was very apparent that he was hungry and he stood by the table and didn't sit down. He literally ate plate after plate after plate [of food]."

Another student in his music class, Marci Dunker, remembers Joshua was always "hiding" from his classmates, never hanging around after class to socialize.

"As soon as the class was over, he'd leave," said Dunker, "and didn't really talk to anybody. I tried to say hi a couple of times, but all he did was look. I just thought it was strange."

Classmate Josh Boldt thought he could be suffering from a serious vitamin deficiency.

"He was really pale, and it was kind of odd," said Boldt. "Really malnutrition-like looking. And on top of that, he always had this depressive aura about him and really kept to himself. He was very enclosed."

Soon after moving to Muir Wood Road, Louise placed statues of Mickey and Minnie Mouse in the yard. Now two of their three vehicles had personalized Disney license plates, and one had a pink Disney car seat. There was also a small stone rattlesnake by the front door, which Louise had bought years earlier at a rattlesnake festival.

Their new neighbors would occasionally see David and Louise or a couple of their older children collecting mail at the communal mailbox across from their house, but no one suspected their new neighbors had twelve children, with another on the way.

"[David] looked like Moe of *The Three Stooges* or Jim Carrey in *Dumb and Dumber*," said Ricardo Ross, whose garden backs up to the Turpins' house. Ross said that he never saw more than one of two Turpin kids at a time, and they only came out if the road was deserted.

"When I went to the mailbox," he said, "they'd wait till I came back in, and that's [when they came out]. They weren't very friendly. They avoided everybody."

Soon after the Turpins arrived, Salynn Simon, who lived across the street, and her small daughter knocked on their front door to sell them Girl Scout cookies. Louise snapped up eight or nine boxes.

"Louise would never open the door all the way," she said, "but I would see children jumping up and down behind her because they were so excited for the cookies. I just thought they were really private."

Another neighbor, Kimberly Milligan, said she rarely saw the children and had no idea there were twelve living there. One night, she saw one of the older Turpin boys rummaging for food in a neighbor's trash can and wondered why.

"I thought they were isolated," said Milligan. "Stand-offish . . . not in a mean way, just 'don't bother me.' I'm in my land, [and] I'm not going to pay attention to you [so] you don't pay attention to me."

Throughout her pregnancy, Louise posted photographs on Facebook, proudly showing off her growing belly. In her final trimester, the forty-seven-year-old expectant mother posted a sideways shot of herself next to a large white crib, wearing a bright pink Mickey Mouse maternity T-shirt that read, EMBRACE YOUR BUMP.

In early 2015, Louise gave birth to her thirteenth child, a baby girl they named Janna. It was their first baby in more than a decade, and some family members questioned it.

"There's many years between the two last ones," said her sister Elizabeth. "And when the family asked about that, [Louise] said, 'I don't know. I just couldn't get pregnant during those years.'"

Over the next few months, Louise sent picture after picture of her new red-haired baby to her and David's families. She and David brought their new baby to Disneyland for photo opportunities. The new mother even donned a low-cut Snow White outfit to pose with her chubby baby and posted it on Facebook.

When Teresa asked Louise to send photographs of her other nieces and nephews, she demurred.

"She told me, 'It's hard to get them all together,'" Teresa recalled. "There was always an excuse."

On March 27, 2015, John Taylor had a party to celebrate his ninety-first birthday. As he stood in his kitchen by his birthday cake in the shape of a cross, with the words HAPPY 91ST BIRTHDAY DAD iced on it, his daughter, Phyllis, and last surviving son, James, sang "Happy Birthday" to him.

"Yeah, light that candle," said Louise's mother. "It's a beautiful cake, isn't it?"

Then James lit a single candle, and it took three attempts for the aging Taylor patriarch, who still had a full head of white hair, to blow it out.

t was in Perris that fifteen-year-old Jordan Turpin decided to finally escape the ruthless tyranny of her parents.
She was fed up with the violence and degradation she'd
endured all her life and wanted to break free. It would
take her two years of careful planning. She knew there
would be dire consequences if Mother and Father ever
found out.

16

"MAY YOU BE BLESSED WITH MORE CHILDREN"

In the fall of 2015, Monument Park was hit by a plague o
mosquitoes after a torrential rainstorm flooded the reten
tion basins surrounding the new development. The mos
quito problem became so bad that residents, fearing the
West Nile virus that had recently caused three deaths in
Riverside County, kept their children indoors.

In early October, more than seventy-five people de
scended on Perris City Hall to demand action. Angry
neighbors told horror stories about the mosquito infesta
tion, comparing it to a Stephen King novel. Josh
Tiedeman-Bell, the Monument Park neighborhood watch
program president, said that he had come home from va
cation to find his walls covered in mosquitoes.

"It's hell living here," he said. "We are miserable."

Perris resident Sheri Fink, sixty-two, who lived just a
couple of blocks away from the Turpins, displayed her
horribly bitten right leg at the meeting, announcing that
she was a "prisoner" in her own home.

Soon after the meeting, a delegation from the neigh
borhood watch arrived at 160 Muir Wood Road, ordering
David Turpin to cut his overgrown grass and weeds in

their front yard, declaring it a mosquito magnet. At nine o'clock that night, neighbor Wendy Martinez saw four of the Turpin kids outside their house. They were on their knees digging up weeds and laying new turf, while their mother watched from the door.

"They were just rolling on the grass," remembered Martinez, who noticed how pale and thin they looked. "Their mother was in the archway, and I said hi. There was no movement . . . like they were told not to talk to anybody. The mom, no movement at all."

Inside, the Turpin house was filthy and stank of human waste. Mother and Father had ordered that all the blinds in the siblings' bedrooms be closed all the time so neighbors could not see the children chained up inside. They were prohibited from opening the blinds or looking out of the windows.

Jonathan, now twenty-two and five foot eight, was chained up far more often than his other siblings. He would later tell investigators how torturous it was being chained up to the rails of his upper bunk bed for several months at a time, especially during one of the frequent lice outbreaks in the house.

"It was hard for him to sleep," said lead investigator Thomas Salisbury, "and hard for him to move, roll over, or itch the lice on his head or scratch his back."

Mother was becoming increasingly violent with the younger children. Jolinda would tell investigators how Mother would lose her temper and hit Jolinda on the head with her knuckles so hard that her mind went blank.

Once, the frail little girl took some clothing and lip gloss out of Mother's room and secretly dressed up in it.

Later, when Jolinda sneaked backed in to return the
items, she was caught and dropped some of the makeup
under the bed. Furious, Mother grabbed her by the hair
and neck, forcing her underneath the bed to retrieve it and
holding her there. There were lots of spiders underneath
the bed, and Jolinda was bitten badly, but Mother
wouldn't let her up until she found the makeup.

That Halloween, Mother and Father brought their thirteen children back to Las Vegas for their third wedding
renewal ceremony at A Elvis Chapel to mark their thirtieth
anniversary. This time, they brought some guests with
them.

Louise had now dyed her hair brown and had a fashionable new cut. She wore a strapless white satin dress
with a peaked bodice and carried a bouquet of mixed
flowers. David wore his usual tuxedo. Their daughters
who had been allowed to bathe for the first time in many
months, wore the exact same purple plaid dresses, with
white tights and white shoes. Their scrubbed-up sons wore
the same suits with purple ties.

"It was like, 'The kids are back,'" said Kent Ripley who
once again officiated as Elvis. "A fun family. Did the
clothes fit? No. They had got a little older and taller
maybe. I don't think they looked any worse. I don't think
they looked any better."

Louise had ordered the "Hound Dog" package, a
slightly more modest affair than the previous one.

As Ripley began singing "Love Me Tender" to start
the ceremony, baby Janna could be heard crying. The Elvis impersonator then escorted the smiling bride down
the aisle past two young couples sitting at the back, who
have never been identified.

"They weren't family," said Ripley. "Sometimes

people just stroll in, but under the circumstances, I don't think [David and Louise] would have wanted them to be there, if they didn't know them."

At the altar, overcome with emotion, David started weeping. But before he could pull a tissue out of his trouser pocket, Ripley had one waiting.

"Have a happy towel, David," he quipped.

As David composed himself, Ripley continued. "Today, we celebrate the moment you truly have waited for . . . thirty years of memories. And if you take today's date and flip it around to thirteen. Yeah . . . there they are."

Ripley pointed toward the thirteen Turpin children in the audience, their new chubby baby, wearing a bright pink chiffon dress, being held by one of her older sisters.

"Your love has grown," Ripley observed, "and so has your family."

David and Louise exchanged marital vows once again as their new baby wailed. Then Ripley summoned ring bearer James to the altar with their wedding rings, which they duly exchanged before slow-dancing to "Can't Help Falling in Love."

Ripley concluded the ceremony by declaring, "It is Halloween Day, the year 2015, and by the power that's vested in me by the suit that I wear today . . . the two of you still will be husband and wife. Together forever, and may you be blessed with more children."

After David French-kissed Louise to rapturous applause, Ripley invited all the Turpin children to the stage to participate in the finale song, "Wear My Ring Around Your Neck."

As their parents snapped their fingers in time with the music in front of the stage, their children posed for photographs. Ripley counted them out one by one.

"It's lucky thirteen," he joked. "But wait nine more months [and] come back."

In December, the Monument Park neighborhood watch held a Christmas decorating contest, with gift cards for the winners. Louise and David decided to enter. Late one night, a couple of the older girls set up a Nativity scene in their front yard, placing a Nativity star in a window and a Santa Claus in a sleigh by the garage.

While they were working, Kimberly Milligan and her son Robert came out of their house across the road to see what their mysterious neighbors were up to.

When she complimented them on their Christmas decorations, the girls went blank.

"They just froze," remembered Kimberly. "They were scared to death, [and] you could tell they were terrified."

When Kimberly said she was just being friendly, the girls turned and went back inside.

A few days later, the Turpins took their four eldest children to Monument Park for the official judging of the Christmas decoration contest. Louise seemed unusually friendly, chatting to her neighbor Salynn Simon about growing up in West Virginia and family life in Texas. She also talked about how proud she was to have thirteen children, whose first names all began with the letter *J*. She introduced Joshua, then twenty-three, and Simon was stunned by how young he looked.

"I told him, 'You look so young,'" she said. "'You look fifteen.'"

Joshua merely smiled and nodded. Louise explained how David always took the older children to Las Vegas for their twenty-first birthdays, and they were continually asked for ID because they looked so young.

Watch program president Josh Tiedeman-Bell saw the

four Turpin children standing in line behind their parents, waiting for hot chocolate and cookies.

"Everybody was super-skinny," he said. "Not athletic skinny [but] malnourished skinny. Their haircuts were all like their dad's. They looked like pilgrims."

To celebrate Christmas, Mother and Father unchained their children, allowing everyone more time out of their bedrooms. For the next week or two, the children would receive what they called "good treatment."

"Mother would buy them good and expensive gifts," said Riverside County deputy Manuel Campos, "[and] try and feed them better. She would spend more time with them and play games with them."

The "good treatment" could last anywhere between two days to two weeks. Then they would chain up the "suspects" again, and life in the house would continue as usual.

The holidays provided an all-too-brief reprieve from the horrendous living conditions the children endured for the rest of the year.

On Thursday, February 18, 2016, Phyllis Robinette died at Princeton Community Hospital at the age of sixty-six. A few days earlier, she had been rushed into hospital with a viral infection and put on life support. Her two youngest daughters, Elizabeth and Teresa, and son Billy all drove from Tennessee to be with her. Over the last few years, Elizabeth had finally forgiven her mother for allowing Papaw to molest her as a little child.

"I always felt like Mommy did her best," wrote Elizabeth. "Even when she let Papaw molest us for money. She needed money to feed us, pay the bills."

On her deathbed, Phyllis asked to Skype Louise so she could say goodbye to her thirteen grandchildren.

"My mom's last request on her deathbed," said Elizabeth, "was to talk to the kids and see them on Skype. [Louise] wouldn't even answer the phone."

"I think she harbored a lot of resentment toward Mommy," said Teresa. "I think she resented the whole family because they kept the secret [of abuse]."

A few hours after their mother was taken off life support, Louise finally called, launching into a vitriolic attack on her siblings.

"She was saying strange stuff," said Elizabeth, "like, 'Mommy didn't love you like she did us. She [doesn't] want you at the funeral.'"

Louise refused to attend her mother's funeral the following Monday, saying that she had a prearranged trip to Las Vegas. But her grandfather John Taylor did attend after agreeing to pay for the service as none of the other family members could afford it.

Just shy of his ninety-second birthday, Papaw walked into the Cravens-Shires Funeral Home in Bluefield, where Phyllis's body lay in an open casket. He went straight over to his granddaughter Elizabeth, assuring her everything was taken care of.

"And he wanted to know," said Elizabeth, "if I'd come over later and give him a tight hug."

17

THINGS 1 TO 13

In early 2016, Jennifer Turpin secretly lent Jordan her cell phone so she could go online and surf the internet. The fifteen-year-old was watching Justin Bieber music videos when Joshua caught her. He reported her to Mother, who flew into a rage.

"Do you want to die?" Mother yelled, grabbing Jordan by the throat and starting to choke her.

When Jordan said she didn't, Mother screamed, "Yes, you do! Yes, you do! You want to die and go to hell!"

When Louise finally released Jordan, her neck was sore for the next two days.

After the choking incident, the teenager considered calling Child Protective Services, which she had somehow found out about. She sneaked out of the house for the first time by herself to summon help. But when she saw Mother's car approaching, she rushed back inside and up to her room.

That April, David and Louise posted a carefully staged photograph of the family outside near the Skydive Perris headquarters. All their children are wearing jeans and red Dr. Seuss T-shirts, numbered Thing 1 to Thing 13, in order of their ages. Their parents also have Dr. Seuss T-shirts, but no visible numbers. Although gamely smiling, all the siblings look emaciated, except baby Janna.

Nine months earlier, the hit TV reality show *19 Kids and Counting* had been canceled after seven years. The TLC cable show followed the lives of devout Baptists Jim Bob and Michelle Duggar, from Tontitown, Arkansas, and their nineteen children—nine girls and ten boys. Like the Turpins, every one of them had a Christian name starting with the letter *J* and were homeschooled.

Louise Turpin was a big fan of the show, which had averaged 2.3 million viewers a week. Now Louise and David saw a void in the reality show market and perhaps thought they could take advantage of it with their thirteen children, telling relatives they were trying for more kids.

On May 12, they updated their Facebook cover photo to a shot of their recent Halloween wedding renewal and posted several others of their smiling children at the ceremony. They also posted a photograph of baby Janna visiting Santa Claus, and of their front yard Christmas decorations, which had been finally removed in late February.

Four days later, Allen Robinette died at the age of sixty-seven at his daughter Elizabeth's home in Cleveland, Tennessee. It was just three months after his ex-wife, Phyllis, had passed away.

Once again, Louise shunned her dying father, refusing to respond to a stream of urgent texts, voice mails, and private Facebook messages from Elizabeth, who'd cared for him in his final days.

"She wouldn't answer me," said Elizabeth. "She knew Daddy wanted to talk to the kids on Skype, and she didn't want to have to tell him no."

John Taylor, Louise's grandfather, was a handsome war hero when he returned to Princeton in 1944, ready to make his fortune.

(Courtesy of the Mercer County Historical Society)

JOHN THOMAS TAYLOR, T/5, U.S. Army, 3rd Armored Div., Expert TSMG, 1st Class Gunner. Silver Star, 5 Bronze Stars, Good Conduct Medal, Purple Heart, Belgian Forragere, American Theater Ribbon, European African Middle Eastern Ribbon, WWII Victory Medal, Combat Infantry Badge.

The Princeton Church of God, where David Turpin first set eyes on Louise Robinette during prayers.

(Courtesy of John Glatt)

David Turpin's yearbook photo from his freshman year at Virginia Tech, typical of the late 1970s, shows no hint of the obsessively controlling man he would become. He graduated with honors, but frequently returned to Princeton to visit his then-underage girlfriend, Louise.

(Courtesy of John Glatt)

In this photo from the 1984 Princeton High School yearbook, Louise Turpin smiles for what would be her last school picture—an image that shows an innocence that is absent in later photos. She eloped with David a few months later and would never graduate. She was sixteen years old. *(Courtesy of John Glatt)*

In early 1990, David and Louise moved into this spacious house at 3225 Roddy Drive in Fort Worth, Texas, with their two-year-old daughter, Jennifer. *(Courtesy of John Glatt)*

David and Louise loved going to Billy Bob's rodeo in the Fort Worth Stockyards. *(Courtesy of John Glatt)*

It was at their new house at 595 Hill County Road in Rio Vista, Texas, that David and Louise started abusing their children as they shut themselves off from the world. Their next-door neighbors, the Vinyard family, eventually gave up trying to befriend the Turpin family. They had no idea of the horrors that were going on behind closed doors. *(Courtesy of John Glatt)*

In June 2010, fleeing from creditors, David and Louise moved their twelve children to Murietta, California, where the torture and abuse escalated.

(Courtesy of John Glatt)

David and Louise forced the children to sleep during the day and stay up all night. Neighbors would see the twelve children marching back and forth for hours in the upstairs hallway.

(Courtesy of John Glatt)

David and Louise loved taking their children out for photo opportunities, which they would then post on Facebook to portray themselves as the perfect family.

(Courtesy of Facebook)

In 2014, the Turpins moved into a model home in a prestigious new development in scenic Perris, California, an up-and-coming bedroom community halfway between Los Angeles and San Diego.

(Courtesy of John Glatt)

The Turpins pose with Mickey Mouse at Disneyland.

(Courtesy of Facebook)

David and Louise and their twelve children pose with Princess Jasmine during one of their trips to Disneyland. According to child-trauma expert Allison Davis Maxon, it must have been terrifying for the children to suddenly leave their dark world of deprivation.

(Courtesy of Facebook)

David and Louise sang and danced with "Elvis" at all their wedding renewals, while their "dazed-looking" children watched *(Courtesy of A Elvis Chapel)*

David and Louise share a romantic slow dance at one of their three wedding renewals in Las Vegas.

(Courtesy of A Elvis Chapel)

In 2013, Louise opened a new Facebook account under her maiden name, prompting speculation that she was seeking sex online.

(Courtesy of Facebook Court)

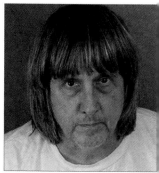

David Turpin's mugshot, taken hours after his arrest in January 2018. *(Courtesy of the Riverside County Sheriff's Department)*

Riverside County District Attorney Mike Hestrin shocked the media when he shared the details of the Turpin children's abuse at his press conference, just days after Jordan's heroic escape.

(Courtesy of David McNew/Getty Images)

Louise seems to be smirking in her mugshot.

(Courtesy of the Riverside County Sheriff's Department)

Scores of well-wishers signed this card of support for the Turpin children, which was left outside 160 Muir Woods Road.

(Courtesy of John Glatt)

David Turpin at his arraignment at the Riverside Hall of Justice.

(Courtesy of Mike Blake / Getty Images)

David's two public defenders, David Macher and Allison Lowe.

(Courtesy of John Glatt)

Louise shares a joke with her defense attorney, Jeff Moore.

(Courtesy of Digital First Media / The Riverside Press Enterprise / Getty Images)

Louise's sister, Elizabeth Flores, and her cousin, Tricia Andreassen, attended a court hearing in March 2018, along with *Dr. Oz Show* crime correspondent Melissa Moore. *(Courtesy of John Glatt)*

Louise also refused to attend her father's funeral, saying it was too short notice. It led to a huge fight with Elizabeth, during which Louise demanded some of her father's personal items.

Furious, Louise sent her in-laws, Betty and Jim Turpin, who did come to the funeral, to confront Elizabeth at the hotel where they were all staying.

"I told them exactly how I felt," wrote Elizabeth. "She wouldn't get anything after the way she treated my parents."

Mercer County clerk Verlin Moye, who was a pallbearer at Allen's funeral, was surprised that neither Louise nor her children attended.

"They were not there," he said. "There were a couple of daughters that lived in Tennessee and their children, but none of his California family."

In their absence, Elizabeth made sure that the recent photograph of his thirteen grandkids wearing their Dr. Seuss T-shirts was placed in Allen's casket.

A few weeks later, David and Louise brought Joshua and several of his older siblings to Mt. San Jacinto College to watch a guitar ensemble perform. The Turpins occupied almost half a row of seats near the stage, dressed identically in blue shirts and tan pants.

"They all seemed well behaved," Mt. San Jacinto student Joe Chermak told the Associated Press. "They were all in uniforms, so at first I thought it was a group of kids coming from another school."

Then, during the performance, the Turpins suddenly all stood up and walked out of the auditorium.

"They left abruptly in the middle of the show," said Chermak. "You could tell from their [arms] they were really skinny and pale."

Joshua, now twenty-four, puzzled his younger classmates. They wondered why his mother still escorted him to class, waiting outside to take him home.

Now in his sixth semester at Mt. San Jacinto College, Joshua was an A student, constantly on the president's honor roll. In his last report for spring 2016, Joshua maintained a 3.93 grade point average, although he never earned a degree.

"[He] talked to himself," said Seraphim Faith (not her real name), who took an a cappella class with him. "He was mentally disturbed. During class, he would get up and just go stand in the hall."

Seraphim later told *Radar Online* that Joshua smelled and his hair looked like he had just gotten out of bed. She once confronted Louise Turpin after he complained to her about not knowing anyone and asked if they could be friends.

One night after class, Seraphim accompanied Joshua out into the parking lot, where his mother was waiting by their van.

"He asked her," said Seraphim. "'Mom, I met this girl, and she doesn't have any friends either. Can we be friends?'"

Louise looked the girl up and down and asked her name.

"I told her my name, and she told him, 'Sure, sure, whatever,'" said Seraphim. "They got in a large van and left. Never showed up again."

That was the last time Joshua ever set foot in Mt. San Jacinto College.

In late 2016, the Reverend Randy Turpin self-published *21 Days of Prayer and Fasting*. The book, which provides a guide to the spiritual enrichment of fasting, credited Jim and Betty Turpin as his "personal mentors in prayer."

In his book, David's brother said that fasting and prayer go hand in hand.

"With prayer we lay hold of the heavenly," he wrote. "With fasting we cast aside the earthly. When we are fasting, we are not fasting *for* ourselves. We are totally *removing* ourselves from the picture. Fasting is not me-centered."

Though there was still no proof of a correlation between the Pentecostal principle and the Turpin children's near starvation, the idea was chilling. Leaving their children at home hungry, Mother and Father would often eat out at one of their favorite Perris restaurants.

"Louise was in here every other day," said Matthew Padilla, who worked at Leonardi's Pizza inside the WinCo supermarket. "Sometimes with her husband. She would order a slice of pepperoni, or a chicken club sandwich with no tomato. We . . . would chat. She was normal, if maybe a bit reserved."

Louise often took two of her oldest daughters shopping with her at Walmart on North Perris Boulevard before stopping off at Taco Bell across the mall for a Burrito Supreme. On one occasion, she was photographed with Joshua and her new baby, eating doughnuts at Krispy Kreme.

Mother was also a regular at Los Primos Mexican Food in Perris Crossing, where she would buy one or two dishes of take-out food.

"She was pleasant enough," remembered Primos' manager, Gabriela Del Toro. "There was absolutely nothing out of the ordinary."

That Christmas, Jonathan, Jolinda, Julissa, and Jeanetta were caught stealing food out of the kitchen and were chained up. Part of their punishment was losing Christmas. While their siblings enjoyed "the good treatment" and presents, the four "suspects" could only watch the fun.

On May 14, 2017, Louise celebrated Mother's Day by giving her daughters a bath. It was their first in a year. One by one, Mother washed their hair and scrubbed their filthy bodies. But after Jolinda got into the bathtub, she asked to use the bathroom.

"Her mom got extremely upset with her," investigator Thomas Salisbury later testified, "and pinched her and . . . picked her up off the ground by the neck."

After their bath, Mother gave them all clean, matching dresses to wear and took them out to pose for photographs, which she later posted on Facebook.

Immediately after returning to the house, Mother handed the girls their soiled clothing to put back on. That would be their last bath for nine months.

After her parents died, Louise almost completely severed ties with her family back east. She blocked her sister Elizabeth on Facebook, rarely picking up the phone if any family member called. But she did call Elizabeth to inform her that she had just bought some "aunt shirts" for little Janna, who had red hair like Elizabeth—but Elizabeth would never get to see her niece wearing them.

"She told me that since I upset her," wrote Elizabeth, "she would never send me those pictures . . . that Janna would never have a relationship with me."

Instead, Louise sent the photos of Janna in her "aunt shirts" to Teresa, writing that she was no longer talking to Elizabeth. This time, Louise severed all ties to Elizabeth and would have nothing further to do with her.

Cut off from her family, Louise went into a tailspin, taking her angst out on her younger children, who were petrified of her. She was constantly in a bad mood and liable to lash out with her fists at any time without warning. And she began chaining up her "suspects" for longer and longer periods of time.

18

"WHERE IS THE KEY?"

On Halloween 2017, Louise dressed up baby Janna in a spooky costume and took her out trick-or-treating. A few days earlier, she had told Teresa how much she was looking forward to it.

"I was talking to her about taking the kids trick-or-treating," recalled Teresa. "I said, 'Well, you're going to have to send me pictures.'"

A few weeks later, Louise sent Teresa photographs of herself and the baby, but none of the other kids.

"I asked, 'Did none of the other kids go trick-or-treating?' And she was like, 'Teresa, they are not into that. They don't want to go anymore. They're too old for that, and since the baby's here, I figured we'd have fun.' I didn't question her any further."

Later, it would emerge that Mother had already started punishing her baby, pinching her and hitting her on the head with a pencil.

In December 2017, Joshua Turpin gave Jordan his old cell phone after getting a new one for Christmas. Although deacivated from making phone calls, it was still able to access the house Wi-Fi and get on the internet. David and Louise were confident that their children were now so well conditioned that they would never use these tools to escape.

Jordan, who had learned about social media from Jennifer, now started setting up various accounts, using the pseudonym Lacey Swan. Her profile picture was a selfie, in which she wore makeup and lipstick.

On December 19, she opened a Twitter account with the tag: @swan_lacey. Her first action was to retweet a post by self-described motivator, influencer, and musician @smthnglikekites that read: "You can't let other people tell you who you are. You have to decide that for yourself." But most of her retweets were about Justin Bieber, whom she still idolized. Jordan followed eighty-eight people on Twitter, more than two-thirds of whom were Bieber fans. She also retweeted posts from animal rights activists, one geared toward protecting elephants.

The pretty teenager also opened an Instagram account and set up her own YouTube channel, where she began posting videos of herself performing songs, secretly recorded in a bedroom, behind closed doors.

"Hello, this is Lacey Swan," she introduced herself in one video. "This is a song I wrote—'Where is the Key?'"

She then launched into a poignant song, apparently about finding the strength to escape the horrific captivity she had endured all her life. In the video, Jordan is wearing a black top, her long hair tied to one side with a red scrunchie, as her high voice soars and she gesticulates wildly.

Lord, I can do it
Pray, pray to the Lord, ask for help while I'm still
    down

So broken down so many times
So scared inside so many times
Where is the key to my heart?
Oh, where do I go from here
Let me through the doors
Where is the key?
Where is the key?
Where is the key?

In another song called "Not Today," Jordan seems to challenge Mother and Father, saying she has finally had enough of their cruelty.

Look at me
Where I am
Standing here
Welcome back
So far what do I see
I see pain that fills me so
I will not go back alive
I will stay until I die
You can take everything I own
But not from today
No, not from today

In a third video, she wears a Rainbow Dash baseball cap and sweatshirt from *My Little Pony* and a brightly colored wig. A large pile of dirty clothes is clearly visible in a corner of the room, and the door is covered in dark smudges.

"This is a song I wrote about two years ago." She sighs. "It's called 'So Weak.'"

The song, sung to a simple electronic accompaniment, has the words, "I'm so weak! So weak! So weak!" repeated over and over.

Another video shows her playing fetch with Sandy, one

of the children's two small Maltese dogs. The frisky white dog seems well fed and nourished, unlike its owners.

Jordan also began chatting online with a young man in India named Nilesh Potbhar. They became friends, and she told him all about her miserable life and her parents. Shocked, Nilesh encouraged her to escape and alert authorities to what was going on.

Over the Christmas holiday period, Jordan was busy posting on social media. Whenever Mother and Father were out of the house, she would sneak out of her room and chat with Nilesh, tweet about Justin Bieber, and post videos of her new songs on YouTube.

For the first time in her life, she felt empowered.

In a new song called "You Blame Me for Everything," she sings about betrayal, apparently about some of her older siblings who spy on her.

> *You are my best friend*
> *I thought I could tell you everything*
> *I thought you were true*
> *I guess I was wrong*

> *You blame me for everything*
> *You blame me in every, every way*
> *You blame me for what to say, what to say*
> *You blame me for everything*

> *I don't understand*
> *If only you could explain*

On December 23, Louise left a message on her half brother Billy's phone, asking about legal problems they were having with their mother's estate.

"I just realized how late it was," she said. "I don't

know what time you go to bed. But anyway, I called the lawyer's office today. Yeah, I wanted to let you know that [I'm] taking care of that this weekend. So, all right, Billy. Love you. Bye-bye."

The next day, he called her back to discuss dividing the money from the sale of their mother's house. At the end of the conversation, Billy asked if he could see his nieces and nephews over the holidays.

"She said she would set up a Facebook webcam soon so I could see the children," said Billy. "But it was all a lie."

On New Year's Eve, Jordan forwarded a message from Justin Bieber to her friend Nilesh, who was now helping her plan to escape her parents' prison.

"Happy New Year to all friends & all in the world," it read. "Everyone lives together in Peace."

Now everything came together for Jordan's escape plans when she got on social media. For the first time in her life, she had found friends outside the house, who she could open up to about her and her siblings' torturous life. They gave her the support and encouragement she needed to summon the strength to finally break out. On January 7, 2018, Jordan posted her final video on YouTube. It was a dramatic song of desperation called "What's Wrong with Me?" It seemed to foreshadow what lay ahead for the seventeen-year-old.

What now?
What do I do?
Look at me
Here I am

Three days later, Louise told Billy that she and David were planning to have their fourteenth baby. He had called about a visit to California he was planning in June, and Louise invited him to stay at her house.

"She said she was busy with homeschooling," Billy said, "and she and David were looking into buying a school bus, because their fifteen-seat van wouldn't fit the fourteenth baby they wanted. I said, 'Are you serious? Why would you want another kid? Haven't you got enough?'"

Now approaching fifty, Louise said she had already consulted her doctor, who told her she could have another child. Besides, she added, they needed an even bigger family to sell their reality TV show.

"The very last conversation I had with her," said Billy, "she did actually say that she [felt] that they would be perfect for TV. She thought the world would be fascinated by their lives. It would make them millions and household names."

Just before the holidays, Northrop Grumman had informed David Turpin that his aerospace engineering job was soon being transferred to Oklahoma City, Oklahoma. It meant yet another move for the Turpins, who spent the holidays packing up boxes of their things for the thirteen hundred–mile move east.

On Saturday, January 13, David and Louise told neighbors they were soon leaving Perris.

"They were getting ready to move," said Ricardo Ross, who lived a few doors away. "They had moving boxes [everywhere]."

For the Turpin children, this meant another new house full of unknown horrors. Jordan and her siblings must have been terrified of what might happen in Oklahoma and whether they could even survive the move. Jordan knew it was now or never. Early the next morning, she slipped out of her first-floor window and set her plan in motion.

PART THREE

THE MAGNIFICENT THIRTEEN

19

RESCUE

In the wake of Jordan Turpin's 911 call, dozens of police officers descended on 160 Muir Woods Road and would remain there for weeks. David and Louise were led out in handcuffs, one behind the other. They were driven to the Perris Police Department to be formally arrested and processed.

When the sheriff's deputies walked into the house, they were appalled at its filthy state and the overpowering stench of human waste. They found the children scattered in different rooms around the house. Jonathan Turpin was still chained up when they walked into his bedroom and freed him. Julissa and Joanna, chained to their bunk beds since October, had already been freed by Jessica on Mother's orders; Jessica had hastily thrown the chains and padlocks into a closet.

Within minutes, agents from both Child Protective Services and Adult Protective Services arrived to look after the children. Officers from the Riverside Fire Department came soon afterward.

"There was a very foul smell inside the residence," said Captain Greg Fellows, the chief of police for the City of

Perris, who was one of the first officers to enter. "It was extremely dirty. Many of the children were malnourished."

About forty-five minutes after the police arrived, the Turpin children were led out of the house one at a time wearing pajamas, one of the older daughters carrying baby Janna. An officer standing in the driveway ushered them into a waiting police van. One of the children who had fallen behind ran to catch up.

They were then driven to Perris Police Department, where officers made them comfortable. A deputy went to get food, as the children said they were starving. Medics treated them with IV drips full of antibiotics, vitamins, and nutrients. Blood samples were taken to confirm they were all David and Louise Turpin's biological children.

Over the next several hours, members of the Child Protective Services and Adult Protective Services gently talked to the thirteen siblings. Although they never mentioned their parents, some did ask about their two dogs, which had been taken to an animal shelter for safekeeping.

At 1:40 p.m., Deputy Manuel Campos walked into an interview room at the Perris Police Department's Detective Bureau, where a nervous Jordan Turpin was waiting. On the other side of the police station, Detective Thomas Salisbury of the Riverside County Sheriff's Department, who had been appointed the lead investigator in the case, was interviewing David and Louise Turpin separately.

Initially, Deputy Campos thought Jordan was only ten years old due to her emaciated body and childish speech patterns. She was filthy.

"She appeared to have the mental capacity of somebody a lot younger than seventeen years old," he later noted. "Her hair appeared to be unwashed. She appeared to not bathe regularly. She had a lot of dirt on her skin. It looked like it was caked on."

During the hour-long interview, Deputy Campos asked if she had any injuries. Jordan tried to show him a scar on her foot, but it was impossible to see through all the dirt caking her skin.

Speaking in simple sentences and struggling to pronounce words, Jordan described her and her siblings' torturous life. She constantly referred to her parents as "Mother" and "Father," explaining they insisted on being called that "as it was more like the Bible days."

Campos asked how she had felt during the escape a few hours earlier.

"She said she was scared to death," he would later testify. "She said it was one of the scariest things she's ever done."

Jordan told Campos she had escaped because she could no longer watch Julissa and Joanna wake up crying in pain from being chained up.

"It was hurting her," said Detective Campos, "and depressing her."

She also revealed that Mother had been in a particularly foul mood that morning, "yelling" at thirteen-year-old Jolinda and telling her she was worse than the devil. That had particularly upset Jordan, who said she was a good Christian.

"She boldly spoke about her love for God," Campos said. "And when she would hear her mother call her or her siblings the devil, it really, really bothered her and hurt her a lot."

Jordan described her disgusting living conditions and her daily routine of spending twenty hours a day in the bedroom she shared with her three sisters, never seeing daylight. She said she slept for more than fifteen hours a day and could not leave her room without Mother's permission.

"She told me she lived in filth," said Campos, "that her room was dirty, and that it smelled really bad. There were often times that she couldn't breathe [and] would stick her head out of her bedroom window."

Jordan said that even altering the permanently closed blinds to open the window was a serious crime, punishable by being beaten or chained up.

"She would be disciplined," said the detective, "in the form of knocking on her head and pulling her hair. She said she would get hit and smacked in the face and pushed. She used the word 'pitching.' Mother would 'pitch' them around the room as she was pulling their hair."

Jordan recounted how Mother had choked her for watching a Justin Bieber video on Jennifer's cell phone.

Although Jordan said she had never been chained up, many of her siblings had been for several months at a time. The chains were only removed so they could use the restroom, eat, and brush their teeth. Jordan also spoke of her recent activity on social media, posting YouTube videos of her songs, and making friends on Twitter.

"She gave a lot of credit to Jennifer," said Campos. "She said that almost everything she knows is because of [her], and she feels like she has nothing in her brain."

The teenager described her life as "nothing," saying Mother had given up teaching them and Father's homeschool was a sham. The detective was shocked by Jordan's lack of basic knowledge.

"She told me that her parents call it 'private school,'" said Campos, "and she did part of the first grade [when she was fifteen or sixteen] . . . She knew we were in the year 2018, and she knew we were in the first month of the year. But she did not know the name of the month . . . the day or the date."

Jordan said she had only seen a doctor once in her life and had never gone to a dentist. She had no friends, besides her new online ones, and spent her waking hours playing with her Barbie doll and writing songs and stories in her journal. She described how the siblings were only given one meal a day, as they weren't awake long enough to eat two. All they ate were peanut butter or baloney sandwiches, or a frozen burrito and chips.

Jordan told the investigator that she had been outside on only a handful of occasions, including Halloween, Las Vegas, and a trip to Disneyland when she was eleven years old.

Toward the end of the interview, the investigator asked if she had ever been sexually abused. Jordan told him about the incident in Murrieta when she was twelve, when her father had pulled her pants down and put her on his lap. She said they were interrupted by Mother's return before he could do anything further, but Father later told her not to tell anyone.

Campos asked Jordan what she thought her father had been trying to do.

"I have no idea of what he was trying to do," she replied.

She told the detective that from then on, Father would try and force kisses on her mouth almost a dozen times over the next four years.

In another interview room, Detective Thomas Salisbury interviewed Jolinda Turpin for more than an hour. A Child Protective Services worker stayed with her in the room.

Jolinda said that before moving to California in June 2000, Mother had homeschooled her, and she had worked her way up to the letter *I* in the alphabet. There had been no further lessons in Murrieta, but in Perris, Mother had helped her progress to the letter *T*.

"She believed she was ready to accelerate past kindergarten," the investigator later testified. "She wanted to accelerate to the first grade because she was tired of doing kindergarten work."

Jolinda told him how angry Mother became if she made the slightest mistake in class, pulling her hair and literally throwing her across the room. At the age of thirteen, Jolinda was virtually illiterate.

"She told me she could recognize some words," said Salisbury. "Any reading that she was able to do was self-taught and with the assistance of her brothers and her sisters."

Jolinda also did not know the difference between a state and a country, and she thought Texas was a country.

She told the investigator how Mother and Father had appointed four of the older siblings as hall monitors to spy on the younger ones and stop them stealing food and sneaking into Mother's room. In return, they were given extra privileges.

"It was Mother's idea," said Salisbury. "To stop the kids from getting candy, things out of Mother's room, and . . . food out of the kitchen area."

Jolinda said she had been born in Texas and was cared for by Joshua after Mother and Father moved out of the trailer. She recalled that it was "filthy, dirty, and smelled bad." She revealed that she'd last had a bath on Mother's Day 2017.

The investigator was sickened to hear Jolinda's descriptions of Mother's violent temper.

"She had been pinched by her mother," said Salisbury, "choked by her mother, and hit by her mother."

Salisbury then interviewed twenty-two-year-old Jonathan. He revealed that Julissa and Joanna had also been chained up when police had entered the house. Mother had accused them all of being "suspects" for stealing food and chained them to their beds.

He told the investigator that he had been restrained in various ways for the last six and a half years. It had started with ropes at the Murrieta house before progressing to bigger and heavier chains when Jonathan was able to escape using his teeth.

Jonathan said Father had chained him up at first, and then Mother had taken over. During his punishments, which could last up to two months, he would be chained up all day and only unchained to relieve himself, eat, and brush his teeth. Often he would be unable to get to the bathroom in time. His wrists and feet had been chained to a safety rail on either side of his top bunk bed so tightly that they were bruised.

Jonathan said that he had completed third grade and was "done with school," and he did not expect to receive any further homeschooling. When asked how many grade levels there were, he guessed ten.

In a third interview room, investigator Brett Rooker interviewed Joanna, fourteen, Jessica, twenty-four, and Joy, twenty. Joanna said that Mother had a terrible temper. She described the incident in the Murrieta house when Louise had thrown her down the stairs after catching Joanna in her bedroom, leaving her dizzy and crying in pain.

Joanna said she had been chained up because she would take things, leaving "dark places" on her arms.

"I asked her to show me her arms," said Rooker. "I saw dirt caked [on] both her right and left arms. There were clean spots on her wrists from where the chains had been."

Her last bath had been on Mother's Day 2017, and she had been chained up since last October. Joanna told the investigator that she had received no homeschooling since the move to Perris almost four years earlier.

"She said they had not completed the first book of phonics," Rooker recalled. "She told me that her, nor her siblings, had completed one full lesson for any of their grades. Mother stopped [and] just gave up."

Joanna said she was "terrified" of Mother, whose hall monitors patrolled the hallway around the clock to stop any-one stealing food or entering her room.

"She said that Mother knocks her on her head," said the investigator, "throws her around the room, pulls her hair."

In another interview room, Riverside County Sheriff's Department deputy Daniel Brown interviewed twenty-five-year-old Joshua, eleven-year-old Julissa, and eighteen-year-old Jeanetta.

During their two-hour interview, Julissa told him that she was always hungry.

Though they usually had jalapeño baloney or peanut butter sandwiches and what she called "freezer food," she said that sometimes they only received bread, and water from the faucet. She would see her parents wolfing down a hearty meal but was too afraid to ever ask for any, because she would be yelled at.

The emaciated little girl said she adored apple juice, but although Mother always had some in the fridge, she was never given any. She described how Mother would buy pies but not allow the kids to eat them, letting them mold and eventually throwing them away.

Julissa, too, had received her last bath on Mother's Day and was covered in dirt. She said that just before Christmas 2016, she and three siblings had been caught stealing food out of the pantry because they were so hungry.

"[They] were not allowed to celebrate with the rest of

the family, but [they] had to watch," said Brown. "They lost their Christmas."

She also told the deputy how Mother often punched her with a closed fist, slapped her in the face, or lifted her up off the ground by her hair. She had learned never to cry out in pain, as Mother "gets real mad . . . and the punishment would intensify." She called it "spankings on the face."

Julissa said Mother had started chaining her to the bedpost for up to four months at a time when she turned eleven. The chains would be wrapped around each of her wrists like bracelets and then around the bedpost. Initially, she was able to stand up in the chains, but when Mother found out, she shortened the chains.

When the officers had arrived, Julissa had been chained up for fifteen days. She said the chains were tight and bruised her, referring to the black-and-blue marks as "indentations."

Deputy Brown asked to see them. He noticed white spots on her arms where the chains had rubbed the dirt away.

At the end of the interview, Deputy Brown asked Julissa who was the big boss in charge. She answered, "Mother."

After the interviews, each sibling showered and was given a change of clothes. Their putrid old ones were collected as evidence. Investigators laid each of the thirteen siblings' clothing and underwear on butcher paper, labeling each one before photographing them. The girls' underwear appeared to be covered in dried blood. All the clothing was "very heavy and soiled" with an extremely foul odor, as they had not been changed in seven months.

Then the Turpin siblings were split up—the six minors

were admitted to Riverside University Hospital System, and the remaining seven were sent to the Corona Regional Medical Center. Later that day, investigator Brett Rooker photographed the adults for injuries and other evidentiary purposes. When they arrived at the medical center, he placed a 5150 hold on them so they could be held for up to seventy-two hours as dependent adults.

"They were all gravely disabled," Rooker later testified. "We asked them what they would do if they went home without their parents, and none of them could answer the question. I didn't feel they were able to care for themselves."

After giving statements at the Perris Police Department and having their fingerprints and mugshots taken, David and Louise Turpin were transported twenty miles north to the Robert Presley Detention Center in Riverside, California. They were each booked on nine counts of torture and ten counts of child endangerment. Bail was set at $9 million each.

The Riverside County Sheriff's Department executed a search warrant for the house on Muir Woods Road, and scores of crime scene investigators arrived to scour every inch, taking photographs and gathering evidence. The whole house stunk, and there was human waste and dirt everywhere.

Officers photographed every room, carefully noting all the chains and padlocks still dangling from many of the bunk bed guardrails. They also found several moldy pumpkin pies on the kitchen counter.

The whole area around the house became a crime scene and was sealed off with police tape. Then officers started canvassing neighbors for any available CCTV footage.

"They wanted to look at our camera because we've got it rolling twenty-four hours," said Ricardo Ross. "You can see the Turpins' backyard from our house."

Another neighbor, Andria Valdez, watched various police officers going in and out of the Turpin house all day. One deputy stayed until 10:00 p.m., and a police truck remained outside all night.

When the seven older Turpin siblings were admitted to Corona Regional Medical Center, they had absolutely nothing. Hospital staff went out to buy their new patients clothes, paying out of their own pockets. All the adults were so underweight that they needed children's sizes.

Hospital CEO Mark Uffer appealed to the Corona Chamber of Commerce for help.

"So we went into action," said Corona chamber president Bobby Spiegel. "We found out that the kids were taken there with limited to no clothing. They needed pajamas that night, and I told my staff, 'You know, it would be nice if we could collect a couple of thousand dollars to go buy them stuff.'"

Within hours, the chamber had dropped off bags of clothing, shoes, toiletries, and games for the kids. From then on, there was a constant stream of care packages for the new patients arriving by the hour.

The seven siblings were placed in their own wing in the hospital, with an around-the-clock guard. They had to be taught basic skills like cleaning their teeth and washing and brushing their hair. They had never seen fresh fruit or vegetables and had to be coaxed into tasting blueberries, strawberries, and raspberries. When they first saw a tomato, they were scared. It was only after a nurse ate one to prove it was safe that they gingerly took a bite and loved it.

20

GOD CALLED ON THEM TO HAVE
SO MANY CHILDREN

Monday was Martin Luther King Jr. Day, a national holiday. It was supposed to be a slow news day, but at 12:30 a.m., the Riverside County Sheriff, Stanley Sniff, posted a dramatic press release online, announcing that David and Louise Turpin had been arrested for the suspected torture and endangerment of their thirteen children. Accompanying the release were the couple's mugshots. This would set in motion global coverage of one of the biggest news stories in years.

Early Sunday morning on January 14, 2018, a 17-year-old juvenile escaped from her residence situated in the 100 Block of Muir Woods Road, Perris and managed to call 911 from a cellular device she found inside the house. The teenager claimed her 12 brothers and sisters were being held captive inside the residence by her parents and further claimed some of her siblings were bound with chains and padlocks.

When Police Officers from the Perris Police Department and Deputies from the Riverside

County Sheriff's Department met with the juvenile, she appeared to be only 10 years old and slightly emaciated. After a brief interview with the female, they contacted 57-year old *David Allen Turpin* and 49-year old *Louise Anna Turpin* at the residence where the teenager escaped.

Further investigation revealed several children shackled to their beds with chains and padlocks in dark and foul-smelling surroundings, but the parents were unable to immediately provide a logical reason why their children were restrained in that manner. Deputies located what they believed to be 12 children inside the house, but were shocked to discover that 7 of them were actually adults, ranging in age from 18 to 29. The victims appeared to be malnourished and very dirty.

All 13 victims, ranging from the age of 2 to 29, were transported to the Perris Station and interviewed. Both parents were detained and transported to the station for further investigation. Child Protective Services (CPS) and Adult Protective Services (APS) arrived to assist in the investigation. The victims were provided with food and beverages after they claimed to be starving.

The six children were eventually transported to the Riverside University Hospital System (RUHS) for medical examinations and were admitted for treatment. The seven adult children were transported to the Corona Regional Medical Center for an examination and admitted for medical treatment.

Both parents were interviewed in this matter and subsequently transported to the Robert Presley Detention Center (RPDC). They were booked for violations of California Penal Code Section

206-Torture and Section *273a(A)-Child Endangerment.* Bail was set at $9,000,000.00 each.

Anyone with additional information regarding this investigation is encouraged to contact Master Investigator Tom Salisbury at the Perris Station.

When reporter Brian Rokos of *The Press-Enterprise,* which covers Riverside County, first saw the press release, he almost put it to the side.

"We get a lot of those," explained Rokos, "and usually we'll take a quick look at them and say, 'Well, we'll get to it at some point.' But in this case we knew that this was going to be a big story, and we needed to get somebody to the house right away."

Within minutes of the release being posted online, Los Angeles–based NBC4 assigned reporter Tony Shin to the story.

"I got a call from my assignment desk," he said, "and they said, 'You've got to go now.'"

When he arrived at 160 Muir Woods Road, things were quiet. Police were still searching the Turpin house, refusing any comment.

"I was one of the first reporters there," said Shin, "and then after about thirty to forty minutes, neighbors started coming out. More media started showing up, and then it became a madhouse."

That Monday, all thirteen Turpin siblings were medically screened to assess what physical and mental damage they had sustained from their years of captivity. Because the doctors and nurses at both hospitals would be the first people the siblings had ever interacted with outside the house on an ongoing basis, a team of positive, upbeat physicians was handpicked to treat them. Dr. Fari Kamalpour, the director of hospitalist program for the Corona Regional Medical Center, was appointed the attending physician for all seven Turpin adults. The center's lead dietary manager, Jenyl Garay, was put in charge of their individual dietary requirements.

But even the well-trained medical professionals were shocked when they first saw the terrible state of their emaciated, stunted patients. All the siblings, except for two-year-old Janna, had suffered severe malnourishment, nerve damage, and mental and cognitive impairment. Many of the adult siblings had muscle loss due to bad diet and lack of exercise. Nearly all of them were between twenty and fifty pounds underweight.

When twenty-nine-year-old Jennifer Turpin was admitted to the hospital, she was five foot three and weighed just eighty pounds. Dr. Kamalpour diagnosed her as suffering from "low cognition, ability to perform mental tasks." She also had severe protein caloric malnutrition and an acute B12 deficiency, causing peripheral neuropathy, which resulted in tingling, numbness, and weakness in her hands and feet.

She was also suffering from cachexia, or a wasting away of her muscles, due to long-term extreme weight loss and loss of muscle tone, as were the rest of her adult siblings. Dr. Kamalpour found that Jennifer and her twenty-four-year-old sister, Jessica, would probably never be able to have children.

Joshua was five foot eight and weighed just 115 pounds. He was diagnosed with severe iron and vitamin D deficiency, as were all but one of his adult siblings.

Jessica, Joy, and Julianne were all severely underweight and suffered from malnutrition, cachexia, and vitamin deficiency.

Twenty-two-year-old Jonathan also suffered from these ailments, as well as "skeletal abnormalities," caused by all the years of being restrained by ropes or chains. He was five foot seven and only weighed one hundred pounds, forty-seven pounds below what he should have.

The only adult who was not underweight was Jeanetta, although she too was diagnosed with slow cognition, neuropathy, severe protein caloric malnutrition, and severe iron and vitamin D deficiency.

Dr. Mark Massi, a pediatrician at the Riverside University Health System, treated Jordan, James, and Julissa, who was in the worst condition of all the younger siblings. Eleven-year-old Julissa had a body weight percentile of just 0.01—compared to a healthy weight percentile between 5 and 85—and a body height percentile of 0.79, well below the normal range of 5 to 95.

Dr. Massi also performed a mid-upper-arm circumference (MUAC) test on her, finding that her mid-upper arms were the same size as a four-month-old baby's.

Julissa was more than fifteen pounds underweight, anemic, and had severe muscle wastage. She had such low potassium and glucose levels her heart was damaged, and extreme malnutrition had caused liver damage. She also suffered from psychosocial dwarfism, or stunted growth, as the result of living in such an abusive and neglectful environment.

Fifteen-year-old James was in the 0.01 percentile for his weight and 1.4 for his height. His muscles were so weak that he had an abnormal gait and difficulty walking. He had a vitamin D deficiency and visible scoliosis, his back curved into an S shape.

James also exhibited disturbing antisocial behavior, telling the doctor that he wanted to kill animals and believed his dreams could predict the future.

The doctor then examined Jordan, who weighed just over ninety-four pounds. She also suffered from protein calorie malnutrition and muscle wasting and had mild scoliosis. Dr. Massi found Jordan to be very childlike for her age, sending her for speech therapy, as she was so hard to understand.

The other three minors were treated by Dr. Sophia Grant, the medical director of the child abuse unit at Riverside University Health System. She found that Jolinda and Joanna suffered from severe malnutrition and muscle wasting. Thirteen-year-old Jolinda, with a body weight percentile of 0.04 and body height of 0.01, was very small and, due to malnutrition, showed none of the normal signs of puberty for a girl her age. Joanna, who had a body weight percentage of 0.01 and height of 0.81, also suffered from vitamin D and potassium deficiencies. In the ten days she spent at the hospital, Joanna would put on almost eight pounds, more than a normal girl of her age would gain in a year.

Dr. Grant also examined two-year-old Janna, who was the best fed of all the siblings. Her body weight percentile was 7.5, and her height was 7.18. The toddler weighed twenty-five and a half pounds when she was admitted and would gain a further three pounds over the next three months.

That afternoon, *The Press-Enterprise* broke the story online with the headline, 13 CAPTIVE SIBLINGS, SOME CHAINED TO BEDS, RESCUED FROM PERRIS HOUSE; PARENTS ARRESTED. Both authorities and neighbors were stunned by the discovery, Brian Rokos reported. He interviewed neighbor Ricardo Ross, who said he was in total disbelief.

"It's very shocking," he said. "Very devastating."

Soon, dozens of people had gathered in groups along Muir Woods Road as a helicopter hovered overhead. A procession of motorists drove by the brown stucco house, where a van and three other vehicles, including two Volkswagens with vanity plates DL4EVER and DSLAND, were parked outside. One had a baby seat in the back.

A dozen television news crews had set up camp by the house. They would remain there for a week. Reporters went door-to-door, speaking to neighbors for any insight into the mysterious Turpin family. But few residents on the street could tell them very much.

"They looked very unnutritioned [*sic*]," said Wendy Martinez, who lived nearby. "Very white, like they never got any sun at all. I mean, they would never come out, and when they did, the lady would stand there watching them."

Neighbor Andria Valdez said her family had joked that the family was just like the fictional Cullen family of vampires from the hit *Twilight* movies.

"They only came out at night," she said. "They were really, really pale."

Inside 160 Muir Woods Road, dozens of crime scene investigators sifted through the thick dirt, collecting piles of forensic evidence that was then packaged up and driven away for analysis. Cadaver dogs were also brought in, searching for human remains.

Officers videoed and photographed every inch of the house. In the garage, they found hundreds of DVDs, alphabetized and stacked up to the ceiling. These included every season of the *Kate Plus 8* reality show, Disney cartoons, and a collection of horror movies, including *Glass House: The Good Mother,* about two seemingly ideal parents who torture and imprison their adopted children.

That evening, all three Los Angeles television networks led off with the sensational story, which would soon go national. They had easily accessed the David-Louise Turpin Facebook page, with all the family photographs of the couple posing with their twelve identically dressed children at Disneyland. There was also stunning video of the Las Vegas wedding renewals, showing the Turpins and their children posing with "Elvis."

"Tortured, starved, and shackled," declared the anchor of NBC4's six o'clock news. "Thirteen brothers and sisters forced to live in filth. Tonight, their parents are accused of unthinkable crimes."

Reporting live from outside the Turpin home, reporter Tony Shin canvassed the neighbors' stunned reactions.

"They say they knew the family was a little strange," said Shin, "but they didn't think anyone was getting hurt."

Julie Olha expressed horror that something like this could have happened in Perris.

"If we had known, we would have turned this in a lot sooner," she told Shin, "because we take care of each other in this neighborhood."

Araceli Olozagaste described David and Louise being led out of their house in handcuffs. She said David had been "crying uncontrollably" while his wife was acting very strange, smirking at the officers and then spitting twice on the ground.

KABC7's newscast broadcast the first reactions from family members. Jim and Betty Turpin had learned what had happened to their grandchildren after getting a call from a reporter at their Princeton, West Virginia, home. When *Bluefield Daily Telegraph* reporter Greg Jordan learned there was a Princeton connection to the story, he found Jim and Betty Turpin's number in the phone book and immediately called them.

"And [Jim] was gracious enough to talk to me for a few minutes," said Jordan. "Of course, he did not believe the charges he was hearing. They were trying hard to contact authorities in California to find out what had been happening with the children."

The elder Turpins told ABC News that they were "surprised and shocked" at the allegations and had last visited their son and his family in California about four or five years earlier. At the time, they appeared to be a "happy family," said the grandparents, although the children seemed thin. Asked why David and Louise had so many children, they said "God had called on them" to do so.

To Greg Jordan, Jim Turpin described his son as "a fine person" who "did an outstanding job." He told Jordan that when he'd last seen his grandchildren, "the kids were fine," Jordan recalled. "They were healthy and nothing was wrong."

It was a brief interview, as Jim wanted to get off the phone so he could get more details from the Riverside County Sheriff's Office.

"He was holding up as well as anybody could," said Jordan. "He wasn't hysterical, but he wanted to get on with the business of contacting the authorities and [talking] to the grandchildren themselves. He didn't believe the charges and wanted to find out what was going on."

A few hours later, Jim and Betty Turpin hired Princeton lawyer Paige Flanigan to represent them.

"James and Betty Turpin had no knowledge of the allegations that have been made regarding this matter," read a statement issued by the Flanagan Law Office, "other than what they have seen in the media. [They] would ask the media to respect their family's privacy at this time as they deal with this difficult situation, and their focus is solely on the safety of their son and grandchildren."

Back in Tennessee, Elizabeth Flores learned what had happened when somebody posted a link to the story to her on Facebook, asking, "Is this your sicko sister?"

"My initial response was, 'Oh my god! Oh my god!'" she remembered. "And I broke down. I knew my sister was strange, but never anything like this. And then not even five minutes later, I had a news reporter calling and wanting to interview me. And it began like that."

Elizabeth called her sister Teresa Robinette and told her to sit down.

"I looked at the news and I just . . . I don't really know how to describe the feeling to you," Teresa told Fox News. "I felt like it wasn't real. Then I just got mad. My next emotion was anger."

When she turned on the television, she immediately saw her sister's and brother-in-law's mugshots.

"That in itself shocked me," she said.

Quickly branded "the House of Horrors," the story of what had gone on behind closed doors at 160 Muir Woods Road spread like wildfire, shocking everyone who had ever come into contact with the Turpin family. Back in Rio Vista, Texas, Ashley Vinyard told a reporter that she finally knew why her old neighbors had been so secretive.

"I wanted to say I'm shocked," she said, "but at the same time, it kind of all adds up when you're looking back."

Her father, Ricky, said he now wished he had alerted authorities.

"I found it very disturbing," he said. "We should have done something. Today I still feel terrible about it. These people are shit."

Elvis impersonator Kent Ripley, who remarried David and Louise three times in Las Vegas—twice with their children present—now found his interactions with the family disturbing.

"I would never have thought this," he said, "and I feel so bad for the children."

Ripley said he hoped that their two visits to Las Vegas had at least been a ray of light in the children's otherwise dark existence.

"Were they free for a moment in the outside world?" he asked. "Do they look back and go, 'Oh, that was great,' or do they look back and say, 'We got punished when we got back to the hotel'?"

That night, A Elvis Chapel removed all videos of the three Turpin marriage renewals from its website, and the David-Louise Turpin Facebook page was taken down.

21

"I WOULD CALL THAT TORTURE"

At 10:00 a.m. Tuesday morning, as police arrived at 595 Hill County Road in Texas with cadaver dogs to search for human remains, Captain Greg Fellows, the Perris chief of police, held a press conference. Scores of reporters and cameramen packed into a conference room at the Riverside County Sheriff's Department.

"First of all," he began, "I'm very saddened to report on such a heartbreaking case."

Captain Fellows recounted how Jordan—whose name he withheld—had dialed 911 early Sunday morning, reporting that she and her twelve siblings were being held against their will, and some were chained up. The deputies and a supervisor had met the girl, who had showed them photos of her two sisters chained to their beds. Then they had gone straight over to 160 Muir Woods Road to conduct a welfare check.

"When they arrived inside the house," he continued, "they noticed that the children were malnourished. It was very dirty, and the conditions were horrific. The biological parents and children were taken to the Perris Sheriff's Station for further investigation."

He emphasized that this was an ongoing investigation and that nothing would be ruled out.

"I wish I could come to you today with information that would explain why this happened," he said with obvious emotion. "But we do need to acknowledge the courage of the young girl who escaped from that residence to bring attention so they could get the help that they so needed."

The mayor of Perris, Michael Vargas, took the podium next.

"I can truly say that I'm devastated at this act of cruelty and heartfelt for the victims," he said. "I can't begin to imagine the pain and suffering that they have endured."

Mayor Vargas thanked the police department for its "swift response," saying he had faith that officers would do a thorough investigation.

"This is a very happy and tight, hardworking family community," he said. "And I know that I speak on behalf of the residents of Perris, that our thoughts and prayers are with the victims as they endure the next few weeks that are coming up."

Next, Dr. Sophia Grant, the medical director of the child abuse unit at the Riverside University Health System, addressed the immediate medical needs of the thirteen victims, including the three siblings she was treating.

"They would require stabilization," she said, "and in cases of starvation, we would have to slowly start to feed them to avoid any problems that refeeding may cause. The long-term needs of these kids are going to be the psychological and psychiatric needs, due to the prolonged periods of starvation and maltreatment."

Mark Uffer took over with an update on the seven adults' progress at the Corona Regional Medical Center.

"It's hard to think of them as adults when you first see them," he said, "because they're small, and it's very clear that they're malnutritioned."

He told the audience that all seven were "stable" and being fed appropriately.

"They're comfortable, and they are in a very safe and secure environment," he said. "They've gone through a very traumatic ordeal. I can tell you that they are very friendly, they're very cooperative, and I believe that they're hopeful that life will get better for them after this event."

Captain Fellows then took a few questions from the bustling crowd.

"Did the parents try and explain what was going on?" asked one TV reporter.

"I can't get into the specific details of the conversation," replied the captain, "but it seemed that the mother was perplexed as to why we were at that residence."

Another reporter asked if law enforcement or Child Protective Services had ever been called out to 160 Muir Woods Road.

"No, sir. We had no prior contacts at that residence regarding any allegations of child abuse or neglect."

ABC7 reporter Rob McMillan questioned whether religion had played any part in it. "I spoke to David Turpin's parents last night," he said. "They were a very religious family. They taught their kids the Bible [and] actually instructed them to memorize large sections of it. Could religion have caused this? Is this some sort of cult or an offshoot of religion that made them treat their children like this?"

"As of right now," Fellows said, "I have no information regarding any religious organization associated with this matter. But again, we're still in the very early stages of this investigation."

A reporter asked for details on how the Turpin siblings had been tortured.

"I can't get into the specifics of that," he said again.

"But if you can imagine being seventeen years old and appearing to be a ten-year-old. Being chained to a bed. Being malnourished and injuries associated with that. I would call that torture."

Reporters then directed their questions to Dr. Grant, asking what was ahead for the children medically, physically, and psychologically.

"Well, you can imagine the post-traumatic stress disorder," she replied, "if you've been deprived of nutrition for a prolonged period of time. If you've been deprived of normal childhood activities, normal interactions, and the people who should have been providing for you have failed to do so, that is going to cause some psychological damage. The psychological support is going to be ongoing and long term."

Asked if there was any hope of full recovery after so many years of physical and psychological torture, she said, "I think there's always hope. But you have to imagine that these kids are going to need a lot of support. This is going to be long term, and they're going to need support and loving, supportive people in their lives to help them try to achieve any type of normal life."

The discovery, first revealed by *Press-Enterprise* reporter Brian Rokos, that David Turpin had been running a private school to keep his children under the radar raised many questions about the lax regulations for homeschooling in California. On Tuesday morning, the California Department of Education issued a statement denying any responsibility for what had happened.

"We are sickened by this tragedy," it read, "and relieved the children are now safe and the authorities are investigating. Full-time private schools are required to register with the state to record their students' exemption from compulsory attendance at public schools. Under California law, the CDE does not have the authority to monitor, inspect, or oversee private schools."

Since the story had broken, Rokos had begun researching private school licensing, discovering that all private schools should receive an annual inspection by the fire department. But in the seven years that David Turpin had registered his City Day School and then Sandcastle Day School, there had never been a single inspection.

The legislation makes it very specific that any day school that files the affidavit, as the Turpins did, would be subject to the annual inspection. "They never did one," Rokos explained. "Restaurants and day care homes have to be inspected, but apparently not private schools."

Local assemblyman Jose Medina decided that it was time to take action and tighten up regulations for private homeschools. The former high school teacher was shocked that David Turpin had been able to hide in plain sight under the guise of running a private school.

"He listed himself as the principal of the Sandcastle School," said Assemblyman Medina, who chairs the California State Assembly's higher-education committee. "That was striking to me. I am extremely concerned about the lack of oversight the State of California currently has in monitoring private and homeschools."

The assemblyman called the CDE and the Office of the State Superintendent, looking for answers. He demanded an investigation into why the Turpin private schools had never received a fire inspection, and he also began drafting legislation to toughen up the regulations for opening a private school and monitoring the schools more closely.

"Perris is a great city and has many, many good things going on," he said. "And I think when they move on past it, as they should, there'll be some good that comes out."

Soon after Tuesday morning's press conference, eighty-one-year-old Betty Turpin gave a series of interviews, defending her son David and daughter-in-law Louise. She told CNN the couple had always been "highly protective" of their children, expressing "total shock" that they now faced torture and child endangerment charges.

"This is a highly respectable family," she said, "[who] had annual passes to Disneyland."

The siblings' grandmother also spoke to *Time,* accusing the media of distorting everything.

"We don't believe anything until we find definite proof," she told reporter Melissa Chan. "It's just a one-sided story. You can't always go with that."

She said her college-educated son had had a good upbringing, and she was very proud of him.

"He's very likeable," she said. "Raised in a Christian home all his life. Gone to church all his life."

To the *Southern California News Group,* she called the whole family "model Christians," saying David shared her Pentecostal faith. She reflected on her own five-day visit to Murrieta six years earlier and said she'd witnessed nothing untoward to raise her suspicions.

"They are *the* sweetest family," she explained. "They were just like any ordinary family, and they had such good relationships. I'm just not saying this stuff. We were amazed."

Their grandmother said she never heard any of the kids argue.

"Some [now] say they were told to behave," she said. "But you take a household of kids over five days, they're going to be themselves. It was wonderful."

Though Betty was a staunch and outspoken supporter of her son, when reporters attempted to contact David's older brother, Dr. Randy Turpin, they were told that he had taken a leave of absence from his position as president of Valor Christian College. In a prepared statement, the Ohio-based college said Dr. Turpin was on a sabbatical while he dealt with "revelations about estranged family members."

"The Valor Christian community joins with millions of Americans who are shocked and saddened by these terrible stories from California and we are praying for the full recovery of all involved."

Soon afterward, David Turpin's employer, Northrop Grumman, issued a formal statement as well.

"We are deeply troubled by the nature of the allegations against Mr. Turpin," it read. "We have no information regarding the case and would refer any inquiries to the authorities."

After press reports that Joshua Turpin attended Mt. San Jacinto College, its public information office also felt the need to speak out.

"Mt. San Jacinto College is aware that one of the children of the Perris couple accused of torture and child endangerment was previously enrolled at MSJC," a statement read. "These allegations are extremely disturbing. We at Mt. San Jacinto College are deeply saddened and horrified to hear of the allegations involving these children. Our hearts go out to the victims."

The college refused to give out any information about the student, citing privacy laws.

On Wednesday morning, Elizabeth Flores appeared on *Good Morning America*. Producers had flown her to New York the night before for an exclusive interview by Robin Roberts in ABC's Times Square studios.

"I know this is a difficult time for everyone," Roberts

began. "It was so hard for all of us to hear about your nieces and nephews. What was it like when you first heard the news?"

"Well, I was shocked," Elizabeth replied. "I was devastated, just like the rest of the world."

As a series of Facebook pictures of the Turpins at Disneyland flashed up, Roberts asked Elizabeth about the summer she'd spent living with the Turpins in Fort Worth back in 1996.

"I thought they were really strict," Elizabeth said, "but I didn't see any type of abuse."

"I heard," Roberts continued, "that your brother-in-law at the time made you uncomfortable. How so?"

"Yes," replied Elizabeth. "If I went to get in the shower, he would come in while I was in there and watch me. And it was like a joke. He never touched me or anything."

When Roberts asked what she would like to say to her sister, Elizabeth burst into tears.

"I want her to know she's still my flesh and blood, and I love her," she said, struggling to compose herself. "I don't agree with what she did . . . and I want her to know that I'm praying for her salvation. But mainly, we want to reach out to the kids . . . to know that they do have family that love them, whether they know us or not."

On Wednesday afternoon, a forensics team from the Riverside County Sheriff's Office removed dozens of boxes of evidence from 160 Muir Woods Road. They also seized two safes and pieces of a bed frame, throwing hundreds of bags of trash into the backyard.

"Our investigators are combing the scene," said Deputy Mike Vasquez of the Riverside County Sheriff's Office, "making sure they cover all the angles."

Since the Turpin siblings' rescue, Muir Woods Road had become a tourist destination. Curiosity seekers lined the road, taking photographs. A steady stream of cars drove slowly past the now infamous Turpin house, with rubberneckers snapping pictures on their cell phones.

"This isn't Disneyland where you take pictures," complained Kimberly Milligan. "Who does that?"

Residents were becoming increasingly upset by all the questions of how all this could have happened without anyone in the neighborhood realizing.

"How could you blame the community?" asked Andria Valdez. "When we were outside, cars would stop and say, 'You didn't know anything?'"

Mayor Vargas went to the Monument Park community's aid, comforting neighbors and urging them to be positive.

"This is something you wouldn't suspect in an urban-type city," said the mayor, who is a former Los Angeles police officer. "It's a fairly new community, so obviously the immediate neighbors were devastated that something like that could happen right underneath their eyes. I don't want to backseat quarterback anybody . . . and put the blame on anybody. This could have happened anywhere."

With global attention now firmly fixed on Perris, Mayor Vargas said his main concern was for his residents.

"It's a very negative thing, and we don't need that in our city, but I wasn't worried about that. I was more worried about the neighboring folks, how they were doing and how they were affected by this."

Dan Brodsky-Chenfeld, who manages Skydive Perris, said the House of Horrors had been on everyone's lips.

"It's only a mile away from here," said the six-time world skydiving champion. "It's insane. It's on the news everywhere. It just really shows you that maybe you want to know your neighbors better."

But along with the backlash came an outpouring of support for the thirteen Turpin siblings from the local community and all over the world. The Corona Chamber of Commerce had donated a bag of new clothes to each of the siblings and opened a fund that would eventually raise more than $200,000 for them.

"The chamber has been given a gift," said president Bobby Spiegel. "It is truly an opportunity for us to do something good, because Corona Regional Medical Center is one of our premier members."

He said everyone in Corona, a forty-minute drive from Perris, had been moved by the siblings' plight and wanted to embrace them.

"I refuse to even call them by their last name," said Spiegel. "The parents, or those idiots who consider themselves parents, don't deserve to have their family name carried on. So we changed the whole thing. When people call in, we refer to them as 'the Magnificent Thirteen,' as we want to be able to speak it into existence that they're going to have a magnificent life. And they'll each be a big contribution to the society."

In the days after the escape, the Chamber of Commerce was inundated with offers of support.

"We were taking two hundred calls a day from people wanting to know how they could help," said Spiegel. "From every tragedy, good things happen, and this horrific situation has brought the best out of so many people."

The Corona Regional Medical Center staff bought each of the seven adults a pair of shoes. These were the first shoes they had ever owned, and they slept in them so they wouldn't be taken away like their parents had always done.

"They were afraid that anything that they got was going to be taken away," said hospital CEO Mark Uffer. "There was always a question, at least from one or two of them, 'Is anybody going to take my things?'"

Uffer promised them that nothing would ever be taken away from them while they were at his facility. During their first few weeks there, the siblings formed close attachments with staff members. It was the first time in their lives they had ever been fussed over and made to feel important.

"They really thrived on the attention from nurses and staff," said Uffer. "When they saw certain nurses, they would run to them . . . a little bit overwhelming when you first experienced it."

On Thursday morning, Taha Muntajibuddin, who had been in Jennifer Turpin's third-grade class at Meadowcreek Elementary School, apologized to her on Facebook.

"Jennifer Turpin was the one girl at Meadowcreek Elementary that nobody wanted to be caught talking to," he wrote. "Every grade level had a designated 'cootie kid' and she held the title for our year."

Describing her as "frail" with "pin-straight hair with bangs," he wrote that she had worn the same purple outfit to school every day and smelled bad. He recalled the entire class "scoffing" at her one day because the teacher had asked her to discard a scrunchie made out of an old Hershey bar wrapper, which she had used to tie her hair back.

After she moved away at the end of the third grade, Taha had forgotten about Jennifer until reading about the horrific coverage of her siblings' escape.

"I can't help but feel an overwhelming sense of guilt and shame," he wrote. "Of course, none of us are responsible for the events that ensued, but you can't help but feel rotten when the classmate your peers made fun of for 'smelling like poop' quite literally had to sit in her own waste because she was chained to her bed. It is nothing but sobering to know that the person who sat across from you at the lunch table went home to squalor and filth while you went home to a warm meal and a bedtime story."

There was an important lesson to be learned from how his third-grade class so cruelly mocked Jennifer.

"A simple act of kindness and acceptance may be the ray of hope that that person needs. Befriend the Jennifer Turpins of the world."

And he wrote that despite "being vehemently vilified by her peers" Jennifer had always maintained a cheerful disposition, which would ultimately prevail.

"That despite being let down by her parents and by her peers alike," he wrote, "Jennifer rose above it all. And I'm going to be rooting for her, as her peer, as her classmate, as her friend. Jennifer Turpin: from 'cootie girl' to 'conquered the world.'"

22

"THIS IS DEPRAVED CONDUCT"

At 11:00 a.m. Thursday morning, Riverside County district attorney Michael Hestrin held a press conference to announce that he was filing seventy-five felony charges against David and Louise Turpin. If convicted of all of them, they faced ninety-four years to life in prison.

To the right side of the conference room stage were two blown-up mugshots of Louise and David Turpin. So many reporters and camera crews were there that some sat on the stage, just feet away from Hestrin.

"What I'd like to do today is first tell you what we've charged and the potential consequences of those charges," Hestrin began, "and then give you a snapshot of some of the evidence."

He then outlined some of the charges:

- Twelve counts each of torture, against all their children except two-year-old Janna

- Twelve counts each of false imprisonment

- Seven counts each of cruelty to a dependent adult, against their seven children aged eighteen and over

- Six counts each of willful child cruelty, against their six minor children

- One charge against David Turpin of committing a lewd act by force or fear on his daughter Jordan when she was under the age of fourteen

All the charges ranged from June 11, 2010, when they first moved to Riverside County, to their arrest on January 14, 2018. Hestrin said he would be requesting bail to be set at $13 million for each defendant—$1 million for each child.

"We're fully prepared to seek justice in this case," he said, "and do so in a way that protects these victims from further harm."

The youthful, collegiate-looking district attorney, wearing a brown tailored suit and glasses, appealed to anyone with any additional information to contact his senior investigator, Wade Walsvick.

"We're asking for the public's help," he said. "Not only here in California but in Texas. Someone must have seen something. Someone must have noticed something. We need your help."

Hestrin then continued by finally revealing some of the heartbreaking details of the case.

"First of all, I want to tell you these individuals sleep all day and are up all night," he said. "All thirteen of the victims, including defendants, typically got to sleep around four or five in the morning."

He went on to specify some of the horrific punishments David and Louise Turpin had employed to condition and control their own children.

"Starting many years ago, they began to be tied up," said the DA. "First with ropes. One victim . . . was tied up and hog-tied. When that victim was able to escape the ropes, these defendants eventually began using chains and padlocks to chain up the victims to their beds. These punishments would last for weeks or even months at a time."

The DA revealed that three of the victims had actually been chained up when police first arrived.

"Circumstantial evidence in the house," he continued, "suggests that the victims were often not released from their chains to go to the bathroom."

He then discussed the escape, which Jordan had been planning with her siblings for more than two years.

"She escaped through a window," said Hestrin, "and took one of her siblings with her. That sibling eventually became frightened and turned back and went back into the house."

The DA told reporters that the "neglect and abuse" had started when the family lived in Texas. At one point, the parents had lived apart from most of the children, occasionally dropping off food. After the family moved to Murrieta in 2010, the abuse and severe neglect intensified.

"All the victims have now been examined by doctors and medical professionals," he said. "All the victims were and are severely malnourished."

He said that twenty-nine-year-old Jennifer weighed just eighty pounds, and thirteen-year-old Jolinda was the weight of a seven-year-old. Several of the victims had suffered cognitive impairment and nerve damage, the result of years of physical abuse. The punishments, he said, included frequent beatings and even strangulation.

None of the victims, said Hestrin, had seen a doctor in over four years and had never been to the dentist. They were allowed to shower only once a year. When the siblings were not chained up, they were locked in different rooms and fed meagerly on a schedule. Although they were not allowed toys, investigators had found many unopened toys in the house, still in their original packaging. To gasps from reporters, the DA explained how David and Louise would cruelly taunt their starving children by leaving scrumptious pies on the kitchen counter. They could see and smell the pies but were forbidden from eating them, having to watch them rot before being thrown away.

"Supposedly homeschooled," he continued, "the children lacked even a basic knowledge of life. Many of the children didn't know what a police officer was."

The only thing the siblings were allowed to do was to keep journals. Hundreds of them were now being "combed through" by investigators for evidence.

"It's a very complex case," said the DA. "It's important that we gather and analyze this evidence. Based on the information I've shared with you today, it's my hope that members of the public will come forward with any information about this family or these crimes."

Hestrin then introduced his director of Victim Services, Melissa Donaldson, to talk about help the children would be receiving.

She told reporters they would need long-term help, and her department would be working closely with Child Protective Services to ensure they were not revictimized.

"We have a crisis response team," she said, "and those victim advocates are specially trained in mass casualty and victimization [and] are ready and serving the victims."

Then DA Hestrin opened the floor for questions. The first was what the lewd act charge was in reference to.

"We're alleging that David Turpin," he said, "touched one of the victims in a lewd way by using force or fear."

Asked if David and Louise were the biological parents

of all thirteen children, Hestrin said it was too early to know, but investigators would certainly be looking into it.

A TV reporter asked why they had done this to their children.

"I don't know that I can answer that completely," Hestrin replied. "But I'll tell you that as a prosecutor, there are cases that stick with you, that haunt you. Sometimes in this business we're faced with looking at human depravity, and that's what we're looking at here."

He was then asked to characterize the type of control the parents put the children under twenty-four hours a day.

"This is severe emotional, physical abuse," he answered. "There's no way around that. This is depraved conduct."

A reporter asked whether the parents were "partly nuts."

"I can't answer that question," replied the DA.

Finally, he was asked how his team of investigators was dealing with this "horrendous case" on a personal level while remaining objective.

"Well, we're not robots," Hestrin said, "and this is difficult for everybody that sees these images and hears these stories. So it breaks our heart. But we're professionals. Ultimately, our job is to go into court and seek justice, and we're going to do that."

Two hours later, David and Louise Turpin were arraigned at the Riverside Hall of Justice. The two defendants were led through a tunnel from the Robert Presley Detention Center, where they had been held since their arrest, into the court across the road. They were already shackled, waist and wrist, at the defense table, when reporters and photographers were allowed in. The defendants both wore black blazers provided by the public defender's office. David, unshaven with shoulder-length dyed blond hair, wore a purple shirt, the heavy chain tightly wound across his paunch.

Each had their own defense team. David was being represented by public defenders David Macher and Allison Lowe, Louise by Jeff Moore of Riverside-based Blumenthal Law Offices. As a public defender, Macher could represent David, but it would be a conflict of interest if his office also represented Louise, so private attorney Jeff Moore would do so. During the seven-minute arraignment, they sat on either side of their lawyers, briefly glancing at each other. To their right sat Riverside County deputy DA Kevin Beecham, who would be the lead prosecutor in the case.

Prior to the arraignment, none of the defense lawyers had met their clients, and as Jeff Moore spoke to Louise at the defense table, she smiled at him. Before the proceedings, Macher asked his new client if his name was spelled correctly on the voluminous charge sheets.

"I don't have my reading glasses with me," David muttered, turning toward Louise and shrugging.

Judge Michael B. Donner entered the courtroom to begin the arraignment.

Macher asked the judge to ban all film or electronic coverage of the proceedings, saying it would harm his client. The prosecutor had no objection, but Judge Donner denied the motion.

"I am told the coverage of this case literally spans the globe," explained the judge, "and that photographs, people's comments, editorials, et cetera, have been out there in the news for a very long time. So I can't find that the electronic coverage of the arraignment today will be as prejudicial as suggested by the defense."

After the prosecution told the judge that it had submitted initial discovery—police records and the siblings' medical records—to the defense, both defense teams confirmed that they had advised their clients of their constitutional rights, asking the court to waive reading of the complaint and enter pleas of not guilty to all seventy-five counts.

The only time the Turpins spoke was to quietly answer "Yes," when Judge Donner asked them if they also waived a speedy preliminary hearing within ten days.

He then continued bail at $12 million each, setting the next hearing for February 23.

Outside the courtroom, Macher conceded that defending David Turpin was going to be a challenge.

"We're going to provide a vigorous defense," he declared. "The case will be tried in court, not in the media."

Louise's attorney, Jeff Moore, was equally aware of the high stakes of the case.

"It doesn't get more serious," he said, "in terms of severity of the conduct being alleged and also the exposure in prison."

A few hours after the arraignment, Louise's half sister McCeary Lee, the daughter of Phyllis and David Lee, and also a former U.S. Marine in Guam, posted an emotional appeal on Facebook to leave her family alone. She wrote that she had not intended to post anything about "this mess," but felt compelled to after the accusations that the family must have known what was going on and had ignored it.

"Yes, we knew David and Louise were a bit odd," she wrote, "but there was no way in hell we knew they were torturing our nieces and nephews. Please leave the kids and us alone. We're reeling from the news just like everyone else and what the kids are going through is unspeakable . . . Additionally, we know just about as much as everyone else does. Asking us questions won't get you many answers."

23

"WE STAND UNITED WITH THE TURPIN CHILDREN"

At 160 Muir Woods Road, a Christmas star still hung in the window, and Louise's prized statue of a hissing serpent remained outside the front door. All day long, people arrived at the Turpin house, leaving candles, stuffed animals, flowers, balloons, and heartfelt notes of love and support for the Turpin siblings.

"The kids are so loved by so many people," read one note. "They will go on to do wonderful and great things."

"God bless," read another. "I pray for nothing but joy for all of you. You're in our thoughts."

"WE STAND UNITED WITH THE TURPIN CHILDREN," declared a third.

Three-year-old Riley Unger, who lives a few doors away, left two of her own teddy bears on their porch for children she had never met.

Neighbor Wendy Martinez told *The Press-Enterprise*, "For me, it's to show a little light in a dark tunnel."

Money was still pouring into the Corona Chamber of Commerce and the Riverside University Health System Medical Center from all over the world, with some donations as high as $10,000.

"Our phones started ringing almost immediately," said executive director Erin Phillips, "with calls from private individuals and organizations wanting to know how they can help. We recognize financial gifts will not eliminate their trauma, but additional resources will be extremely important in helping these victims adjust over time."

The Chamber of Commerce had now received $65,000, and the Riverside University Health System, where the younger siblings were being treated, had collected almost $200,000.

"Someone at the hospital mentioned how good it would be for educational purposes for them to have an iPad," said Corona Chamber president Bobby Spiegel. "So I went to my Rotary Club and said, 'Does anyone know anyone in the computer business?' Then one lady says, 'I'll donate one.' And in less than a minute, thirteen people's hands went up to buy an iPad."

Several days after the Chamber of Commerce fund was launched, a homeless man approached Spiegel outside his office.

"He reaches into his pocket," said Spiegel, "and pulls out two dollars and thirty-eight cents, probably everything he had. And he says, 'I want you to tell the kids that the world is watching and they love them.' And I still tear up over it, because that is the good that has come."

Although he had never met the seven Turpin adults, Spiegel received regular reports on their progress at Corona Regional Medical Center. He had also received many offers of free dental care for life for the children.

"The boys got haircuts for the first time," he said. "They had long, long hair . . . Captain Kangaroo is what the dad looks like."

Joshua and Jonathan donated their hair to Locks of

Love, a nonprofit organization that make wigs for cancer
victims.

The medical team treating the seven Turpin adults at Corona Regional Medical Center soon found themselves becoming personally involved with their patients. They
empathized with the older siblings and were horrified to
see firsthand what they had suffered. Hospital CEO
Mark Uffer told ABC News of one twenty-four-year-old
nurse, the same as age as Jessica Turpin, who was
shocked to see her emaciated body.

"It becomes very personal to you," explained Uffer.
"And it hurts to see what [one] human being can do to
another human being. So it does stay with you."

Everyone on the team treating the older siblings had
been affected, with many reduced to tears.

"I don't think there's any of us," he said, "that are involved or have spoken to them or interacted with them
that slept much in the last week, because you wake up in
the middle of the night worrying about them."

All the physicians treating the Turpins had been carefully chosen to develop a bond and a trust with them to
help them heal physically and mentally.

"We are the first stage of their introduction to the outside world," explained their primary physician, Dr. Fari
Kamalpour.

Child trauma expert Allison Davis Maxon agreed that the
Turpin siblings would need ongoing love and support
from trusted people who care about them in order to help
them overcome the relational trauma and intense deprivation they had suffered.

"Healing takes time and is a process," she said. "You

can't go back and erase early deprivation, neglect, and trauma. We're wired from the moment we enter the world to get our needs met through human connection. And early deprivation starves all aspects of our social and emotional development, especially impacting brain development. Think about how we learn language—we learn that through relationships; we don't learn that in isolation.

"When children, especially at early ages, experience severe deprivation, they don't learn this 'dance of attachment.' They may struggle to learn how to communicate their needs and/or feel valuable enough to get emotionally close to others. So what you'll see is a social, emotional awkwardness or a stuntedness. They may struggle in being able to read and attune with what other people are feeling, being in awareness of what they themselves are feeling, and why they are feeling it. Being able to communicate their emotional and attachment needs, thoughts, and feelings to other people requires basic trust, self-awareness, and a willingness to take a risk."

The process of treating the siblings would be a long one, Maxon said, as their physiological systems and development had not progressed in a normal way.

"Childhood development occurs sequentially," she explained. "Children first learn to sit up, then crawl, then stand, then walk, and then run. Our social-emotional skills are similar in that children first learn to make sounds, then words, then string words into sentences, then identify what they need or what they are feeling. And then they communicate what they are feeling to people they trust.

"Our brains and bodies are built to develop and learn like that. So when windows of opportunity diminish or close, the next part of what we need to learn can't sit on top of a particular skill set or competency, because we were deprived of the experiences needed to master or

learn those skills. So children who have experienced extreme and chronic deprivation can be fifteen years old or
twenty years old and in some ways emotionally and socially function like they're three or five or eight years old.
It's not something you can just bounce back from."

On Friday, the Riverside County District Attorney's Office announced that it would seek a criminal protective
order barring David and Louise Turpin from any further
contact with their children. This would prevent the
Turpins from communicating with their children to try to
pressure them in any way before the trial.

That night, the City of Perris held a neighborhood
watch meeting to help residents cope with the Turpin
case. More than fifty residents gathered in Monument
Park, just a short walk away from the now-notorious
Turpin house.

"We tried not to let that get out publicly," said Mayor
Vargas, "because we wanted to focus just on the community members of that neighborhood. But the press was
there. They got hold of it right away."

At the meeting, Perris city officials assured residents
that although it was an appalling situation, they would
have to move on.

"Like you," said city manager Richard Belmudez, "we
know that these two individuals don't define the 74,998 individuals who live in this community."

Captain Greg Fellows of the Riverside County Sheriff's Department urged residents to volunteer for community service to ensure this never happens again.

"You would be surprised," said Fellows, "that the extra
eyes and ears you have [can] make a significant difference in your community."

At the end of the meeting, there was a solemn procession to 160 Muir Woods Road for a vigil, where residents lit candles and sang "Amazing Grace."

Later that night, ABC's *20/20* broadcast a special on the Turpin case, retracing David and Louise's life back to Princeton, West Virginia. Riverside County DA Michael Hestrin gave an exclusive interview for the program, revealing new details about the case.

"You've got parents who are torturing their children," he said. "Causing them pain. Causing them suffering over a prolonged period to time through malnourishment, through physical abuse, through psychological abuse. It's horrific."

Elizabeth Flores was also featured, describing their childhood back in Princeton, West Virginia, as "a pretty normal life." But when prompted, she did open up about the darker parts of her and Louise's past.

"There was sexual abuse by a family member," she admitted. "A close family friend, not our parents. We were not allowed to talk about it. And I'm not making excuses for my sister, but I think that may have been an [underlying] issue."

Elizabeth said that both Louise's and David's families had attended the same Pentecostal church in Princeton.

"I've known David all my life," she told *20/20*'s Elizabeth Vargas. "My parents and his parents were pretty close. We all attended the Princeton Church of God for years and years and years."

The show turned to Louise and David's time in Texas, where they had had most of their thirteen children. Ashley Vinyard, whose brief friendship with Jennifer and Joshua was ended by their mother, recalled the day they all moved into a double-wide trailer at the back of the house. She never saw them again.

"The secrecy just grew and grew," she said. "One day they just vanished."

Billy Baldwin, who bought the Turpin spread after it was foreclosed on, said the house was left in a disgusting mess. He also showed some Polaroid pictures that he had found, pointing out a rope hanging off a bed rail in one of the children's bedrooms.

"But we didn't have no idea what was going there," he said. "I really feel bad that something like that would happen."

The special followed the Turpins to Southern California, focusing on their trips to Disneyland.

"She was obsessed with Disneyland," said Elizabeth. "Her whole marriage they've had season passes and go regularly. They were obsessed with Disney and Mickey Mouse."

The show also screened video clips from one of the Turpins' three wedding renewal ceremonies in Las Vegas.

"It was a fun wedding," said Elvis impersonator Kent Ripley, "because I got to see smiles on their kids' faces."

Mike Clifford Sr., who lived opposite the Turpins in Murrieta, California, said he often saw the siblings after midnight, marching back and forth in single file. He thought it was some kind of therapy.

At the end of the show, DA Hestrin once again appealed for anyone who knew anything to contact the newly set up Turpin tip line.

"We want to know anything and everything," he said. "These alleged crimes were committed in a closed house, in a closed room under cover of darkness. But someone must have seen something, and we're asking for the public's help."

————————

On Sunday, January 21, one week after the escape, Jim and Betty Turpin attended a service at the Princeton Church of God. Afterward, they met with Pastor Ray Hurt for counseling.

"[David's] family, his mother and father, are very faithful, very solid citizens," said Dr. Hurt. "And their concern has been primarily for their grandchildren, because through the years they've been kept apart from them. They haven't been able to get very much response from their son and daughter-in-law."

The grandparents told the pastor about their last family visit to Murrieta.

"They said they did not notice any behaviors in the children out of the ordinary," he said. "They acted happy. Now, of course, the Turpins are elderly and only there for a few days. And they're not trained professionals in terms of psychology, so they might not have noticed anything."

The Church of God pastor also emphasized that David and Louise Turpin's treatment of their children had absolutely nothing to do with Pentecostal teachings.

"We consider children a gift from God," he said, "to be nurtured and cared for. We stick to a pretty strict admonition of care and love for children. I don't know where they came up with their ideology, their thinking. Something happened to them after they left here, obviously."

24

FAMILY SECRETS

On Monday, January 22, Teresa Robinette was the special guest on *Megan Kelly Today*. In front of a studio audience, an emotional Teresa said David and Louise were now dead to her after what they had done.

"Let's talk about Louise," said Kelly. "There was abuse in your family. In the wake of this discovery, can you tell us a little about that?"

"A very, very close family member that we should have loved and trusted abused my mother," said Teresa, tearing up. "And then me and Louise and Elizabeth and a few of our cousins. That was ongoing for me and my sisters . . . and my mother still took us around this person a lot."

Kelly asked if she had ever publicly outed the man responsible.

"No," Teresa replied. "The adults in our family protected him because he was family . . . but it was always a dark family secret that he did this."

Teresa told Kelly about Louise and David's trip to Alabama and their sexual experimentation. Teresa said that, growing up, Louise had never smoked a cigarette or drank alcohol because of her strict religious beliefs. But when she turned forty, she and David stopped going to church, began drinking, and had an open marriage.

At the end of the interview, Kelly asked what Teresa hoped would happen with all her nieces and nephews.

"My main hope is that I can put my arm around them," she replied, "and just tell them they have family that love them. That's not deranged. That this is what it's supposed to be like."

On Monday afternoon, a Canadian skydiver died after colliding with another jumper and crashing into the roof of a house less than a mile away from Muir Woods Road. When the reporters camped outside the Turpin house learned the news, they rushed to the scene of the accident, giving residents a brief respite from the constant media presence.

"That was the only time they left," said resident Donald Kick. "The chute didn't open, and he must have collided with his friend. All of a sudden they were onto the next thing. So if it bleeds, it reads."

That same day, Dr. Randy Turpin contacted Child Protective Services in California, expressing interest in adopting some of his younger nieces and nephews. He even posted a video message online for the siblings saying, "I'm looking forward to having you join us."

But when CPS returned his call, there was no answer, and he'd hired an attorney to field media inquiries.

Since his brother's and sister-in-law's arrests, the president of Valor Christian College had kept a low profile, refusing to give interviews. But a 2011 photograph on his Facebook page showing Randy's and David's families together at Disneyland had been discovered and shared by the media, along with the caption: "A memory that I will hold to for the rest of my life. It was so great being with you guys."

His book *21 Days of Prayer and Fasting* had also received extensive publicity in light of the malnourished condition the Turpin children had been found in.

Church of God pastor Ray Hurt said he knew Randy and was familiar with his religious work.

"His family seems very well balanced," said Dr. Hurt. "So what's going on with David is a complete anomaly."

Dr. Hurt insisted that fasting was always done in a biblical context and never forced on anybody.

"And so I would think, knowing Randy the way I do," said Dr. Hurt, "that his approach to fasting had absolutely no connection with anything that went on out there. I mean, they're in complete different contexts."

On Wednesday, David and Louise Turpin were back in Riverside Superior Court to hear Judge Emma Smith's ruling on the prosecution's motion to stop them from contacting their children. Before the hearing, public defender Steve Harmon had filed a motion claiming the "extraordinary" media coverage of the Turpin case could poison a future jury pool and requesting a change of venue for the trial.

At 1:30 p.m., the press was allowed to enter Judge Smith's courtroom, where Louise and David were already sitting at the defense table, shackled at their wrists and feet. Defense lawyers had visited the Turpins' home and collected clothes for them to wear at the hearing. David was wearing a gray suit with a purple shirt and tie, and Louise had a white button-down shirt and jacket, her frizzy graying hair falling over her shoulders. At one point, she looked at her husband and smiled.

Deputy district attorney Kevin Beecham began by explaining that prosecutors had had to divide the thirteen children over two protective orders, since there were so many of them.

Then, as David and Louise Turpin looked on without a hint of emotion, Judge Smith read out her three-year protective order.

"You must not harass, strike, threaten, assault, follow, stalk, molest, destroy, or damage property of the [victims]," she told them. "Disturb the peace of, keep under surveillance or block the entrance of the protected people. You must not try to, or actually get their addresses. You must have no personal, electronic, telephone, or written contact with any of the people listed . . . except through their lawyer.

"And finally, you must stay at least one hundred yards away from all of them at all times, other than court proceedings, where everyone is ordered to be present. Okay, all right?"

The two defendants nodded. Judge Smith ordered them to be back in court on February 22 for a felony settlement conference to discuss the attorneys' preparedness for a preliminary hearing. After the hearing, Louise grinned at her attorney.

Outside the courtroom, David Macher told reporters that he had already begun his investigation into the case, refusing to elaborate further.

A Riverside County public guardian had been appointed to care for the seven adult Turpin siblings, as they were unable to take care of themselves. They would eventually move into a supervised living facility. The six minors, who had asked to remain together, had already been discharged from the hospital and split up to live in two foster homes.

"You have two different agencies overseeing the children," said *Press-Enterprise* reporter Brian Rokos. "The public guardian has oversight of the adults, and the Department of Social Services has oversight of the minors."

Teresa Robinette told *Inside Edition* that she did not want the six underage siblings to be kept apart.

"That's the worst-case scenario," she said. "We would like to get family members of ours together to make sure that each one of these kids is placed with a blood family member. That way, even if they are scattered, they would still be with our family and they would still have a connection for life."

On January 27, the two-week anniversary of Jordan's escape, DA Michael Hestrin appeared on the local KCBS News for an investigation update.

"We're working around the clock to leave no stone unturned," he said.

The DA theorized that the Turpin family had been able to fly under the radar so long because of their nocturnal existence.

"These crimes," he said, "by their very nature, happen behind closed doors and in dark places, and they go undetected."

He was then asked how the victims were progressing, both emotional and medically.

"They're doing well," he replied. "They're relieved. They are being well fed and being well cared for. My sense is that they've got the best professionals looking after them, not just their physical well-being but their mental and emotional well-being."

Hestrin again said that he believed the hundreds of journals the siblings kept over the years would provide "significant" evidence against their parents at trial.

"You have to sit back for a second," he said, "and think how rare it is to have evidence directly of what a victim in a case like this went through."

The day after David and Louise Turpin were ordered not to have any contact with their children for three years, Austrian kidnapping victim Natascha Kampusch gave an interview saying the siblings should be able to confront their parents. Now thirty, Natascha had been snatched off a Vienna street at the age of ten by Wolfgang Přiklopil. She then spent eight years as his hostage in a secret cellar under his garage. Finally, she ran away and alerted authorities, but Přiklopil committed suicide by jumping in front of a train before he could be arrested.

Kampusch, who has written several books about her ordeal and participated in a documentary, told *The Sun* that it would be a vital part of their healing process for the Turpin children to interact with their abusers.

"It is important that they have contact with their parents," she said, "and the ability to visit them in prison. They will need to find a way to either forgive them or leave them behind."

Being able to tell their parents that they either hate them or forgive them would be very therapeutic, she said. "It will help them begin a process where they can cope with the whole situation and get more stable. The children will need closure."

25

LEARNING TO FLY

Since the Turpin children's rescue, Elizabeth Flores and Teresa Robinette had been speaking candidly to the media about their sister Louise's tragic childhood. Their first cousin Tricia Andreassen had also been a victim of her grandfather's abuse as a child. She had grown up with the three Robinette sisters but lost touch with the family after leaving home.

Then in 2012, Tricia reconnected with Elizabeth on Facebook, and they began to rebuild their relationship. In the twenty-five years since leaving Princeton, West Virginia, Tricia had become an author, life coach, and motivational speaker. She calls herself "an Unstoppable Warrior."

Since Louise's arrest, the cousins had become even closer, finding freedom after years of being instructed to remain silent about their childhood abuse. In the foreword to Elizabeth's memoir, which Tricia published, she wrote that God had given her a mission to help Elizabeth tell her story.

"My life calling was putting me front and center to raise my own voice," she wrote, "and share it along with Elizabeth."

On her Facebook page, Tricia posted photographs of herself and Elizabeth on the sets for *Good Morning America, ABC World News Tonight,* and *The Dr. Oz Show.*

"My beautiful cousin [Tricia]," Elizabeth commented, "friend, mentor, coach, and most of all my ROCK!"

On Monday, January 29, Elizabeth appeared on *Dr. Phil,* talking about how Louise had changed after eloping with David.

"When she left home, she wanted to put everything behind her," Elizabeth told Dr. Phil, "including our family, because of our history of abuse as children."

However, when Dr. Phil asked her for more details, she remained vague. Elizabeth emphasized the abuse was by a "family member" and not her parents, without elaborating further.

But the next day, Elizabeth and Tricia appeared together on *The Dr. Oz Show,* where they tearfully unmasked the family member who had molested them all.

During the highly emotional interview in front of a studio audience, Elizabeth spoke in detail about the abuse. She theorized that it could have led to Louise abusing her own children so many years later.

"I feel that a sense of control [is] maybe what she wanted," said Elizabeth. "She never had control in her life growing up. And she didn't have friends in school [and] was made fun of a lot. That's where Disneyland and everything comes in."

Elizabeth said although she and her cousins had all gone through the same abuse, they were nothing like Louise.

"Can I ask you about the family abuse?" said Dr. Oz.

"A very, very close family member that we were with daily abused all the cousins. And it was just swept under the rug, I guess. If it came up, it was like we were lying."

Elizabeth told him they had all been groomed by their abuser, who would provide cues before it happened.

"It was like, 'We've got to go in the other room, you've got to give me a big hug,'" said Elizabeth. "And we knew what that meant."

Tricia added that she had told her parents about the abuse, but they did nothing about it.

"So all of us girls were trained," Tricia said, "to be fake or not to come forward."

Elizabeth said their abuser was "very wealthy," using his money as a bargaining tool.

"He was the family leader," she said. "When my mom needed money, she ran to this person."

"Was this person her father?" asked Dr. Oz gently.

"Yes," Elizabeth admitted. She broke down in tears as Tricia gripped her hand in reassurance.

"Your grandfather?"

"Yes."

Elizabeth told Dr. Oz how her grandmother had once caught him raping Louise on the couch, which had led to their divorce.

"She took a frying pan after him," she sobbed. "And she still didn't report it, because the thing was that we had to keep our family name. It was a very small town, so everybody knew him. My grandfather would throw money at her as long as he got what he wanted."

A *Dr. Oz* producer had tracked down John Taylor, now ninety-three, and asked for his comments.

"No, I don't think they were sexually abused when they were little," he told the producer. "I'm sure they weren't."

That night, the Perris City Council discussed the House of Horrors, praying for the thirteen children's recovery.

"Our hearts and prayers are with that family," said

Mayor Vargas, "with those kids as they continue to progress in their therapy. It's been an extremely tough month for all of us."

The council also donated $10,000 to the Perris Victims of Neglect Fund.

On Wednesday, the Corona Chamber of Commerce hosted a "dine-out day" to raise money for the Turpin siblings. More than three dozen restaurants participated, donating 20 percent of their takings that day to the children's fund. More than $400,000 had now been raised, with contributions coming from as far away as Italy.

Amy Duggar King, a cousin of the stars of the reality show *19 Kids and Counting,* announced that she wanted to adopt all thirteen of the Turpin siblings. Ironically, this was the show that David and Louise had always dreamed of emulating.

"I would love to show them true love and have a beautiful life and provide a secure and stable home for them," Amy tweeted. "Anyone who can hurt animals and starve, torture children in any way needs to be hung by their toenails. Watching the news just breaks my heart. God can restore what the devil has stolen."

During their long years of incarceration, the Turpin siblings had passed the time by writing songs and singing to one another. Mark Uffer would often bring his acoustic guitar into their wing at the Corona Regional Medical Center and play them music. A drummer in a local rock band, Uffer thought music would be great therapy to help them heal.

"Music is very soothing and a great hobby," he told *People* magazine. "It takes you to a quiet place."

One particular favorite of the older siblings was John

Denver's "Take Me Home, County Roads," which they would sing along to.

"They all have good voices, beautiful voices," said Uffer, "and the tears started running down the nurses' faces."

After learning that the Turpins were big John Denver fans, the late singer's estate sent over a box of his complete discography.

Uffer contacted the Fender guitar factory, which is located in Corona, asking if it could donate some guitars to the siblings. The legendary guitar maker was only too happy to oblige, sending over thirteen acoustic guitars.

After they were delivered to the hospital, staff lined them all up against a wall, labeled with each siblings' name. The kids were then brought in and given the guitars. They were overjoyed and overcome by the gifts.

"The sight would have brought you to your knees," said Uffer. "They all wanted to love you and hug you and say thanks. They are very appreciative."

Before being rescued, none of them, except Joshua, had ever seen a real guitar before, except on television or in the movies.

"To [see them] actually physically hold a guitar," reflected Uffer, "was heartwarming to watch. They didn't know what to do with it, but they liked the sounds it made."

They immediately started guitar lessons, held in a hospital conference room, and had sing-alongs. Another favorite was Tom Petty's "Learning to Fly," the emotional, optimistic lyrics really resonating with them all.

"They fell in love with the song," said Uffer. "They seem to understand it."

Wednesday, February 14—Valentine's Day—marked the one-month anniversary of the children's escape. To celebrate, the Turpin siblings all received special gifts from the Corona Chamber of Commerce.

Chamber president Bobby Spiegel had received a call from a woman in North Carolina who had just started her own porcelain doll business.

"She said she'd like to send a couple of dolls," said Spiegel. "And I said I need ten. And so she hung up the phone and prayed."

The woman, who makes collectable religious dolls, emailed all her customers and vendors asking for money to buy supplies. Within a day, they had donated enough for her to make each of the Turpin girls her own personalized doll.

"They're beautiful," said Spiegel, "and we gave them to the girls on Valentine's Day, and they fell in love with them."

But the chamber did not forget the three boys, who had already grown out of the clothes bought for them a month earlier.

"One of the best blessings is that they're being nourished with good food and exercise," said Spiegel. "So the pants that we had bought them early on don't fit them, and we went out and bought them each three new pairs of pants for Valentine's Day."

Staff at the Corona Medical Center had also set up an outdoor area, where the siblings could exercise and play soccer and basketball. They were eating well for the first time in their lives. They loved lentil soup, fish, and lasagna, but still couldn't tolerate burritos.

The siblings delighted in making personalized bracelets for hospital staff, using lettered beads to spell names and funny messages.

"They would take the stretchy twine they make bracelets out of," said Uffer, "and would make one for me saying, 'Outstanding CEO' or 'Coolest CEO ever.' We had lots of donations of crafts, people sending Play-Doh, crayons, and coloring books."

They also left Post-it notes in various staff offices to show their appreciation. They would write things like "We love you" and "Thank you for taking care of us." They even left one for the hospital CEO with a picture of a horse and the message, "Green Acres is the place for Mark Uffer."

"They do have a good sense of humor," said Uffer. "They are very loving, [and] you can tell they are hungry for attention."

One morning, someone snuck onto the Turpin property and stole one of David Turpin's cars. A few hours later, his Volkswagen Beetle disappeared too. Then someone slashed the tires of the Turpins' Chevrolet van. Riverside County Sheriff's Department soon arrested a twenty-nine-year-old drifter for the theft of the Volkswagen. The first car stolen has never been recovered.

A month after their lives had been turned upside down, Muir Woods Road was slowly returning to normal for the Turpins' neighbors. Since the arrest, the street had been besieged by media from all over the world. A dozen television trucks had occupied most of the available curb space, and residents could not step outside without reporters questioning them about the Turpin family.

Neighbor Kimberly Milligan said her street had become "an amusement park."

"The morbid curiosity," she said. "That's what's most disheartening. It's tunnel vision to that house and not respecting everyone else."

Wendy Martinez told *The Press-Enterprise* that this "will be a scar on our neighborhood forever. Every car that passes is a stare-down."

Outside 160 Muir Woods Road, the motley collection of balloons, candles, and flowers was still growing. Among the dozens of moving messages left on the porch, one from another abuse victim stood out.

"Sweet children," it read, "I come from an abusive childhood as well. I learned to trust God and truly rise above it. This is now your story to help other kids recover from something similar too. The road is long and painful, but you will rise and be strong from it. Trust the Lord and keep your faith in him."

On Friday, February 16, DA Hestrin announced his intention to put some of the Turpin siblings on the stand to testify against their parents if the case went to trial.

Speaking at the Corona Chamber of Commerce's monthly meeting, he said that over the next few months, his highly trained victim advocates would be helping the Turpin children become acquainted with the court process.

"When you have a child victim," he explained, "you just can't put that child on the witness stand like you would an adult. They've got to understand and feel comfortable with the process."

Hestrin said that the Turpin siblings would likely go to court several times before they testified, to meet the judge and familiarize themselves with the courtroom and experience sitting on the witness stand.

"It's traumatizing," explained Hestrin. "Imagine a child who's been abused by a parent, victimized by a caregiver, and now we're going to ask [them] to come into court and relive that crime in front of a jury. In front of strangers. Imagine having to recount the most painful moment of your lives, when you were the most vulnerable, having to talk about it in public, and be questioned about it and have your credibility questioned."

The DA said he had personally prepared child victims for court before and would always tell them never to look at their abusers as they testify.

"[I told them] 'You can look at me, and we're going to talk,'" said Hestrin. "'Look me right in the eye, and we're going to have a conversation, just like we're doing right now.' And it would start to get these kids to feel comfortable. Get them to be able to talk and to testify in what would otherwise be an impossible situation."

Meanwhile, a Riverside County probate judge had appointed attorneys Jack Osborn and Caleb Mason, of the Los Angeles–based law firm of Brown, White & Osborn, to represent the seven adult siblings. "[This] is a new experience for them," said Osborn, "understanding that they do have rights and they do have a voice."

The attorneys told CBS News that their new clients were all progressing well at the Corona Medical Center, although their discharge had been put on hold after a flu outbreak.

The siblings were using their new iPads and catching up on *Harry Potter* and *Star Trek* movies. For the first time in their lives, they had the freedom to spend their time however they wanted. "That's a big deal," said Osborn, "deciding what they're going to read, deciding what they're going to wear. These are all decisions they make every day that are new and empowering. It's been more like being on a cruise ship than at this hospital."

Although the six younger and seven older siblings had not seen one another since their escape, they communicated daily on Skype. The older ones wanted to go to the beach or to the mountains or watch movies, said Osborn, and would like to eventually attend college and have careers.

"They all have their own aspirations and their own interests," he explained, "and now they may have an opportunity to address those, which is really exciting."

Corona mayor Karen Spiegel, married to Chamber of Commerce president Bobby Spiegel, told *People* magazine that she received daily progress reports on the older siblings from their nurses.

"They are warm and loving kids," she said. "Even though they're adults, we keep calling them kids; they just have some growing up to do."

On Friday, February 23, David and Louise Turpin were back in court, where they were each charged with three additional counts of child abuse. Louise was also hit with another felony assault charge.

"Further investigation has led us to amend the complaint," explained Riverside County DA spokesman John Hall. "It could add more time to the exposure they are facing."

David, who was in shackles and wearing a black suit with a blue shirt, had had his hair trimmed since the last hearing. Louise, in a navy blue suit, seemed unusually animated, swiveling and rocking in her chair as she glared at reporters.

Both sets of lawyers told Judge Emma Smith that their clients pleaded not guilty to all the new charges. Prosecutor Kevin Beecham told the judge that he would only call police officers to the stand if the case went to trial to avoid the children having to testify.

With the preliminary hearing—where it would be determined if there was sufficient evidence to proceed to trial—scheduled for May 14, defense attorney David Macher argued that he may need more time to prepare.

"Given the voluminous discovery in this case," he said,

"including audio and video statements, significant physical evidence, I am skeptical of being ready on May 14. I'm willing to set that date as a good faith date and will make the effort to be ready, but I don't know that we can."

"Your skepticism is noted," said the judge, setting another status hearing for March 23.

26

"SHE'S LIVING IN A FANTASY WORLD"

Three days later, *The Dr. Oz Show* flew Elizabeth Flores and Tricia Andreassen to California to visit Louise and David Turpin behind bars. They were picked up at their hotel by the show's crime correspondent, Melissa Moore, the daughter of Keith Jesperson, the notorious "Happy Face Killer." After surviving the trauma of growing up with her father, who was convicted of killing eight women and is now serving three life sentences in Oregon's state penitentiary, Moore wrote a book and became an advocate for the relatives of other serial killers.

As the cameras rolled, she assured the women that she understood what they were going through. "When I was about fifteen years old," she told them, "I had to go see my dad in jail, and I remember I didn't sleep all the night before."

On the drive to the Robert Presley Detention Center, Moore asked Elizabeth why she wanted to visit her sister in jail.

"Nothing changes the fact that she's my sister," replied Elizabeth, "and nobody in the world is supporting her. And I don't support what she did, but I do support the fact that she's still a human being."

Still, she was very nervous about seeing Louise, afraid to look her in the eye and see "pure evil," or that she had been brainwashed by David.

"I really believe he's almost like a puppeteer," said Tricia. "Like, 'If I do these things, I will get more of what I want and he won't bring his wrath onto me, because we'll be partnered up as a team.'"

As they arrived at the jail, Moore asked Elizabeth what she most wanted to ask Louise.

"Could she tell me why," said Elizabeth. "What was she thinking? What led to this?"

More than two hours later, Elizabeth and Tricia emerged from the jail, looking stunned. They said Louise was in complete denial.

"She's living in a fantasy world," said Elizabeth. "I kept thinking, *Am I going to see evil in her eyes?*"

Louise had cried at first but was happy to see them. She never once asked about her children and appeared to think she had done nothing wrong.

"As I was talking to her," said Elizabeth, "I realized that it's all fantasy. She's living in a movie. She's rewriting her own story."

The next day, Melissa Moore drove them back to the jail, this time to visit David Turpin. According to Elizabeth, Louise had asked them to go and see him, as she felt bad that he never had any visitors.

Elizabeth said the idea of seeing her brother-in-law again made her sick. "I do wish Louise would not have asked me to do this."

Added Tricia, "I feel like I'm going to see a sadistic person."

But after their visit, they had totally changed their opinion of David Turpin.

"He knew he had done wrong," Elizabeth explained. "He was remorseful. He cried the entire time. It wasn't fake."

She said David had broken down and sobbed uncontrollably at one point, even apologizing for watching her in the shower so many years earlier.

"It was like I was looking at a little boy that was ready to confess everything he had done. He kept saying, 'I wish I could tell you about what we've done. What happened.' But he'd been advised not to."

The next day, they were scheduled to visit Elizabeth's nieces and nephews at the Corona Regional Medical Center. Before leaving the hotel, Moore filmed them putting the final touches on pillows they'd made for each of the seven siblings. They had embroidered uplifting messages on them, like "Let Your Light Shine."

But when Elizabeth and Teresa arrived at the hospital, they were turned away at the front door. They left the pillows with the siblings' attorney, Jack Osborn, expressing their disappointment at not being able to see the children.

Moore then drove them to Perris to see the infamous House of Horrors for themselves.

"I feel like it's a nightmare I can't wake up from," said Elizabeth on the drive over. "Every step is so nerve-racking."

After being filmed walking up to the front door and reading some of the messages left outside the home, Elizabeth broke down in tears.

"What hurts so bad is everybody else cared more about the kids than their parents," she sobbed. "The kids just wanted help. They just wanted somebody to reach out. What they endured was hell for so long. Their cries nobody heard."

On March 2, world-famous cellist Yo-Yo Ma played a
private concert for all thirteen Turpin siblings at the Corona Regional Medical Center, after hearing about their
love of music and being moved by their tragic story. It
was the first time all the children had been together since
the escape, an emotional moment for everyone.

"They were just really amazed," said Mark Uffer, "awe-
struck by the level of the talent. They really enjoyed it."

Ma, who was in California at the time for a concert at
the Hollywood Bowl, did not respond to media requests for
comment or mention it on his official website. The private
concert was arranged by the Corona Chamber of Commerce after Ma said he wanted to do something special
for the Turpin children.

"He decided he wanted to go and visit with the kids,"
said Bobby Spiegel, "and just interact with them a little
bit. And it was beautiful. One of the kids said, 'Hey, this
is great, but who are you?' They had no clue."

Four days later, *Good Morning America* (*GMA*) revealed
that Jordan Turpin had been active on social media before
her escape, posting a series of videos on her own YouTube
channel and posting to Twitter and Instagram under the
alias Lacey Swan. In the segment, promising "a new look
inside the House of Horrors," *GMA* reported that her last
video was posted just a week before she escaped. Clips
were shown of Jordan singing several of her songs, her
face blurred out.

As soon as the story broke, YouTube and Instagram
immediately took down all her accounts, but her Twitter
remained.

The Riverside County District Attorney's Office refused to confirm or deny the videos were posted by one
of the Turpin daughters.

"There has been a recent media report about one of the victims in the David and Louise Turpin case being on social media," read a statement issued by the DA's press office. "Our office has not commented on that report nor will we be confirming or commenting on it as this continues to be an active investigation."

In the first week of March, ninety-three-year-old John Thomas Taylor gave a brief telephone interview. He said he was aware that Louise had been arrested for torture and neglecting his great-grandchildren.

"No, I don't know anything about it," said Taylor. "I just know they're in trouble. I've seen that on the news. They have been prosecuted, and that's all I know."

When asked about the growing allegations of sexual molestation leveled at him by his female family members, he was noncommittal, though he'd previously denied the claims to the *Dr. Oz* producer.

"Well, I don't need to be interviewed [about that]," he said. "I can't understand what you're saying, [and] you don't need to know what my business is."

Suddenly, he announced that he had made a will three years earlier and was leaving everything to his only surviving son, James.

"I ain't leaving the grandchildren nothing," he snapped, hanging up.

27

A NEW LIFE

On Thursday, March 15, the seven Turpin adults were secretly whisked away from the Corona Regional Medical Center, where they had lived for two months. Their attorney, Jack Osborn, and their public guardian escorted them to a rural house at an undisclosed location to begin the next stage of their recovery.

"The adult siblings want to be known as survivors, not victims," said Osborn, adding that their pet dogs would soon be joining them.

Their nurses and doctors, who had all formed close emotional attachments with the siblings, threw them a going-away party before they left.

They dined on pizza and sandwiches, and then a karaoke machine was brought in so the siblings could sing their favorite songs.

"They love to sing," said Mark Uffer, "and love to interact with people. They can sense people that actually care for them, so they were very attached."

During their two-month stay at the hospital, the seven siblings made a deep impression on everybody they met.

Despite all the years of abuse and neglect, they were still capable of feeling love and returning it.

"That is what is so heartbreaking," said Uffer. "We only read what the parents allegedly did to them. [When you] interact with them on a day-to-day basis, you find it really hard to understand how seven young adults and six children could have been abused yet so capable of giving love back."

The siblings and hospital staff were emotional when it came time to say their final goodbyes.

"This has been their home away from wherever they were at before," said Uffer. "It was a very touching experience for all of the staff, so [the goodbye] was a little bit tough. If you asked the nurses, they would all tell you it was a life-changing experience."

At the end of the party, the siblings gave each of the staff presents they had made to show their gratitude.

"It was like a birthday party environment," said Uffer. "They made gifts for each of us, little crafts for each one of us. They made bracelets out of beads that they gave to the nurses. They had little scrapbooks that they wanted us to all write messages in before they left so they had something to remember us by."

The nursing staff were also given personalized bracelets the siblings had lovingly made as mementos.

"They gave them from their hearts. That is all they had to give. They truly loved the people they were interacting with over the last two months."

Leaving the hospital was a very traumatic moment for the siblings. When the public guardian arrived to collect them, they cried. And when they were taken to the vehicles to take them to their new home, they kept sneaking back into the hospital.

"They were tearful," said Uffer, "and I think a little bit

afraid. I told them we weren't going to say goodbye—we are going to say, 'Until we meet again.' We are hopeful it wasn't a goodbye."

The location of their new home is such a closely guarded secret that no one at the Corona Regional Medical Center has been told where it is. Mark Uffer had wanted to have the nurses and physicians, whom the children now trusted, continue their treatment out of the hospital, but the public guardian and their appointed attorneys immediately cut off all communication.

"It is a little bit disturbing for us," said Uffer. "We were hopeful we could do a transition with them and get them to their new place, and wanted to send the nurses and therapists out to make sure. But we have no idea where they are."

The hospital CEO said he was also concerned because it could be years before the siblings are ready to live on their own.

"They have to learn basic skills," he said. "Shopping, cooking, laundry, things that we all take for granted. I don't think they have those basic skills yet. It's going to take some work."

While their stay at the hospital had helped heal some of their physical wounds, child trauma expert Allison Davis Maxon observed that the Turpin siblings would now move on to the complicated process of healing emotionally and mentally.

"Trauma, neglect, and deprivation hits us typically on three general levels," Maxon explained. "You have the body—how it's going to hit our physiological system. Extreme neglect may cause some permanent physical issues that the kids may have. They may have medical issues or diseases that weren't treated. Things that occurred from starvation and extreme neglect.

"Then you have their psyche. Their mind. *Why did it happen to me? Was it my fault?* Children often think like that. So how their minds heal from this will be important to address in therapy. How they tell the story of their life and what happened to them is critical in their healing from these events."

Finally, there was the emotional piece of the healing puzzle.

"You have children," she said, "exposed to tremendous amounts of distress, pain, trauma, violence, and torture. So emotionally, they have accumulated a tremendous amount of toxic stress and pain that needs to be addressed as well." One positive, said the trauma therapist, was that the siblings all went through the nightmare together. This would be an important part of their healing journey.

"They probably had a level of trust within their bonds with each other," she explained. "So while they didn't trust their parents most likely, they might have developed that trust with their older siblings. And vice versa.

"They can develop some of those [emotional] skills, because you have older kids taking care of younger kids. And as they're healing in the outside world, the relationships they develop with folks over time, and building intimacy and authenticity into those relationships, they can develop an ability to trust. They can experience and learn that not all humans are the same as their mom and dad."

According to Maxon, the abrupt removal of the siblings from the connections they'd made at the hospital could be detrimental to their healing.

"Children who have horrific childhood experiences with both parents can develop loving, trusting relationships with people who are there for them on an ongoing basis over their life span. It doesn't happen quickly, and it shouldn't. What they are going to need are folks permanently committed to them," Maxon said. "Not a lot of temporary people rotating in and out of their lives, but people that are very committed to them and their healing over the long haul. And that's really healing that relational dance and what we call the *corrective experience,* making sure they have access to meaningful, long-term, safe, loving, and healing relationships."

The day after the older siblings were discharged from Corona Regional Medical Center, senior investigator Wade Walsvick interviewed Jordan Turpin, who was now living in a foster home. Jordan told him about her miserable life in Murrieta, saying she barely received any education.

"She equated her level of education to that of a first grader," said Walsvick.

The investigator, trained in questioning child abuse victims, said Jordan had accused her father of sexually assaulting her at the Murrieta house. Giving more detail than she had earlier, Jordan said it happened during Thanksgiving 2013, when she was only twelve. Father had been sitting in a recliner in the upstairs TV room, when he beckoned her over.

After he pulled her pants down, she pulled them back up, saying she didn't like that. But he pulled them down again, lifted her up, and placed her on his lap. At that point, they heard Mother coming up the stairs, and he let her go.

"She said her father directed her not to tell anyone," said Walsvick. "She described it as one of the worst days of her life."

Jordan said that she was so upset, she decided to kill herself. She went into the bathroom and filled up the sink, planning to drown herself. But then she changed her mind.

Three weeks later, Walsvick interviewed the oldest siblings, Jennifer and Joshua Turpin. Jennifer told him she had reached third grade at Meadowcreek Elementary in Fort Worth before her parents had taken her out of school. Jennifer said Mother had eventually presented them with high school diplomas.

"She said it wasn't real," said the investigator, "because you just simply ordered it online, which is what her mother did for her. She said that's for homeschoolers."

The investigator also asked her whose idea it was to start chaining up the children as punishment.

"She told me it was her father's idea to utilize chains," Walsvick later testified. "He said, 'Things were going to continue to keep missing in the house if we don't chain all of them.'"

Jennifer said that Mother had opposed it, only wanting to chain up "suspects" who had stolen food or other things.

When Walsvick interviewed Joshua, he was extremely agitated.

"To say that he was nervous and anxious would be an understatement," said the investigator. "Joshua could barely speak at some points of the interview."

Joshua described the different levels of punishment his parents had inflicted on the siblings, and their progression over the years.

"The low threshold would be slapping, knocking on the head, hitting, and/or throwing across the room," the investigator testified. "And he made a point to explain to me that being pushed was not as simplistic as it sounds. If you were pushed by either his mother or his father, it threw you to the ground or across the room. It was to that degree."

The next level of punishment would be whipping with a belt. It would start with the leather end, but his parents soon progressed to using the buckle end, which would break skin. If a sibling continued to disobey after that, their parents would use a paddle and then an oar to beat them on the lower back, buttocks, and legs.

"He described the oar as the worst of the worst," said Walsvick.

"Joshua said his parents also beat them with what he called 'a switch,' which was a metal tent pole wrapped in fiberglass, with metal tips on the end that would break the skin. [His parents] would both implement and utilize these devices. He preferred it if his mother would do it [as] she did not have the strength [his father] did."

If these punishments still did not work to curb their behavior, they would be caged up like animals. Mother and Father used two types of cages while they lived in the trailer in Rio Vista, Texas. The first, a metal-framed cage with a thick pegboard siding, could hold two offenders. At the bottom, there was just enough space to slide food inside. But they stopped using it after Jonathan managed to escape.

Then Mother and Father brought in a three-by-three-foot dog cage, which Joshua referred to as "a common shepherd dog kennel."

"That would be locked with an additional lock and key," said the investigator. "You cannot stand up in it and you cannot escape from it."

His parents had once locked him in the cage for a day, Joshua said, after Mother caught him watching a *Star Wars* movie.

Joshua also explained that they had moved into the double-wide trailer in Rio Vista after their house had become uninhabitable. Soon afterward, Mother and Father left, moving into a more comfortable apartment with their two youngest children, Jolinda and Julissa.

"They abandoned the children for . . . three years," explained the investigator, "[to live] in an apartment approximately fifty miles away."

Joshua said that their parents had left him and Jennifer in charge of their eight younger siblings, changing their diapers and feeding them. Father occasionally came by with food, but they never saw Mother. However, they continued to control their children over the phone, ordering Joshua and Jennifer to punish their siblings for any misdeeds or risk being put in "time-outs" in the cages themselves.

During the interview, Joshua struggled to explain how he had once tried to rebel. But he was so overcome with emotion that he could not finish telling Walsvick the story.

"I chose to take the correct path to keep my siblings alive," Joshua said.

On Friday, March 23, David and Louise Turpin were back in Riverside County Superior Court for a felony settlement conference to discuss the exchange of discovery and other issues. A few minutes before the hearing started, Elizabeth Flores, Tricia Andreassen, and Melissa Moore arrived with Denise Perdoux, an attorney from *The Dr. Oz Show,* and waited outside the courtroom. They were allowed in to take their seats before the press entered.

Inside, David and Louise Turpin were already at the defense table with their respective attorneys. For the first time, neither of the defendants were shackled.

Before the hearing began, Judge Emma Smith summoned all the attorneys into her chambers for a conference. Alone at the defense table and just three feet apart, the defendants smiled at each other. Louise whispered something to David, but a female bailiff ordered her to be quiet. She smiled at her sister and cousin, who sat in the back row of the public gallery directly behind her.

During the five-minute hearing, a representative of

Riverside Adult Protective Services handed over two boxes of evidence containing information about the seven adult siblings. It was immediately sealed by the judge.

After court adjourned for the day, reporters and TV crews besieged Elizabeth and Tricia outside the Riverside Hall of Justice, shouting questions about Louise. At one point, a tearful Elizabeth had a panic attack and had to sit down on a bench to recover. Once she regained her composure, she was escorted to a waiting car by Tricia and Melissa Moore.

Outside his law offices, defense attorney David Macher was asked about Elizabeth's recent announcement that she was writing a book and the ongoing coverage on Louise from *The Dr. Oz Show*.

"Isn't that nice. Family," he said. "It does sound like people are trying to turn it into a reality show and make a profit off it."

Two weeks after the seven adult Turpin children moved into their new home, their attorney, Caleb Mason, gave *People* an update on their progress. Their main priority, he said, would be to get an education.

"They are all bright and articulate," said Mason, "and incredibly eager to study. The thing they want more than anything else is an education."

The attorney said a local university was drafting an educational plan to help them get their GEDs or high school diplomas.

"That is what we are trying to remedy right now," explained Mason. "They do not want to be sequestered doing their education online. They want to get the same sort of education as anyone else. We are hoping that we can find them, within the next couple of years, sitting in a college campus taking notes like anybody else. They have the same . . . educational aspirations as any other group of young adults."

Mason said it had been inspirational to witness the siblings adapting to their new lives after leaving the hospital.

"It is pretty new and different," he said, "and, I think, quite extraordinary to have some freedom, really for the first time, and experience life outside the type of constraints they had experienced. It is an extraordinarily positive thing for them, and it will take some time to get used to. They are moving to the next phase of their journey, which is actually beginning to rejoin the community."

The siblings' transition into the outside world would deliberately be slow, to help them acclimatize.

"Eventually, they are going to be just regular people, going to classes, getting jobs . . . and you would never know," said Mason. "The problem is that they have been through some unparalleled trauma, so it is going to take a little time. But I think they are very resilient, and they are going to ultimately be fine."

The Dr. Oz Show flew Elizabeth Flores and Tricia Andreassen back to Princeton, West Virginia, to film a two-part special tracing the Turpin family roots.

On March 27, John Taylor had turned ninety-four. Days later, his granddaughter and grandniece arrived at his house in Bailey Hollow Road to finally confront him about his sexual abuse—"the original House of Horrors," as Melissa Moore described it.

From the car, Tricia spotted their grandfather outside in the backyard, pottering around.

"Oh my god!" cried Elizabeth. "My heart is racing."

Then Tricia got out of the car to confront him. She marched up to the front door and knocked, and Taylor opened the door and let her in. Half an hour later, she came out again, a blank look on her face.

Three weeks later, in front of a studio audience, Dr. Oz asked Tricia what had happened inside the house.

"I told him that I was Patty," she said, "and he remembered me. And I said, 'I'd like to address something with you right now. No matter what you say, I forgive you.'"

As the studio audience listened in rapt attention, Tricia explained that she had been "armored up" with her Bible, asking him about what he had done to Louise and other female family members.

"He had the opportunity to share that," she explained, "and he said, 'I don't remember what you're talking about.' He denied everything."

Tricia announced that she soon would be filing a criminal complaint against him.

"I'm going to press charges," she declared to the applause of the audience. "It's time for me not to live in the past."

Ten days after *The Dr. Oz Show* aired, John Taylor died at Princeton Community Hospital of natural causes. In his obituary posted online by the funeral home, he was saluted as a highly decorated war hero and the former owner of the Shell station on Athens Road.

"John proudly served his county in the United States Army," it read. "During his time in the Army he was awarded two purple hearts; Silver Star; five bronze stars; Good Conduct Metal [sic] and French Fortiche metal [sic]. John was also the Past State President Purple Heart; Past Commander of the VFW, Mercer County Veterans Counsel, Member of the American Legion and DAV and was Chaplain for the Military funerals. John was also a member of the Church of God."

No mention was made of his granddaughter Louise or her children.

On April 9, Riverside assemblyman Jose Medina introduced a bill into the California State Assembly to tighten up regulations for homeschools. It was a direct response to the Turpin case and the lack of oversight it highlighted.

"I think it was clear [from the incident in Perris] that we don't have a lot of information on homeschooling in the state of California," Medina explained.

But the assemblyman knew it would be a difficult bill to get passed, as homeschooling was such a controversial subject.

"I call it swimming upstream," he said, "struggling to make it to the finish line—to make it to the governor's desk. That's the process."

In an editorial in *The Californian*, homeschooling advocate Maximo A. Gomez took issue with Medina's bill, labeling it progressive socialism.

"No doubt everyone . . . has heard of the tragedy in Southern California in which home-schooling parents were arrested in January for the psychological and physical abuse of their thirteen children," he wrote. "Louise and David Turpin were charged with multiple felony counts of torture, child abuse, abuse of dependent adults and false imprisonment. Now, the state of California, but principally . . . Assemblyman Jose Medina, [is] endeavoring to paint every home-schooling parent with the same brush. Every home-schooling parent in California has suddenly been transformed into a sexually depraved, masochistic, cultist, gun-toting nut job."

At the Assembly Education Committee meeting on Wednesday, April 25, Medina argued against this claim.

"I do not see a problem in the homeschool community," he told the committee. "I respect parents as educators, being an educator myself. This bill is not an attempt to in any way attack homeschooling."

But after a three-hour debate, Medina's bill died without a vote even being taken. Hundreds of homeschool parents and students from all over California had written to their assemblymen, opposing the bill.

After the meeting, Medina vowed to continue his fight to make homeschools more accountable. If they were, he said, "perhaps what happened with the Turpin family could have been avoided."

At the end of April, Teresa Robinette announced that she was writing "a tell-all book" about her family, to compete with her sister Elizabeth's *Sisters of Secrets,* about to be published.

After the Turpin story first broke, Elizabeth had posted on Facebook that she had started writing her childhood memoir two years earlier.

"It went into editing the same week the news hit," she wrote.

One of her Facebook friends then asked if Teresa was also participating in it.

"No," replied Elizabeth. "I'm an author. Teresa doesn't write books."

On April 28, Teresa and her half brother Billy Lambert appeared in a two-hour Oxygen cable special called *The Turpin 13: Family Secrets Exposed.* Hosted by Soledad O'Brien, the show retraced David and Louise's life in West Virginia, Texas, and California.

Teresa said she had talked to her nieces and nephews since their escape, and they remember all their Skype sessions with her.

"It was the best phone conversation I've ever had in my life," she told O'Brien. "It was a very happy conversation. But as soon as I hung up, the tears came."

Louise's youngest sister, now thirty-seven, said she would love to adopt two of the siblings, and Billy wanted three.

"I feel like I could do that fine," he said. "If I could get three of the kids, I would love to try and help in any way I can."

In an interview on Fox News to promote the special, Teresa revealed that Louise had called her several times collect from jail since her arrest.

"I wasn't planning on talking to her," she said. "I'm still pretty mad. But I did accept one collect call from her . . . a month ago."

Teresa refused to reveal the details of their conversation, saying she wanted no further communication with her sister.

"She's tried to call me several times since then," she said. "I have not accepted them because I am not paying to talk to her."

On Friday, May 4, David Turpin was hit with an additional eight counts of perjury, one for each of the years he'd filed a private school affidavit with the California Department of Education. He now faced a total of fifty felony charges.

At a brief hearing at Riverside Superior Court, the two defendants were again unshackled. David did not enter a plea to the new charges but was expected to do so at the next status hearing on May 18. Judge Emma Smith also agreed to postpone the preliminary hearing until June 20 to give the defense more time to prepare.

Outside the courtroom, deputy public defender David

Macher said his client still had the presumption of innocence to the new charges, as well as the older ones.

The following week, Macher filed a motion known as
a demurrer, objecting to the eight new charges of perjury
against his client. Macher argued that the perjury charges
were unrelated to the other charges, as they didn't involve
force, violence, or the physical neglect or abuse of David's
children.

Deputy district attorney Kevin Beecham disagreed,
filing a response in superior court.

"The falsity of giving education to multiple children,"
it stated, "is directly connected to the commission of neglecting children, as children require education in order
to eventually become independent. Therefore, the lack of
educating children is directly connected to them becoming dependent adults."

Arguing against the motion in court on May 18, Macher
told Judge Bernard J. Schwartz—who had taken over the
case from Emma Smith—that the new perjury charges
bore no relation to the other crimes his client is accused
of.

"A falsehood regarding education, if there is a falsehood," he argued, "is not part of an atmosphere. It's simply a misstatement written in a document."

Addressing Beecham's filed response, Macher told the
court that lack of education does not necessarily lead to a
dependent adult.

"A gentleman named Abraham Lincoln," he said,
"spent less than twelve months of his life in a classroom,
and he did rather well for himself. And there are other examples as well. So there's no linkage . . . and I would ask
the court to sustain the demurrer."

Beecham took the floor for his rebuttal. "Abraham Lincoln was educated," he began. "That's a difference with
what's alleged here, is that there are seven dependent adults

that were not educated, not homeschooled, and didn't go to school."

The deputy district attorney said their lack of education had created "the atmosphere of neglect that led to dependency," and all the crimes were connected.

Macher then apologized to Judge Schwartz for not using the word *autodidact* in his initial argument.

"I have to bring that up," he told the judge, "because the opportunities do not come up frequently to say President Lincoln was an autodidact. That means a self-taught person. And I'd submit—"

"All right," interrupted the judge. He had already reviewed the defense's motion and made a decision. He said that the defendant's "purported falsity" had prevented the Department of Education from checking on his children's well-being and taking them to a proper school.

"And as a result," said Judge Schwartz, "there was what's been described as a 'prolonged neglectful atmosphere in an uneducated environment' that led to them becoming dependent adults. I think that, on its face, is sufficient to overcome the demurrer."

David Turpin then entered not guilty pleas to the eight counts of perjury, and Louise pleaded not guilty to three charges of false imprisonment and one of assault.

28

"MY TWO LITTLE SISTERS
ARE CHAINED UP!"

By 8:30 a.m. on Wednesday, June 20, Riverside Superior
Court's Department 44 was packed with reporters and curious members of the public for David and Louise Turpin's
preliminary hearing. Judge Bernard Schwartz was only
allowing cameras to be used when he was not in the
court, and no photographs or audio recordings could be
taken during the proceedings.

At the defense table sat David Turpin, his white hair
now cropped to over his ears and brushed forward. He
was wearing a baggy blue shirt and a white, blue, and
yellow checked tie. A few feet away sat his wife, wearing
the same loose-fitting dark suit and white shirt. Neither
were shackled, and both had exceedingly long, well-
manicured fingernails. Deputy public defenders David
Macher and Allison Lowe whispered to David Turpin,
while Louise smiled at Jeff Moore.

To their left, at the prosecution table, sat deputy DA
Kevin Beecham and his cocounsel, Kim DeGonia, as
well as the lead investigator, Wade Walsvick.

Judge Schwartz entered the courtroom, and the preliminary hearing began.

"With regard to the Jane and John Does," Beecham told the judge, referring to the thirteen children, "we will be referring to them with their first name."

Then the people called their first witness, lead detective Tom Salisbury of the Riverside County Sheriff's Office. He told the court that there were two separate recordings of Jordan Turpin's 911 call on January 14, 2018. She had first gotten through to the California Highway Patrol at 5:50 a.m. in the morning, before being transferred to Riverside Sheriff's Department dispatcher, Kelly Eckley, three minutes later.

Jordan's harrowing twenty-minute 911 call was then played in the courtroom. Louise wiped away tears, while her husband studiously took notes on a yellow legal pad.

In the high, quivering voice of a ten-year-old, Jordan misspelled her name as T-U-R-P-E-N, and when asked for her street address, she gave the zip code instead.

"I've never been out. I don't go out much," she told the dispatcher. "I live in a family of fifteen people, and my parents are abusive; they abuse us, and my two little sisters are chained up. They will wake up at night and they will start crying. And they wanted me to call someone and help them. I wanted to call y'all and help my sisters."

She said one of her brothers was also chained up to a bed.

Asked if there was any medication in the house, Jordan replied, "I don't know what *medication* is."

No one went to school, she told the dispatcher.

"A fake school is set up," she said. "I haven't finished first grade, and I'm seventeen."

She had no idea of her mother's age or much about her, except that she didn't like any of her thirteen children except the two-year-old.

"Mother takes care of her right," said Jordan.

Gaining composure, Jordan listed the ages of all her siblings, from the youngest to the oldest. She revealed that her parents had left them alone in a trailer in Texas for four years before they came to California.

She told the dispatcher they lived in filth and sometimes she struggled to breathe. Asked when she had last taken a bath, Jordan replied, "About a year ago."

At the end of the call, she mentioned that Mother and Father were the only people who ever came to the house, and the rest of their family didn't know them. Her aunt Elizabeth had asked to see them, she said, but her mother wouldn't allow it.

After Jordan's 911 call was played, neither the prosecution nor defense had any questions. Detective Salisbury was excused, subject to recall later in the hearing.

Then deputy DA Beecham called his first witness, Deputy Manuel Campos of the Riverside County Sheriff's Department. The deputy had responded to Jordan Turpin's 911 call and later interviewed her at Perris Police Department.

"First, I want you to describe to the court what her appearance was like," said Beecham.

"Jordan appeared to have the mental capacity of somebody a lot younger than seventeen years old," he replied.

Defenders Jeff Moore and Allison Lowe both objected, and Judge Schwartz sustained it, ordering the deputy's answer to be stricken from the record.

"Going off, visually, what she looked like?" Beecham clarified.

"She was wearing a pink hat," said the deputy, "had a jean jacket and blue jeans and white shoes. Her hair appeared to be unwashed. She appeared not to bathe regularly. She had a lot of dirt on her skin. It looked like it was caked on. And she had an odor emitting from her body, that of one who doesn't bathe regularly."

Then Beecham asked how she referred to her parents during the interview.

"*Mother* and *Father*," Campos replied. "She said she was taught to address them that way because it was more like the Bible days."

"Did you ask her how she felt when she initially left the house?" asked the prosecutor.

"Yes," he replied. "She said she was scared to death. She said it was one of the scariest things she's ever done. She said she couldn't even dial 911 because she was so scared, she was shaking."

Jordan told him that she couldn't stay in the house any longer, watching her chained-up sisters crying in pain.

"She said it was hurting and depressing her," he told the judge, "and she couldn't stand to watch it anymore. The morning she escaped, she said everyone was crying. She said Mother was yelling at everybody. She was half-asleep. And Julissa had told her that Mother had . . . told her she was worse than the devil."

Deputy Campos said he asked Jordan some very basic questions, and she did not even know the date.

The prosecutor then asked if Jordan had told Campos how long she had been planning her escape.

"Two years," answered Campos. "She was trying to get ahold of a cell phone."

"How did she get a cell phone?" asked the prosecutor.

"Her brother had received a brand-new cell phone and got rid of his old [one]," said Campos, "and she was able to get that old cell phone."

The deputy testified that prior to the escape, Jordan had photographed Joanna and Julissa in chains on the cell phone to prove what was going on in the house.

"On the subject of chains," said Beecham. "Did Jordan

tell you . . . how tight those chains were on Joanna and Julissa?"

"Objection!" shouted Jeff Moore, springing to his feet. "Calls for speculation."

"Overruled," said the judge. "You may answer."

"She talked about a time where Julissa and Joanna slipped their hands out of the chains," said the deputy, "and because of that, Mother put the chains tighter. The chains would leave marks around their wrists."

Then Campos told the court about Jordan's daily routine. She spent twenty hours in the bedroom she shared with three of her sisters and was only allowed out with Mother's permission to eat, use the restroom, and brush her teeth.

"Did Jordan tell you the reasons why [her little sisters] were in chains?" asked Beecham.

"Yes," said the deputy, "because they were stealing candy from the kitchen."

The prosecutor showed Campos a photograph of Jordan's bedroom, asking him to describe it.

"To my left, I see two bunk beds," he replied. "And then to my right, I see another set of bunk beds with the top mattress on the floor."

"And what do you see on that mattress?" asked Beecham.

"Two padlocks," Campos said.

He testified that Jordan had told him that the children only received one meal a day: either a peanut butter sandwich, a baloney sandwich, or a frozen burrito. "She had constantly been eating peanut butter sandwiches for five years," he said, "and she can't eat peanut butter anymore, because she starts to gag and throw up. [By then] she was only eating the burrito."

The deputy then described how Mother had "choked"

Jordan when she was fifteen for watching a Justin Bieber video on Jennifer's cell phone.

"Her brother [Joshua] found out she watched the video and told Mother," he said. "And Mother choked her because of that . . . and said very hurtful things."

"Did she tell you what hurtful things Mother said to her?" asked Beecham.

"Yes, [while] Mother was choking her, she told her, 'Do you want to die?' Jordan said that she responded by saying, 'No.' And Mother [said], "Yes, you do! Yes, you do! You want to die and go to hell!'"

The deputy then told the court how Jordan had accused Father of attempting to sexually assault her when she was twelve. He had only stopped when Mother came up the stairs.

"She immediately jumped off," said Deputy Campos, "pulled her pants up, and then Mother walked in. [Later] her father told her she'd better not tell anyone what happened."

"Did Jordan tell you whether there was any other incidents of inappropriate or attempted inappropriate contact between her and her father?"

"Yes," replied the deputy. "She said that Father would try to force kisses on her mouth."

"How many times was that?"

"She estimated ten times," said the deputy.

Finally, Beecham asked if Jordan had mentioned leaving her room to socialize with her siblings.

"Yes," replied the deputy. "When Mother and Father were not home and they would all come out of their rooms."

Moving on to the Turpins' time living in Texas, Beecham asked, "Did she ever tell you about a time period in which her parents did not live with her?"

Defender Allison Lowe immediately objected, telling the judge that anything that happened in Texas was
not relevant to any of the charges.

"Are you going to go into incidents that occurred in
Texas?" asked the judge.

"Yes," said the prosecutor.

"What's it being offered for?"

"Well, one of the elements that we have to prove is dependency," explained Beecham. "I think what happened
in Texas is relevant to how the adult children became dependent adults. In addition, I think it shows the conditioning and the intent on the part of the defendants with
regard to torture."

Judge Schwartz ruled that the court could consider evidence from Texas, although the Turpins couldn't be
charged for anything that occurred there, as it was out of
jurisdiction.

Defense attorney Macher wasn't pleased with the
ruling. "Now, Judge," he said, standing, "given your ruling, I want to ask for a mistrial, if this was a trial, so I
guess I'll ask for a mis–preliminary hearing. And that the
court declare this hearing over and we can start again at
another time without that evidence. I feel very strongly
that that is so prejudicial, that we cannot get a fair preliminary hearing with that evidence in."

Judge Schwartz noted the defense's objection but
said he would allow Texas evidence in the preliminary
hearing. He promised to reconsider when it came up
again in pretrial motions if the trial went ahead.

The prosecutor again asked Deputy Campos if Jordan
had mentioned a time when she didn't have any parents
living with her.

"Yes," he answered, "between the ages of six and nine."

"Who took care of her?"

"Her siblings," said the deputy. "And I believe she specifically named Joshua."

"Did she tell you whether she saw her mother from the age of six to nine?"

"She said that she did not," he replied.

The prosecutor finally asked if Jordan had witnessed Mother inflicting any abuse on two-year-old Janna.

"Yes," said Campos. "She said Mother would hit her on the head with a pencil and that she had also pinched her."

In cross-examination, Allison Lowe asked if Jordan had spoken about opening various social media accounts, including Instagram, Twitter, and YouTube.

"Yes," replied the deputy.

"And, in fact," said the defender, "she told you that she also uploaded YouTube videos of herself singing?"

"That is correct," he said.

"She did have friends on social media, because she told you about some of them, correct?"

"She spoke about one friend, yes."

"And do you recall also that she discussed making another friend, who was going to assist her with making music videos?"

"Yes."

Lowe asked if he was aware there was also a landline in the Turpin house.

"I believe one of the other children that I spoke to did tell me that they had a landline in the house," Campos said.

"And Jordan did tell you that when Mother and Father were gone," asked Lowe, "that she would come out of the room to hang out with her siblings?"

"Yes."

Lowe began asking pointed questions, attempting to

show that her client, David Turpin, was rarely at the house and that Louise administered all the punishments.

"Did [Jordan] tell you how many hours her father was gone during the day?" asked Lowe.

"She said he was always gone working," Campos answered.

"And do you recall us talking about rules, in terms of them having to sit in their room, not go outside, et cetera?"

"Yes."

"Did Jordan tell you who enforced those rules?"

"She said Mother."

"And I just wanted to clarify," said Lowe, "that when you talked about punishments for disobeying, that being knocking heads, pulling hair, smacked in the face, et cetera, when Jordan described those incidents to you, she would say Mother did them. Correct?"

"That is correct," replied the deputy.

"She never described being struck or physically hit by her father?"

"Correct."

"Because her father was at work?"

"Correct."

"Let's talk about the chains," Lowe continued. "Jordan mentioned three of her siblings that had been chained. She herself had never been chained. Is that correct?"

"Yes."

"And do you recall Jordan saying that Father [had] not chained up anyone himself?"

"Yes, I do."

Prosecutor Beecham objected, arguing that Jordan had only spoken from her personal knowledge.

"Well, I assume it's based on what she told you she saw," said Judge Schwartz. "She may not have seen everything. But based on what she saw, she never saw Father do that?"

"That's correct," said the deputy.

Lowe then addressed the allegation of sexual abuse against her client. Campos said Jordan had told him about the incident after he and a CPS worker had asked if there had been any inappropriate touching in the household.

"And her response was, she thinks her father has tried?" asked Lowe.

"Yes," said the deputy.

"Now, what she described to you was that her father was in the TV room in a recliner, and that he pulled down her pants?"

"Yes."

"She demonstrated for you that when he pulled her into his lap, that it was to his left leg, his left thigh. Somewhere halfway in between the knee and the hip area. Is that correct?"

The deputy said she had demonstrated with her hands but had not been specific with where his leg had been.

"Okay, did Jordan ever clarify, when she said that he pulled down her pants, whether or not that encompassed her underwear as well, or was it just her pants?"

"She just said her pants."

"Okay. And besides pulling down her pants and sitting down on his lap, did she describe any other sort of touching?" Lowe asked.

"No."

"To be clear," she continued, "she didn't describe him touching her chest area. Correct?"

"That is correct."

"She didn't describe him touching her genital area?"

"That is correct."

"Or her buttocks, for that matter?"

"Correct."

"And she described that her father was clothed during this incident. Correct?"

"Yes."

"And what she told you was that she immediately stood up and pulled up her pants, correct?"

"Yes."

"She said she didn't like that?"

"That is correct."

"And her father never said anything during this actual incident. Correct?"

"Just that she'd better not tell anybody," said the deputy.

She then moved on to the claims Jordan had made about her father trying to kiss her.

"I think you used the words *forcible kissing*," Lowe said. "But to be clear, she said that she believed he tried to kiss her mouth on several occasions. Is that correct?"

"Yeah," replied the deputy. "She did use the word *force*. She said, 'He would try to force kisses on my mouth.'"

"But he never actually accomplished that. Correct?"

"She said he would just try. She didn't specify whether he was successful or not."

"Did she provide any sort of demonstration as to what this would encompass?"

"No, she did not."

"Did she ever provide a specific time frame as to when any of these incident occurred?"

"Yes," Campos said. "She said when she was twelve, and the last time being when she was fifteen or sixteen."

After a short recess, Louise Turpin's attorney, Jeff Moore, began his cross-examination. He first asked Deputy Campos about the "choking incident." The deputy confirmed that Jordan couldn't remember if Mother had choked her with one or both hands.

"You asked her if she had lost consciousness during the incident. Right?" asked Moore.

"Yes," Campos answered.

"And she told she hadn't?"

"That is correct."

"And she actually volunteered that it didn't make a place, and the word she used was *place*. Correct?"

"That is correct."

"Did you interpret that to mean *bruise*?"

"Yes," he replied, "or some type of injury, yes."

The deputy said that Jordan was unable to estimate how long Mother had choked her for.

"But what she said was," said Moore, reading from his notes, "'Do you want to die?' And I said, 'No.' And she said, 'Yes, you do. Yes, you do.' She said, 'You want to die and go to hell.' I know it lasted that long. Right?"

"That is correct."

"Well, her description gives you a couple of pieces of information, right?" Moore said. "It gives you kind of an estimate of how long it lasted, more or less?"

"Yes."

"Long enough for a short exchange of words from both persons. Right?"

"Yes."

"It also tells you that she was able to verbalize while she was being choked, doesn't it?"

"Yes," conceded the deputy.

After the midmorning break, co-prosecutor Kim DeGonia recalled lead detective Tom Salisbury to the stand. He had interviewed both defendants at Perris Police Department the day of the escape.

DeGonia began by asking about his hour-long interview with thirteen-year-old Jolinda a few hours after the rescue.

"Did the two of you speak about her education?" asked DeGonia.

"That prior to moving to Murrieta in June of 2010, that she was being homeschooled," said the detective. "And that they had worked their way up to the letter *I* of the alphabet. But since that time, her mom had done a little bit of additional homeschooling with them at the Perris house, and that she had worked her way up to the letter *J* or *T*. She couldn't remember which one."

"What did she believe was her grade level?" she asked.

"Well, she wanted to . . . accelerate to the first grade, because she was tired of doing kindergarten work."

"Did she indicate how Mother would react if they would get questions or answers wrong while doing the kindergarten curriculum?"

"Yes," he replied. "If they didn't do straight lines or stay within lines, Mother would pull their hair and throw them across the room."

"When you were speaking to her," asked DeGonia, "did you notice her inability to understand basic words, like the word *estimate*?"

"Yes. There were a lot of words that she had problems understanding. And she self-admitted that she even had a problem with the word *said,* s-a-i-d."

The detective also said Jolinda, who was born in Texas, did not know whether it was a state or country.

"Did she call Texas a country?" asked DeGonia.

"Yes."

The prosecutor also asked what Jolinda had told him about the hall monitors who Mother used as her eyes and ears. He said that her two oldest siblings, Jennifer and Joshua, acted as hall monitors, as well as her older sisters Julianne and Jeanetta.

"And did she indicate . . . why there were hall monitors in their home?"

"Yes," Salisbury answered. "To stop the kids from

getting candy [and other] things out of Mother's room, and to . . . stop the kids stealing food out of the kitchen."

Then DeGonia asked what Jolinda had said about her early life in Rio Vista, Texas. Salisbury replied that she knew she had been born in Texas and had lived in a trailer with her siblings.

"[It was] without her parents present," said the detective. "Mostly her older brother Joshua cared for them and the trailer was filthy, dirty, smelled bad." Jolinda told Salisbury that she hadn't bathed since May 2017.

DeGonia then asked what physical abuse Jolinda had suffered.

"Pulling and yanking of the hair," he replied. "And in addition to that, she had been pinched by her mother, choked by her mother, and hit by her mother."

Jolinda had also told him how Mother would get angry and hit her on the head with her knuckles.

"Did Jolinda indicate to you whether she had been choked by Mother?" asked the prosecutor.

"Yes," Salisbury said. "She was taking a bath, and it wasn't until she got into the tub that she realized she had to go to the bathroom. And her mom got extremely upset and pinched her. [She] placed her full hands around Jolinda's neck and picked her up off the ground."

DeGonia then turned to the lead detective's interview later that day with Jonathan, who had been chained up when the police had first arrived.

"Did he know whether anyone else, other than himself, was chained?" she asked.

"Yes, he did. He knew that he, along with his two younger sisters, Julissa and Joanna, had been chained up. Told they were 'suspects,' quote, unquote."

"When you said they were 'suspects,'" asked DeGonia, "what did he tell you about that?"

"We talked a lot about suspects," said Salisbury. "He said that was a term that Mother used. They were suspects of stealing stuff and being disrespectful to their parents and siblings."

The prosecutor asked what Jonathan had done to become a "suspect."

"The original thing," said the detective, "was he took his older brother's camera and hid it in the trash can, and it later got thrown out. And then . . . he was a suspect of stealing food."

The detective said Jonathan had been chained up on and off for six and a half years—first with ropes in the Murrieta house and then chains in Perris.

"So ropes first to restrain, and then chains?"

"Yes."

"Did he know why Mother and Father switched from ropes to chains?"

"Objection," said Lowe. "Misstates the testimony and assumes facts not in evidence."

"Overruled," said Judge Schwartz.

"When they tied him with ropes," explained the detective, "he was able to escape using his teeth. And so they switched to what he referred to as small chains. And then when he was able to slide those off the bed rail, they used thicker, heavier chains."

Salisbury testified that Jonathan told him Father had first chained him up, and then Mother had taken over. When officers arrived at the house, the detective said, they had found Jonathan chained to his upper bunk bed. He had been there for a couple of weeks but had previously been chained up to two months at a time.

In cross-examination, Allison Lowe returned to the detective's testimony that Jolinda had difficulty understanding certain words.

"And I think one of the examples you used was *estimate*?" she said.

"Yes."

"But overall," she continued, "isn't it true that she understood the questions you were asking her and provided appropriate responses?"

"Yes."

"In fact, you told her that she was very articulate. Isn't that correct?"

"Yes," answered the detective. "I tried to encourage the kids during the interview."

"Did Jolinda ever tell you about any injuries that were caused by her father?" asked Lowe.

"No," Salisbury said.

29

"SHE WAS TERRIFIED OF HER MOTHER"

After breaking for lunch, the preliminary hearing continued and the prosecution called its third witness, investigator Brett Rooker of the Riverside County Sheriff's Department. Under Kim DeGonia's direct Rooker testified that he had interviewed Joanna, Jessica, and Joy Turpin at the Perris Police Department on the day of their escape. The prosecutor began by asking about any abuse Joanna had suffered after moving to California.

"She said that when she was about eight or nine, living in Murrieta," said the investigator, "that she was thrown down the stairs by her mother."

"Did she indicate whether, after she was thrown down the stairs, she had injuries?"

"She said her neck and back hurt," replied Rooker, "and that she was dizzy."

The prosecutor asked why Mother had thrown her down the stairs.

"She was caught in her mother's room by her mother. [Mother] became very upset and threw her around the bedroom and was yelling at her. And then when she stood up, she pushed her down the stairs."

"Did she indicate to you," DeGonia continued, "whether or not she's been abused in any other way, physically, by Mother or Father?"

"She said that she was chained up."

"What did she tell you about that?"

"She said that the chaining started because she would take things and that she would have dark places on her arms from the chains."

Rooker had asked Joanna to show him the "dark places."

"She lifted up her sleeves on her jacket," he recalled. "I saw dirt caked on her arms." He said she had been chained up since the previous October.

The prosecutor then showed Rooker a photograph of Joanna's arms a few hours after the rescue.

"And what are we looking at here?" she asked.

"The inside of her left forearm," he replied. "And you can see that there's clean spots on her wrists from where the chains were."

Then the prosecutor showed him a photograph of the fourteen-year-old's right forearm, with a similar clean ring around the wrists where the chains had been.

"Did she describe for you how often she would take a bath?" asked DeGonia.

"She told me that the last time she had had a bath was about eight months prior to that, [on] Mother's Day."

"Now, did Joanna speak to you about whether or not any of the siblings would stay up all night and monitor the hall?"

"Yeah," Rooker said. "She said that Julianne and Jeanetta would stay in the hallway. And . . . since they moved to Perris, somebody would be up all hours day and night, watching them to make sure nobody stole food or snuck in Mother's room."

"Did she indicate how she felt about Mother and Father?"

"She said she was terrified of her mother," he replied. Joanna told him that Mother physically beat her, pulling her hair and hitting her on the head.

"Did she indicate anything to you about the blinds in their bedroom?" DeGonia asked.

"Yes," Rooker replied. "She believed that when the chains started, Mother had closed her window and adjusted the blinds so that nobody could see in."

The prosecutor then questioned him about the photographs of the six minor siblings' clothing taken at Perris Police Department. Rooker said that he had actually picked the items up to pose for the police photographer.

"How did they feel?" asked DeGonia.

"They were very heavy and soiled," he answered.

"How did they smell?"

"Putrid. All the clothing was difficult to lay out."

"Why so?"

"Just because of the smell."

"Was it dirty?"

"Extremely."

The investigator testified that he had later gone to Corona Regional Medical Center to collect and photograph the seven adult siblings' clothing.

"Did you notice the same smell, odor, the dirty clothing, on the adults as you did the minors?" asked DeGonia.

"Yes," Rooker replied.

The investigator told the court that after talking to the seven adults, he had placed an involuntary 5150 hold on them for their own safety.

"They were all gravely disabled adults," Rooker testified.

"Objection, Your Honor," said attorney Macher, rising to his feet. "That states a conclusion."

"Sustained," the judge ruled. "'Gravely disabled adult' is stricken."

The investigator then testified that he had received police academy training on dealing with adults that were a danger to themselves or others.

"I've 5150'd numerous people," he said. "And that day, they were evaluated not just by me but by the other investigators in his case. We all decided that just based on their diminished capacity, their lack of education . . . they were [unable] to care for themselves in any way. So I placed a 5150 hold on them so that they could get the care that they needed."

"At that point," asked the prosecutor, "were the adult Turpins then admitted to Corona Regional?"

"Yes, ma'am," he replied.

In cross-examination, David Macher asked if Joanna had been crying during the interview.

"She was crying," Rooker said. "She said she was scared."

"And did she tell you she was afraid for her parents?" asked Macher.

"Yes, she did."

Then David Turpin's lead attorney continued his strategy of mitigating his client's role in what had happened.

"Did Joanna tell you that David Turpin was always at work?" he questioned.

"Yes," replied Rooker.

"Did she tell you that when he [was] home on the weekends, he and Louise were gone all day?"

"Yes."

"Did she tell you that David Turpin did not do anything to her?"

"I don't believe she used those exact words," Rooker said.

"Okay," pressed Macher. "Did she indicate that David Turpin hurt her?"

"No."

"Now, did she indicate that her parents argued?"

"Objection," said DeGonia. "Relevance."

"Overruled," said Judge Schwartz. "You may answer."

"I don't recall."

Then Macher asked if Joanna had mentioned how several of the adult siblings had been allowed to watch television.

"She said the older ones that helped Mother were able to watch television," Rooker replied.

"Did she tell you that Jessica and Joy always go with Louise when she leaves the house?"

"Yes."

"And she said that her brother Joshua goes to college?"

"Yes," he replied.

"All right," said the defender. "And you inquired about sexual abuse?"

"Yes."

"And was her answer negative?"

"Yes."

Kim DeGonia had no redirect questions, and Rooker was excused.

The next witness was Deputy Dan Brown of the Riverside County Sheriff's Office, who had interviewed Julissa, Joshua, and Jeanetta a few hours after their rescue. He spent just under two hours with eleven-year-old Julissa, who told him about the siblings' diet.

"She was always hungry," said the deputy. "They would have lunch and supper at the same time as one meal. It would be either peanut butter sandwiches or jalapeño baloney sandwiches and then some sort of freezer food."

"Did she indicate whether or not sometimes they received just plain bread?" asked DeGonia.

"Yes, she did," he replied.

"Did she indicate whether or not Mother and Father ate different than they ate, 'they' meaning the Turpin children?"

"Yes, the parents ate different food," Brown said. "She said specifically that the parents would eat Jersey Mike's, pizza, french fries."

"But the children would not. Correct?"

"Correct."

Then the prosecutor asked what Julissa had told him about pies.

"She stated that Mother would purchase pies," said Brown, "and either leave them in the fridge or in the pantry. They would wait until they got moldy, and then she would throw them in the trash."

"Did Julissa indicate whether or not she wanted to eat those pies?"

"Yes, she did."

Julissa also told Brown she'd last had a bath on Mother's Day of 2017.

"Her mother washed her hair, [and] she washed the rest of her body. She changed her clothing to go out for Mother's Day and then immediately upon returning back home, she [had] to put the same dirty, soiled clothing back on."

"When [was] the last time Julissa had her sheets changed?" asked DeGonia.

"Christmas 2016," replied the deputy.

"And you interviewed her on January 14, 2018?"

"That is correct."

The prosecutor then asked if Julissa had mentioned a special punishment for the siblings during the Christmas holiday.

"Prior to Christmas," answered Brown, "her and several of her siblings [were] stealing food out of the pantry because [they] were so hungry. They lost Christmas."

"And did she indicate what it meant to 'lose Christmas' in the Turpin household?"

"You were not allowed to celebrate with the rest of the family, but you had to watch."

"So Julissa, along with a couple other siblings, their punishment for stealing food and being hungry was they lost their Christmas?"

"Objection," Jeff Moore interrupted, "argumentative and leading."

"It is leading," said the judge. "Sustained."

The prosecutor then asked when Julissa had first been chained up.

"Around the age of eleven," said Brown, "was when her mother started chaining her by her wrists."

"And what was she chained to?"

"Her bedpost. Her mattress was on the ground, and she would sit on the ground and have the chains wrapped around each wrist like a bracelet, and then also around the bedpost."

The deputy said that Julissa was able to lie on her back while she was chained up and was initially able to stand up.

"Once her mother found out that she was able to stand up while chained," he said, "[she] threatened to shorten the length of the chain. She was chained as deputies arrived at the residence."

"Did she indicate how she became unchained when deputies arrived at the residence?"

"Yes. Her older sister Jessica ran to the bedroom and quickly unchained her."

Brown said he had inspected Julissa's arms for what she called "indentations."

"So when she pulled her sleeves up," he said, "there were white spots . . . on her wrists from where the chains had actually rubbed the caked-on dirt off."

"Did she indicate how many days straight she had been in chains?"

"At that time, she said fifteen."

"Did she indicate if she had been chained up prior to those fifteen days?"

"Yes," said the deputy. "She had been chained up two times previously, anywhere between two months and four months."

DeGonia moved on to what Julissa had told him about what she referred to as "spankings on the face"—being slapped across her face near her eyes.

"Did she indicate who did that, Mother or Father?"

"She said Mother."

"Did she indicate whether or not Father was present for these 'spankings on the face'?"

"She said Father was aware and did nothing to stop it."

"[Did] she indicate her feelings toward Mother and Father?" asked the prosecutor.

"She said she was equally as terrified of Mother as she was of Father."

In her cross-examination, David Turpin's lawyer, Allison Lowe, asked Deputy Brown if he recalled Julissa saying that "Father has never attacked us."

"Yes."

"And do you remember asking Julissa who runs the show? Who's the big boss?"

"Yes."

"And what was her answer?"

"Mother," replied the deputy.

The prosecution's fifth witness was Patrick Morris, a supervising investigator with the District Attorney's Office. He had been called to testify about the Turpin children's physical and mental conditions, having interviewed the medical professionals who had treated them.

DeGonia asked Morris to discuss his interview with Dr. Mark Massi of the Riverside University Health System, who treated the six youngest siblings.

"Did Dr. Massi indicate any type of physical issues with Julissa?" she asked.

"He described her as perhaps the most severe of the siblings as far as her condition," said Morris. "She had what he described as severe protein calorie malnutrition, coupled with a condition known as *cachexia,* which is muscle wasting."

The investigator said that the eleven-year-old's mid-upper arms were the size of a four-month-old baby's.

"She was underweight for her age," he continued. "He said that her height had stunted due to malnutrition. She was forty-six pounds . . . at least fifteen pounds underweight. She had inflammation and liver damage due to malnutrition. She also had . . . psychosocial dwarfism, [which] is a stunted growth or development, that's a result in living in an abusive or a neglectful environment."

The investigator said that Dr. Massi also found that fifteen-year-old James suffered from many of the same ailments.

"He said his overall retarded development," said Morris, "could be due to malnutrition, psychosocial dwarfism, or a combination of the two. But either way, he said his growth was stunted, and it was still abuse."

Dr. Massi said James also had some psychological problems as a result of neglect.

"He exhibited antisocial characteristics," said Morris, "specifically mentioning that James talked about wanting to kill animals [and] believed his dreams could predict the future."

As for Jordan, the investigator said Dr. Massi had sent her for speech therapy, as she was so hard to understand.

"And he attributed that to lack of socialization and isolation," said Morris. "He also did express that he was concerned about her ability to integrate into society, because she seemed very childlike for her age."

Morris testified that he had also interviewed Dr. Sophia Grant, who runs the child abuse unit at Riverside University Health System. She had examined Jolinda, finding that she too was suffering from severe malnutrition and muscle wasting. And at thirteen years old, she still had not started puberty.

"She would have expected her to have some kind of breast development," the investigator explained, "and she hadn't exhibited that."

"And did she attribute that to anything regarding her health?" asked DeGonia.

"Malnutrition," Morris replied.

"What did Dr. Grant have to say about Janna?"

"She said [the two-year-old] was better fed than her siblings, but still not enough."

In cross-examination, David Macher just asked a few questions about two-year-old Janna, the best-fed of all the siblings.

"According to your report," said the defender, "Janna did not suffer from severe protein malnutrition. Is that right?"

"That's correct."

"And she did not suffer from vitamin D deficiency?"

"Not that they discussed with me, no."

"Okay," said the defender. "And that she did not suffer from a low potassium level?"

"Not that they discussed with me."

Then Macher commented on how all the siblings had gained weight in the hospitals and were doing well.

"And you wrote in your report that all of the minors were responding vigorously to treatment. Is that what the doctors told you?"

"In a general sense, yes," replied Morris.

As Jeff Moore had no questions, Morris was excused, and the judge recessed for an afternoon break.

When the court reconvened, deputy DA Kevin Beecham called his sixth and final witness, his senior investigator, Wade Walsvick. Beecham began by asking Walsvick about Joy Turpin's journal, in which she'd recorded the date the Turpins had moved to California.

"She indicated they crossed into California on June 4 of 2010," Walsvick said, adding that they had moved into the Murrieta house eight days later.

Beecham then questioned him about the eight affidavits David Turpin had filed with the California Department of Education for the City Day School in Murrieta and the Sandcastle Day School in Perris. He asked him to read to the court the affirmation that Turpin had signed for the 2010 school year.

"This is a private full-time school," read Walsvick, "that offers instruction in several branches of study required to be taught in public schools of the state, that offers this instruction in English, and that keeps attendance records."

Walsvick confirmed that the address of the City Day School was 39550 Saint Honore Drive—the Turpins' home in Murrieta—and that the defendant had signed it.

"And what is Mr. Turpin's title, according to this form?" asked Beecham.

"His title is the principal," replied Walsvick.

The investigator said that Turpin had filed the affidavit

THE FAMILY NEXT DOOR 269

online under the penalty of perjury, signing it electronically. He had filed identical ones each October for the next seven years.

Investigator Walsvick said he had also interviewed Jennifer, Joshua, Jeanetta, Jordan, and Julissa about the education they had received at their father's private day school.

"Jordan referred to it as homeschooling," said Walsvick. "She said it would happen occasionally, and they would go for [extended] periods of time with nothing—no education, training, or anything from her mother."

"Did she give you an idea of what 'extended periods of time' was?" asked the prosecutor.

"Years."

"So during the times that they weren't attending school or being taught . . . where would all the siblings be?"

"She actually used the word *nothing*," said Walsvick. "At the Murrieta address . . . her mother directed them to vacate their bedrooms and sit on the floors upstairs [in the hallway] throughout the entire day."

"Did she tell you why they had to sit in the hallway during the day?"

"Yes. She said her mother made it crystal clear that they were not to be seen by the neighbors, because they were supposedly in school, and they were not."

Walsvick said he had also interviewed Jennifer, who had attended elementary school up to third grade in Fort Worth, and she described her siblings' education as "minimal."

"It would go for brief days," said Walsvick. "Very short periods of time. And then lapse for upwards of several years, prior to having again a couple of days' worth of lessons. And that would be it."

"And we know that she never finished high school, correct?" asked Beecham.

"She never went past the third grade."

"Did she tell you whether she was ever able to really socialize with anybody outside her family?"

"She did," he replied. "Only in a secretive capacity while online."

"But socializing as in . . . actually having a flesh-and-blood friend. Did she have any of those?"

"None."

The investigator had also interviewed Dr. Fari Kamalpour of the Corona Regional Medical Center, who had treated the seven adult siblings.

"Now," asked Beecham, "specifically with regard to Jennifer, what was her . . . height and weight upon admission?"

"Jennifer was five foot three inches and weighed eighty pounds," he said. "She was approximately thirty-five pounds underweight for her age, sex, and height."

"What was the chief diagnosis for Jennifer?"

"She was described as suffering from low cognition, ability to perform mental tasks. She was also suffering from severe protein caloric malnutrition."

Dr. Kamalpour told Walsvick that Jennifer had a severe B12 deficiency and cachexia, or muscle wastage. The prosecutor asked if the doctor had detailed the effects of severe malnutrition associated with cachexia.

"She began by describing the effects on adult females, specifically their ability to reproduce," said the investigator. "And then she specifically identified Jennifer and Jessica as probably never being able to bear children."

Then, to audible gasps from the public gallery, the prosecutor showed the court the two photographs Jordan had taken of her two younger sisters chained to their beds.

"What is this?" asked Beecham.

"It is a picture of Joanna, the fourteen-year-old female, in chains, sitting on her bed."

The prosecutor then displayed another photo.

"That is a close-up photograph of Joanna's wrists," Walsvick said, "showing the bruising and indentation caused by the chains."

"Nothing further," said the prosecutor.

In cross-examination, David Macher asked if Jordan Turpin had told him that at one point her mother cooked meals and taught them, but then things had gone downhill.

"That is correct," said Walsvick.

"Okay," Macher continued. "She also told you that when the family lived in Murrieta, Louise Turpin made all the decisions?"

"Yes," he replied.

The defender then asked if Jennifer had witnessed domestic violence when she was younger.

"She did."

"And she also told you that David Turpin promised to stop, and he kept that promise. Isn't it correct?"

"That is correct."

Then Macher turned his attention to the seven adult siblings' medical records, asking if Dr. Kamalpour had told him some of them suffered from neuropathy.

"Correct," said Walsvick.

"Did she tell you that can be reversed with vitamins and improved diet?"

"I believe she did," he said.

"Now, Dr. Kamalpour talked to you about the phrase *severe iron deficiency*?"

"That's correct."

"Is that another term for anemia?"

"Can be, yes."

"And can anemia be treated with iron supplements

and improved diet?" asked Macher. "Did Dr. Kamalpour tell you that?"

"I don't believe she said that to me. But I do know that, yes."

"Thank you, sir. Nothing further."

At 4:30 p.m., the prosecution rested their case. As both sets of defense lawyers had decided not to call any witnesses, Judge Schwartz recessed for the day. Final arguments would start the next day at 10:00 a.m.

30

"CRUEL AND UNUSUAL PUNISHMENT
AND EXTREME PAIN"

At 8:30 the next morning, all seven adult Turpin siblings attended a secret probate hearing in the Riverside Historic Courthouse. Fifteen minutes before the hearing, a sheriff's deputy ordered *Press-Enterprise* reporter Brian Rokos to vacate the hallway so the siblings could enter unseen.

Probate hearings are normally open to the public, but this one was closed. It had been called to decide whether the Riverside County public guardian would continue as conservator to care for the seven siblings. Two deputies were stationed outside the courtroom to stop anyone entering.

After the hearing concluded, bailiffs cleared the hallway so the Turpin siblings could leave via an underground garage without being photographed. Then they were driven away to their undisclosed new home in the rural countryside.

Just a few blocks away, David and Louise Turpin were being brought into Department 44 of the Riverside Supreme

Court for closing arguments. The three defense attorneys had filed a motion to strike all the highly damaging testimony about the abuse in Texas from the day before. Deputy DA Kevin Beecham addressed the judge, arguing that the incidents in Texas played a crucial role in what happened later in California.

"So the physical abuse in Texas," he said, "started with slapping, hitting, throwing around the room. And it aggravated to belts, leather end, and then . . . the buckle end." If the belt wasn't "correcting the disobedience," David Turpin would beat his own children with an oar, a wooden paddle, or a metal switch. Once the family moved into the double-wide trailer, because their house had become uninhabitable, David began keeping his children in cages. Then he and Louise had abandoned them for nearly four years.

"This is like a *Lord of the Flies* analogy," Beecham told the judge, "where these children are just left to fend for themselves during the most tender years of their lives."

But even though they were now living fifty miles away, the defendants were still able to order some of the older siblings to punish the younger ones by caging them.

"It's unimaginable that they had so much control over their children," said Beecham, "while they were out of the house or out of the trailer."

Once they moved to California, he told the judge, David Turpin no longer physically abused his children as he had in Texas. However, the prosecutor argued, this was because he had more control over them than ever before.

"He did initiate the chaining," said Beecham. "It was his idea to do all the chaining of the kids. But the reason why he didn't physically abuse them, why he wasn't using an oar or a switch, maybe even a buckle end of the belt, is because he didn't need to. He conditioned the children over the years, over decades of physical torment and abuse, all stemming from Texas. He conditioned them in a way that's unimaginable."

The prosecutor said that the children could have run away in California but had been brainwashed by all that had happened in Texas.

"There was apparently a landline in the house," said Beecham. "They could have called for help. Sure, at any time when one of the select few were outside the house with Mother, they could scream for help. But they were conditioned—conditioned from what happened in Texas. Conditioned by abandonment."

Even during the years apart from their parents, the siblings were forced to obey them.

"And if they didn't obey," said Beecham, "they were imprisoned. They were put in cages. And this is only after that they were abused physically to an extent that's unimaginable."

He told the judge that when Jennifer had tried to run away in Texas, she was unable to survive on her own.

"And what good did it do her?" he asked. "She tried to get a job, but she had no driver's license. She had no real prospects. No socialization whatsoever. So what did she do? She called her mother, and her mother came, picked her up, and took her away."

Once again, the prosecutor showed the court the two harrowing photographs Jordan had taken of her two sisters in shackles.

"Looking at Julissa, age eleven," he said. "Extremely pale, skinny, emaciated, with chains. The kids were imprisoned in Texas, and they were imprisoned in California. And her other sister Joanna. Dark, sunken eyes. She's fourteen, and she looks like she's seven years old."

He then showed the court photographs of the children's putrid clothing that hadn't been changed for months.

"Dirt caked on them," he said. "They weren't allowed to take baths. They got used to this because of Texas. Because in Texas, they were getting left to fend for their own selves."

When David Turpin came home from work, he would see his children in this terrible state, wearing heavily soiled clothing that stunk.

"All this stemming from the conditioning in Texas," he told the judge. "Texas is extremely relevant. Not only is it relevant, it's extremely probative because of the intent of both Mr. and Mrs. Turpin. What they did. How they did it. How they schemed in Texas. The level of abuse in Texas mirrors that of the abuse in California. It shows that both of these defendants have intent; the intent to cause cruel and unusual extreme punishment and pain and suffering to those poor thirteen kids here in California. It shows that they had knowledge of the conditioning of these kids."

The prosecutor explained that he had concentrated on David Turpin's role, as his attorneys had attempted to minimize his part in what had happened.

"Mr. Turpin initiated the chaining," he said. "He wanted to chain all the children. It was his idea. He wanted all the kids to be chained. When he'd come home, he would see the status of [his] children: hungry, skinny, dirty, smelly, not leaving the house, coming into the kitchen one at a time to stand and eat."

Beecham reminded the judge that for eight years running, David had submitted forms to the Department of Education, stating he was running a private day school for his children.

"He actually lists the grades of all the children," Beecham said, "of all the children attending school. He's not merely sitting idly by. He is a direct perpetrator of the neglect, of the abuse."

The prosecutor described the physical damage inflicted on the children as torture and argued that David Turpin was criminally culpable.

"We're talking about eleven of the twelve kids on the torture counts having muscle atrophy, muscle wasting away," he told the judge. "They are emaciated, incredibly underweight. The adults . . . were on average thirty-two pounds underweight. We had many of the minors within a 0.01 percentile of [the] body weight they should be at. Point zero one. That's incredible.

"At the very least, he facilitated the abuse. And the direct, natural, and probable consequence of that, to the point where they are so emaciated, so malnourished to the point of cachexia, is great bodily injury. They endured extreme pain and suffering as a result."

Then David Macher stood up to argue against allowing the Texas evidence into the preliminary hearing. He began by labeling the prosecution's claim of the children's conditioning in Texas as "an interesting theory," devoid of expert testimony.

"I mean, I'm not a psychology expert," he told the judge. "Are we talking Stockholm syndrome? Are we talking some other kind of psychological conditioning? I have no idea."

Macher said that the prosecution's unproved theory was reason enough to strike the Texas testimony.

"The Texas evidence is inflammatory," he told the judge. "Once you've heard it, it's difficult to forget it. I believe the Texas evidence, based on Mr. Beecham's argument, needs to go out. It is not relevant."

The defense attorney called it "highly prejudicial," saying it would deprive his client of the right to have a fair preliminary hearing. "As the court knows," said the white-bearded attorney, "I'm fond of quoting Shakespeare, the speeches of Abraham Lincoln. But in this case,

I think a scene from a Russian novel . . . Fyodor Dostoevsky's *The Brothers Karamazov* is particularly appropriate."

He explained that in the novel, one of the three brothers, Ivan, tried to reconcile the existence of a benevolent, all-powerful God with all the evil in the world. But Ivan, who framed evil as the suffering of children, was unable to do so. So he turned his back on God and religion.

"Now why do I bring this up?" asked Macher. "I bring it up because, as Mr. Beecham has eloquently described it, in this case we see the enormous suffering of children. It's cataloged for years. We're not here to defend the conduct. We're here to determine what this conduct means. Where does it fit in the corpus of the criminal law?"

As David and Louise Turpin looked on dispassionately, Macher told the court that it was only natural to protect innocent children from harm.

"They are innocent, vulnerable, and undeserving of any evil," he said. "Evil inflicted upon children is so unacceptable to all of us that it may help to explain the interest in this case. But that's just a guess, and it's not the truly important point. The more important point is that our horror at the suffering of children presents a risk today right here in this courtroom. Crimes against children trigger outrage and anger. And in those circumstances, emotion—my emotions, the court's emotions, Mr. Beecham's emotions—can overcome our ability to reason. And reason is the life of the law."

He then urged the judge to dismiss all the torture changes against his client.

"I think the word *torture*," he argued, "is very similar to the suffering of children. I think it elicits a powerful and visceral reaction in us. That's important. It's important because, like the suffering of children, the word *tor-*

ture tempts us to step away from reason and follow instinct."

The attorney said that torture was inapplicable in the cases of Joshua, who went to college and watched television with his parents, and Jessica and Joy, who went out shopping with their mother.

"Jordan described these two as, quote, 'their real children,'" he said. "Jennifer, the oldest of the Turpin children, had social media accounts. She helped Jordan set up online accounts. For these four, I think dismissal of the torture charge is an easy call."

He then told the judge that Louise Turpin was far more culpable for what had happened than his client.

"It's my view that this is a particularly malevolent intent involved with torture. And it can be argued, I suppose, that Louise had that intent. My client, David Turpin, there's very thin evidence as to what he did in California. He worked a lot. He was gone a great deal. Julissa indicated she could not recall a single abusive incident when Mr. Turpin was at home."

Macher conceded that there was some evidence that his client had suggested the chaining, but called it "hearsay twice removed." And he acknowledged that when his client came home, he must have seen how thin his children were and how they were dressed.

"A blind man would know that there was something wrong in the house," said Macher. "But was he aiding that? I don't think the evidence is there because he was not at home, according to Julissa, at any time that an abusive incident took place . . . So I believe Mr. Turpin could only be convicted of torture on an aiding and abetting theory."

Then Macher turned his attention to the seven counts of abuse of a dependent adult, saying none of the siblings over eighteen fit this description.

"They are not dependent adults simply because they don't have a driver's license," he argued. "They are not dependent adults because their education has been woefully neglected. A dependent adult, as I understand it, is someone with physical or developmental disabilities. And we don't have that here."

The attorney then asked the judge to dismiss some of the counts, as they were outside the statute of limitations, and others because the older siblings were treated far better than some of the younger ones.

Allison Lowe then took over to address the charge that David Turpin had committed a lewd act on his daughter.

"Like Mr. Macher, I think," she began, "if we take emotion . . . and speculation out of it, then the elements haven't been proved here."

Lowe told the judge that neither the intent nor the force elements of the charge existed.

"The evidence presented here," she said, "is devoid of clear sexual intent as required. The defendant must commit the act with intent of arousing, appealing to, or gratifying the lust, passions, or sexual desires of himself or the child."

The attorney said the court had heard two different versions of what had happened from separate officers. One had said Jordan's pants were pulled down once, while the other said twice. Nevertheless, she said, the evidence showed it happened very quickly and nothing sexual was said.

Lowe said that the officers who questioned Jordan had never asked how far her pants were pulled down and if any underwear had been removed.

"She never described any removal of actual underwear," said Lowe, "or something more extensive. As the court knows, there's been no allegation of touching of genitalia of either party. There's no described attempt at groping beyond seating her down on his left leg. We know that Jordan told law enforcement, based on the evidence presented, that she got up on her own, pulled up her pants. And this happened before Mother entered the room, and no attempt was made to prevent that from happening."

There was "very thin evidence," she argued, that her client had subsequently forced kisses on his daughter and for how long.

"I would ask the court to discharge [the] count," she said.

Finally, Louise Turpin's attorney, Jeff Moore, addressed the judge, saying that he was in an "embarrassing position," as his arguments had already been presented to the court by Mr. Macher.

"First, I want to make it clear," he said, "that I'm not submitting, as a wink, concession that the elements have been met."

He asked the judge to reduce the assault charge—that his client had choked Jordan as punishment for watching a Justin Bieber video—from a felony to a misdemeanor.

"I believe it would be appropriate based upon the testimony at prelim," he said.

In rebuttal, prosecutor Kevin Beecham argued that the defendant could have caused her daughter great bodily harm. He said he could have understood Mother's reaction if her daughter had been setting the house on fire.

"But Jordan, at age fifteen," he said, "watching a Justin Bieber video, being choked and threatened. For Mrs. Turpin to make the statement, 'Do you want to die? I'm going to kill you!' and 'You're going to hell!' Jordan was actually afraid [and] really believed she was going to die. I think that defeats any real justification to lower [the felony charge] to a misdemeanor. Not only that, Jordan said it didn't just hurt for a minute, but it hurt for two days."

The prosecutor also argued that the seven older siblings were certainly dependent adults who could not look after themselves.

"It's obvious," he told the judge. "The fact that they became dependent adults after decades and decades of abuse, no expert's needed at this time to show that they were conditioned."

He said officers had placed a 5150 hold on the seven adult siblings, as it was obvious they could not care for themselves.

"It's not because they didn't have a driver's license," he explained, "or they didn't hold a job, or because they were uneducated. It's because, again, they were conditioned to such a point, desocialized to such a point where we have a seventeen-year-old that presents like a five-year-old. We have a twenty-nine-year-old with a third-grade education [who] weighs eighty pounds.

"So after years and years and decades of, again, conditioning and torturous intent by the defendants, they unfortunately became dependent adults."

31

"THERE'S A PLETHORA OF EVIDENCE"

Judge Schwartz began his summation by addressing the defense motion to strike all Texas evidence from the record. He explained that a preliminary hearing was different from a trial, as a jury may have difficulty separating what happened in Texas and in California.

"And obviously, in front of a jury," said the judge, "there may be severe prejudice with respect to listening to additional acts that were purportedly committed by Mr. and Mrs. Turpin."

Judge Schwartz said that it would be decided later in pretrial motions whether or not the Texas evidence would be admissible at trial.

"Is the evidence relevant?" asked the judge. "I think it's extraordinarily relevant. And it's prejudicial. But I think it is probative to the grand story that is being told in the evidence that unfolded yesterday."

He said that the evidence clearly met the legal requirements of torture: an infliction of great bodily injury to cause cruel, extreme pain and suffering.

"There is a plethora of evidence in that regard," said the judge, "beginning with the feeding of the children.

They ate twice a day for a while and then it was once a day."

He said that their extremely limited diet of peanut butter and jalapeño baloney sandwiches led to malnutrition and anemia.

"There's very little food value in those items," he said. "And the repetition of the food—I think Jordan's statement was that she got to a point where she couldn't even digest the peanut butter anymore because she was so sick of it. So clearly, the children were not fed appropriately."

Then Judge Schwartz addressed the various punishments the defendants had inflicted on their own children after moving to California.

"There was various hitting, slapping, hair-pulling, throwing around the room, pushing, which was described as not just a push but a severe push causing a substantial distance between the person inflicting that act and the child. And of course the chaining, which would occur for weeks, maybe months at a time, left some bruising on the children that were chained."

Judge Schwartz said he was astounded at the lack of medical care and that none of the children had ever seen a dentist.

"The lack of socialization," he said, "the lack of allowing the children to go out and play with other children and even, for that matter, socialize with each other. And we know what negative effects that has on the upbringing of a child, and the ability to be able to function in society.

"The lack of education," he continued. "It was clear that these children were not being educated. One of the children got to the letter *I,* and I think she was around fifteen years old."

The judge then spoke on the deplorable conditions the Turpin siblings lived in.

"The court saw the exhibits that were shown," he said.

"The soiled underwear that they wore for many, many months and other clothing that was not washed. The bedsheets were not washed for upward of two years. And just the idea that they lived in that kind of environment . . . I think Jordan had testified that in spite of her warnings not to look out the window, she actually had to stick her head out of the window to get away from the odor to allow her to be able to breathe."

Judge Schwartz said that this had resulted in severe physical damage to the children, including malnutrition, cachexia, psychosocial dwarfism, scoliosis, and stunted growth.

"And so clearly, the infliction of great bodily injury occurred to each one of these children to various degrees. In some instances, some of these things will be fixed. I know they were fed and gained weight. But some of these things are not going to be fixed in the medical conditions that they have."

Although Louise carried out most of the physical punishment in California, Schwartz said her husband had done nothing to prevent it.

"So here we have clearly Mother, or Mrs. Turpin, inflicting much of the corporal punishment causing great bodily injury. But Mr. Turpin, either directly as a perpetrator or as an aider and abettor, clearly had a duty to ensure that these children were cared for in a proper manner. And it's clear to the court that he failed in that duty. The court thinks that the elements of torture have been met as to Mr. Turpin."

He then turned to the charge that the defendant had committed a lewd and lascivious act on his then twelve-year-old daughter.

"Court heard evidence yesterday that, according to Jordan, Mr. Turpin told her to come over, pulled her pants down. There is one version where that is all that occurs.

The other version is that she pulled them up and he pulled them back down."

Either way, said the judge, he used some degree of force to pull her pants down, as well as then picking her up and placing her on his lap. And she was only able to get away when Mother came home.

"What is of significance to the court," Schwartz continued, "in its consideration of this count is the kissing. [It] certainly shows the intent . . . of Mr. Turpin and why he may have done this activity for some sort of sexual gratification. Also, what was of significance to the court was him telling her after the fact, 'Don't tell anyone.' Why would he say that if nothing happened, or if it was an activity that was completely innocuous? Mr. Turpin is her father. He's in a position of trust and in a position of power over her, especially in this case where there is such tight control over the children."

The judge then addressed whether the seven older siblings were dependent adults. He said it was only "common sense" for the deputies to put a 5150 hold on them, because of their lack of education and inability to care for themselves.

The only one of all the charges against the defendants Schwartz was not convinced of was that of child endangerment on two-year-old Janna.

"It's true that she lived in an environment that was horrific," he said, "one that obviously she wasn't even aware of. But there was testimony that she was cared for properly. There's no evidence that she was subjected to any of these kinds of physical abuse or emotional abuse."

The judge then dismissed that single charge against both defendants before moving on to the twelve charges of false imprisonment.

"It's clear to the court," he said, "that there were two kinds of false imprisonment that were ongoing in the case. One was the chaining, the physical chaining of the children. But the other was just simply the inability of the children to be able to leave the house."

He noted that even when some of the older siblings did leave the house, they went with Mother and were never allowed to be alone. And most of the time they all had to remain in their bedrooms, only coming downstairs to eat.

"It was compelling to hear Jordan's 911 call yesterday," said the judge. "To talk about the fact that she barely, if ever, was able to get out of the house. She didn't even know her own address. She knew nothing about the neighborhood, because she basically had never been out of the house."

He also addressed defense attorney Jeff Moore's request to lower the choking charge against Louise Turpin to a misdemeanor.

He noted that after Mother told Jordan she was going to die, the young teenager believed she would. And that "quite severe" physical force had been used, which hurt her neck for two days.

"[This] is sufficient to show that this was infliction of force likely to cause great bodily injury and may have caused great bodily injury."

Finally, Judge Schwartz addressed the eight counts of perjury against David Turpin regarding his nonexistent private school.

"The documents submitted by David Turpin in the private homeschool affidavits," said the judge, "basically says that the children are getting full schooling as if they were in public school. And the reality here is they were getting no schooling, or virtually no schooling. These children were left unattended for their ability to be able to learn and be educated during the formative years of their life. And so it's clear to the court . . . that the schooling was not being given to these children in accordance under the law."

Schwartz ruled that there was probable cause to believe both defendants had abused and tortured twelve of their thirteen children. He ordered them to stand trial on more than four dozen felony counts each.

He set an arraignment date for Friday, August 3, with a trial date within sixty days of that.

"Is that acceptable to you, Mr. Turpin?" asked the judge.

"Yes, sir," David replied.

"And Mrs. Turpin?"

"Yes," she said in a soft whisper.

Then the defense attorneys asked Judge Schwartz to seal the audio recording of Jordan's 911 call and the two photographs she had taken of her sisters in chains.

"We've had enough adverse publicity in this case," said David Macher. "I don't think we need more. I don't think we need those photographs to be circulating."

Later, the District Attorney's Office announced that it would not release the audio tape or the two photographs, as it was a pending criminal case.

Outside the court, *Press-Enterprise* reporter Brian Rokos asked David Macher if he planned to request a change of venue and move the trial out of Riverside County.

"Probably," he replied, "if we go to trial."

EPILOGUE

At 8:30 a.m. on Friday, August 3, 2018, David and Louise Turpin were back in Riverside County Superior Court for their rearraignment. Before the proceedings began, Judge Bernard Schwartz was handed a written request on behalf of the thirteen Turpin children, for their birth certificates, IDs, and a camera that had been seized by police. It was a sign that they were trying to move on with their lives. As neither prosecutors nor the defense lawyers opposed it, the judge signed an order to return their personal items. Then he adjourned the arraignment for a further four weeks.

On August 31, Judge Schwartz denied a motion by Defense Attorney David Macher to sever David Turpin's eight perjury charges from the other forty-one. Deputy District Attorney Kevin Beecham told the judge that his sham home school was an integral part of the neglect the seven adult children had suffered, rendering them unable to care for themselves. The judge agreed.

"The lack of education is part and parcel to the entirety of the case," he said.

Then both the defendants reentered pleas of not guilty to all eighty-eight charges against them.

At their next court appearance on October 5, Jeff Moore announced that Louise had now been diagnosed with histrionic personality disorder, asking the judge to release her from jail to undergo mental-health treatment under a pretrial diversion program.

"The actions that underlie the charges," explained Moore, "were motivated or caused by the mental-health disorder. Mrs. Turpin does not pose a threat to the public. She is amenable to treatment in a noncustodial setting."

Deputy DA Beecham argued that the defense had not established that the personality disorder was responsible for Louise's actions. "She is an unreasonable risk to the public," he told the court.

Judge Schwartz agreed and turned down the defense request.

At the end of November, Judge Schwartz set a trial date for September 3, 2019.

On Friday, February 22, 2019, David and Louise Turpin dramatically agreed to plead guilty to fourteen felony counts each, including torture, false imprisonment, and child endangerment. The couple had originally faced nearly fifty counts each, but prosecutors had agreed to drop many of them.

At the hearing, Louise cried and dabbed her eyes as she admitted to each charge while David appeared stoic without a hint of emotion. The couple now face spending the rest of their lives behind bars.

Under the reduced charges, the Turpins each admitted to at least one crime for each of their twelve children. No charges were ever filed for their now three-year-old daughter.

"Those pleas will result in life sentences," declared Riverside County District Attorney Mike Hestrin at a press conference after the hearing. "I think it's fair that the sentence was equivalent to first-degree murder."

Two months later, on Good Friday, April 19, 2019, David and Louise Turpin were sentenced to life in prison with the possibility of parole after twenty-five years. During the emotional hearing, Jennifer and Joshua Turpin stepped out in public for the first time to deliver heart-wrenching impact statements to their parents. They were comforted by a Labrador support dog called Raider.

"My parents took my whole life from me, but now I'm taking my whole life back," said Jennifer, now thirty, in a shaky high-pitched voice. "I saw my dad change my mom. They almost changed me, but I realized what was happening. I fought to become the person I am. I'm a fighter, I'm strong, and I'm shooting through life like a rocket."

Then Joshua, now twenty-seven, walked up to the stand and thanked his parents for teaching him about God and faith. Now at college studying to be a software engineer, he told them that he still has nightmares about being chained up and beaten.

"That is the past and this is now," he told the court. "I love my parents and have forgiven them for a lot of things that they did to us. I have learned so much and become independent."

Joshua also read out a statement from his sister Jessica.

"Although it may not have been the best way of raising us," it said, "I'm glad that they did because it made me the person I am today."

David Turpin's attorney then read out his statement to the court.

"I never intended for any harm to come to my children," it said. "I'm sorry if I've done anything to cause them harm. I hope and pray my children can stay close to each other since their mother and father cannot be there for them."

Finally Louise Turpin addressed the court.

"I want them to know that Mom and Dad are going to be okay," she declared, dabbing her eyes with a tissue. "I'm blessed to be the mother of each of them. I also want them to know I believe God has a special plan for them. I'm sorry for everything I've done to hurt my children. I love my children so much."

Before handing down sentence, Judge Bernard Schwartz told David and Louise Turpin, "Children are indeed a gift. They're a gift to their parents, they're a gift to their family, to their friends, and they're a gift to society. They are a gift to their parents in the sense that a parent should be joyful of firsts in their child's life. The first day of school, first date, first graduation, first job, marriage. All of those things should be enjoyed by the parents and child alike."

Judge Schwartz told the defendants that their "selfish, cruel and inhumane treatment" of their children had permanently altered their ability to learn and thrive.

"It delayed their mental, physical, and emotional development," he said. "To the extent that they do thrive, and we've learnt today that a couple of them are, it will be not because of you both but in spite of you both."